CW00740920

Popes, Cardinals and War

*'Cursed be he that keepeth back his sword from blood.'*

*Jeremiah, XLVIII, 10*


*'Then Simon Peter having a sword drew it, and smote the high priest's servant, and cut off his right ear.'*

*John, XVIII, 10*


*'"Oho!" said Stalin [to Pierre Laval in Moscow, May 1935]. "The Pope? How many divisions has he got?"'*

*Joseph Stalin, 1935, quoted by Winston Churchill,* The Second World War, *vol. 1:* The Gathering Storm *(London, 1949), p.121*

# Popes, Cardinals and War

THE MILITARY CHURCH IN RENAISSANCE
AND EARLY MODERN EUROPE

D.S. Chambers

I.B. TAURIS

LONDON · NEW YORK

Published in 2006 by I.B.Tauris & Co. Ltd
6 Salem Road, London W2 4BU
175 Fifth Avenue, New York NY 10010
www.ibtauris.com

In the United States and Canada distributed by Palgrave Macmillan,
a division of St. Martin's Press, 175 Fifth Avenue, New York NY 10010

ISBN 10: 1 84511 178 8
ISBN 13: 978 1 84511 178 6

A full CIP record for this book is available from the British Library
A full CIP record for this book is available from the Library of Congress
Library of Congress catalog card: available

Typeset in Stone Serif by Dexter Haven Associates Ltd, London
Printed and bound in Great Britain by CPI Bath

# Contents

# List of illustrations

# List of abbreviations

| | |
|---|---|
| *AHP* | *Archivium Historiae Pontificiae* |
| ASDM, AMV | Archivio Diocesano, Mantua, Archivio Mensa Vescovile |
| ASF MAP | Archivio di Stato, Florence, Medici avanti Principato |
| *ASI* | *Archivio storico italiano* |
| *ASL* | *Archivio storico lombardo* |
| ASMn, AG | Archivio di Stato, Mantua, Archivio Gonzaga |
| ASMil, Sforzesco, PE | Archivio di Stato, Milan, Fondo Sforzesco, Potenze Estere |
| ASMod, Estense | Archivio di Stato, Modena, Archivio Estense |
| *ASRSP* | *Archivio della società romana di storia patria* |
| ASV | Archivio di Stato, Venice |
| *AV* | *Archivio Veneto* |
| b. | busta (box file) |
| BAV | Biblioteca Apostolica Vaticana |
| BL | British Library |
| BMV | Biblioteca Marciana, Venice |
| BUB | Biblioteca Universitaria, Bologna |
| c. | carta (page) |
| cart. | cartella (box file) |
| *DBI* | *Dizionario biografico degli italiani* |
| *DHGE* | *Dictionnaire d'Histoire et de Géographie Ecclésiastiques* |
| *DMS* | *Diarii di Marin Sanudo* (ed. F. Stefani, R. Fulin et al., 58 vols, Venice, 1879–1902) |
| *EHR* | *English Historical Review* |
| esp. | especially |
| *GSLI* | *Giornale storico della letteratura italiana* |
| n.s. | new series |
| obv. and rev. | obverse and reverse |
| | Migne, Paris, 1844–64 |

| Pastor | L. Pastor, *Geschichte der Päpste* (many volumes and editions); translations cited, either *History of the Popes* or *Storia dei Papi*, with editor's or translator's name and publication date. |
| *PL* | *Patrologiae cursus completus. Series latina*, ed. J.-P. |
| *QF* | *Quellen und Forschungen aus italienischen Archiven und Bibliotheken* |
| repr. | reprint |
| *RIS* | *Rerum Italicarum Scriptores*, ed. L. Muratori and revised by later editors |
| transl. | translation |

## ACKNOWLEDGEMENTS

In the first place I owe thanks to Lester Crook for suggesting that I turn into a book a lecture I gave at the Anglo-American Historians' Conference in London in July 2000 (the conference's theme that year was 'War and Peace'), and for his thoughtful comments, as well as those of his editorial colleagues and of an anonymous outside reader. I am deeply grateful to friends at the Warburg Institute, particularly to Elizabeth McGrath and Magnus Ryan for reading the first version of the text and making many valuable suggestions and corrections, to Jill Kraye for bibliographical advice, to Ian Jones for his ready opinions and much help concerning photographs, and to Jenny Boyle for her endlessly patient support and cheerful reassurance over word-processing problems, real or feared. For points of information and friendly interest I should also like to thank Stefan Bauer, John Law, Letizia Panizza, Marco Pellegrini, Guido Rebecchini, Rodolfo Signorini and Marcello Simonetta. It is sad that there was no possibility of discussing the book with John Hale, to whose memory I dedicated the original lecture, nor with Nicolai Rubinstein, although he was asking about it not long before he died. Finally, it remains for me to thank my wife Tatyana, who pointed out many infelicities of syntax and punctuation; also Serunchik and Grunya – for their 'endurance'.

# CENTRAL ITALY AND THE LANDS OF THE CHURCH

**Papal lands shown white**

n.b. Frontiers are only approximate and often changed

REP. OF VENICE

Venice

A D R I A T I C   S E A

R. Mincio
Oglio
Mantua
**MARQUISATE**
Po
Ostiglia
Rovigo
Piazenza
**OF MANTUA**
Mirandola
**DUCHY**
Parma
S
I
Reggio
Carpi
Finale
N
Ferrara
Modena
Po
**OF**
Castelfranco
Cento
Argento
E
Reno
Bologna
Lugo
Ravenna
**MILAN**
Imola
Faenza
Manfredi
Forlì
Cervia
Forlimpopoli
Cesenatico
Spezia
Brisighella
Bertinoro
Cesena
Carrara
REP. OF LUCCA
Rimini
**REP. OF**
Marciano
Pistoia
Sarsina
**S. MARINO**
Montefiore
Pesaro
REP. OF LUCCA
**REP. OF**
Fano
Lucca
Urbino
Mondolfo
Florence
Montefeltro
Senigallia
Pisa
Mondavio
Ancona
Arno
Corinaldo
Jesi
**F L O R E N C E**
Nidastore
Osimo
Anghiari
Castelfidardo
Volterra
Arezzo
Gubbio
Fabriano
Montefano
Recanati
Siena
Cortona
Città di Castello
Macerata
**REP. OF**
L.
Tolentino
Trasimene
Nocera
Mogliano
Fermo
Pienza
Camerino
**SIENA**
Perugia
Assisi
Montalto
Piombino
Spello
Foligno
Varano
Offida
Grosseto
Montefalco
Trevi
Ascoli
Pitigliano
Castro
Ombrone
Orvieto
Todi
Norcia
Tronto
Elba
Spoleto
Terni
Teramo
L. Bolsena
Narni
Montefiascone
Rieti
Viterbo
Aquila
Caprarola
Pescara
Chieti
Nepi
Civita Castellana
Corneto
Mentana
**K I N G D O M**
Civitavecchia
Bracciano
Vicovaro
Tagliacozzo
Ceri
L.
Arezzano
L.
Sulmona
Tivoli
Cave
Genezzano
Fucino
Civitavecchia
Zagarola
Palestrina
Paliano
a
Sangro
**ROME**
Marino
Anagni
Sora
**O F**
Ostia
Tiber
Ferentino
Arpino
Velletri
Frosinone
Ceprano
Pontecorvo
Nettuno
**N A P L E S**
Terracina
Gallucio
Gaeta
Volturno
**Benevento**
0  25  50
km
Naples

**M E D I T E R R A N E A N   S E A**

# Preface: Italy and history

The theme of this book is emphatically not the history of Italy, but, since the papacy's engagements in war – and popes' and cardinals' personal participation in it – were to a large extent happening there, some introductory guidelines over the many centuries to be covered, particularly over the central period of the fifteenth and sixteenth centuries, may be of help. Even so, readers may have to bear allusions in the text to unfamiliar and under-explained persons, places and events, and may still remain baffled by the complexities of Italian medieval and early modern history. Unfortunately, no attempt to present a history of Italy ever seems quite to succeed; those multi-volume series written by numerous different authors invariably frustrate the reader by the variety of approaches and too little precise detail.[1]

One starting point would be to present this theme of a belligerent papacy in its Italian background as a struggle for physical survival. The bishopric of Rome, with its primacy over the Church, or over the world as some proponents were to claim for it, and its sacred associations with St Peter and countless martyrs, had its base halfway down the Italian peninsula. This was a highly vulnerable location. Italy was subjected to foreign invaders in every century of the Christian era, from every direction in turn, and the problem of dealing with aggressive invaders has had much to do with forging the papacy's often warlike standpoint. For the earlier period, up to the twelfth century, this is briefly illustrated in Chapter 1, but it is important to stress from the outset two important points.

The first important point is that the Bishop of Rome, like other medieval bishops, possessed from time immemorial local estates and castles, but in addition claimed much more widespread temporal possessions, thanks to political 'donations' and their successive confirmations. The first and most famous of these was the donation allegedly made by the Emperor Constantine I some time after his conversion to Christianity and the decision to remove the capital of the empire from Rome to Byzantium (henceforward Constantinople) in 326–30. It supposedly gave to the Pope imperial rights and possessions in Italy, as well as lordship over all islands, but there is no doubt that the basis of this was an eighth-century forgery, and later donations, more modest and not always consistent with each other, were more authentic.

Among the most significant of these donations was that of Pepin the Short, King of the Franks, dated to the year 751 and later confirmed by his son Charles I (Charlemagne). This deed underlines the close bond forged between the papacy and the new dynasty of Frankish kings, former 'mayors of the palace' to the Merovingians. Sole king of the Franks since 770, ruler of roughly the eastern half of modern France and parts of western Germany, Charlemagne expanded his power on a vast scale. His many wars, against Moors in Spain (continuing the efforts of his father and grandfather), against pagan Saxons, Avars, Slavs and others in central Europe, and against Lombards in Italy, coincided well with the interests of the papacy. He was (as Einhard, his contemporary biographer, records) extravagantly devoted to the see and shrine of St Peter, and avowed himself to be the Pope's military protector against all secular enemies, including the violent people of Rome, leaving the Pope free simply to pray and serve the faith. Charlemagne was in return rewarded with the title of 'Emperor Augustus' (no apologies to Constantinople) and crowned in Rome by Leo III on Christmas Day 800.

In practice, this condominion of world authority, and the separation of papal and imperial functions, did not work smoothly after Charlemagne's death (814). His inheritance was subdivided, and the titles of 'King of the Romans' and (when crowned) 'Emperor', though not filled at all for considerable periods, were to pass to other Germanic dynasties; some holders, particularly Henry IV of the Franconian line in the later eleventh century, claimed superior divine authority and defied the papacy over major Church appointments and other matters. Nevertheless, roughly from Charlemagne's time, it became widely known, if not always accepted, that there were papal legal claims to rights in much of Umbria, southern Tuscany and Campagna ('from Radicofani to Ceprano'), and east of the Appenines, in the former Greek Exarchate of Ravenna, a region called 'Pentapolis' which included the Adriatic coastal strip from Rimini to just north of Ancona and the Marches (borderlands), the region still called 'Marche' today. Originally the three Marches of Fermo, Camerino and Ancona, by ca. 1100 all three were known simply as the March of Ancona. The papal claims extended also over much of present-day Emilia-Romagna even as far north as Bologna and Ferrara. Some serious efforts were being made by the popes to realise such territorial rights until the emperors of the Staufen dynasty, first Frederick I Barbarossa (reigned 1155–89), challenged them by force and, supported by armies that represent the last of the great Germanic invasions of the peninsula, tried to reimpose direct imperial authority in Italy.

By the early thirteenth century, under Pope Innocent III, during a hiatus in imperial potency, a more coherent 'papal state' with some recognised boundaries and institutions of government was emerging in central Italy. The map attempts to explain the region under discussion, which was of relevance from the thirteenth to the nineteenth century. From 1278, when the Emperor Rudolf of Habsburg finally conceded papal claims in Romagna, this turbulent province, also the neighbouring March of Ancona, became the special target of papal attempts at recuperation and consolidation. It would, however, be wrong to suppose that all papal claims of secular jurisdiction, taxation and service, etc. were exactly defined, or that they applied with equal force all over a large region of central Italy, or that local warlords and others readily conceded obedience to Rome. This was no modern state yet, no equivalent to the contemporary strong monarchies of France or England. Force of tradition and forceful possession counted more than written deeds of donation. Indeed, a remark attributed to Pope Julius II in 1512 probably expresses what for centuries remained the prevailing assumption of the papacy and its supporters, that the legal rights of the Church were so ancient that it would be shameful to dispute them.[2]

The second point, which relates closely to the first, is that since 1059 the papacy had established a special relationship or feudal dependency over the southern half of Italy, which in less than a century was upgraded into a kingdom. It was bestowed on the most recent and successful of foreign invaders, a Norman dynasty, who did the work of subjecting Greeks and Lombards on the mainland and Arabs in Sicily. The papal purpose was to obtain security and a reliable source of military protection. In practice this was not always forthcoming; and after the Staufen inherited the southern kingdom through marriage, and from

1230 onwards became mortal enemies of the papacy, the prospect looked bad. However, to obtain the fall of the Staufen the papacy in 1263 conferred the kingdom on a branch of the Capetian dynasty, kings of France, in the person of Charles I, Duke of Anjou. This 'Angevin' dynasty continued to rule the kingdom (it was always known simply as 'il Regno') till the early fifteenth century, although Sicily from 1282 split away to be ruled by the kings of Aragon, by conquest but also by claim of heredity from the Norman–Staufen line. The kingdom continued to be of vital importance to the papacy.

Of course the reality of power, or at least of economic power, in thirteenth- and fourteenth-century Italy, indeed in all Europe, lay in the expanding and prosperous northern cities of Italy – above all in Milan, Venice, Genoa and Florence. For them the temporal preoccupations of the papacy were only of relative interest, though northern banking firms, particularly those of Florence, would for long act as the papacy's creditors and revenue collectors. An irregular pattern emerged that divided Italy on pro-papal lines ('Guelf', Angevin, civic constitutional) – a notable example being Florence – and pro-imperial lines ('Ghibelline', aristocratic, tyrannical), such as Milan, which was controlled by the Visconti dynasty. There were factions in many cities that represented conflicting interests and exploited these supposedly irreconcilable party labels, although the affluent maritime republics, Venice and Genoa, did not fall into either camp. Most cities – excluding Florence, Venice, Genoa, Siena and Lucca, which retained varying forms of elective institutions and some respect for the rule of law – developed into signorial regimes, under the rule of one man, or one family. Such a regime often grew out of some form of civic appointment, which was by vote or acclamation made into a permanent 'captaincy', at best a semi-benevolent tyranny.[3] Ferrara had one of the most long-standing of these regimes, ruled since 1240 by the Este dynasty; Mantua, under the Gonzaga family since 1328, was another example. This pattern also applied to the relatively small towns and their adjacent territories within the papally claimed regions of central Italy. By the fourteenth century, when the papacy – although based at Avignon from 1309 until 1377 – made strong efforts to impose control on these regions, its military legates often had to compromise with the strongmen, warlords or local dynasties in effective control there. They might be recognised as papal 'vicars', conditional on payment of tribute and military service; it was thus that turbulent and in some cases former 'Ghibelline' clans, such as the Montefeltro, with their lordship centred on Urbino in the Marche, the Malatesta of Rimini, the da Varano of Camerino, the Baglioni of Perugia and others, were accommodated. But as they tended to become hereditary and virtually independent, prospering as *condottieri* (mercenary military captains under contract) in the fifteenth and early sixteenth centuries, papal policy changed to attempting a more direct control, sometimes by family alliance, sometimes by force or the threat of it. A special case was Bologna, a city in a key position, since it controlled one of the main routes over the Appenines to Tuscany. There in the fifteenth century a local family, the Bentivoglio, came to challenge or uneasily to share the government of the city with papal legates; the total control of Bologna came to be an overwhelming priority for the papacy.

The idea of the ultimate sovereignty of the emperor, a figure elected by a small number of German princes and prince-bishops, was never eliminated from northern Italy – and in 1310–13 Henry VII of Luxembourg led a last military invasion – but the subsequent election of Lewis of Bavaria was disputed and not recognised by the new pope, John XXII (pope 1316–34). The authority of the empire was still further degraded; its role in Italy became even more nominal, becoming little more than the theoretical source of civil law and right to bear titles of honour. In practice the neighbouring monarchy of France had a much stronger impact on the peninsula throughout the later medieval period, and not least upon the papacy, when transferred to Provence (1305–77).

The condition of the southern kingdom remained crucial. The relative stability of Angevin rule there was shattered, as was much else in western Europe, by the schism in the Church, caused by the rival papal elections in 1378 of Urban VI and Clement VII. Urban was recognised throughout Italy, except by Giovanna I in Naples. Urban backed a cadet line of the family in the person of Charles of Durazzo, Giovanna was murdered, and Clement, who was recognised in France, backed for the kingdom Louis, Duke of Anjou and Count of Provence. Having two separate 'Angevin' branches claiming the kingdom greatly complicated the picture, though it was the Aragonese line ruling Sicily and aspiring to the mainland kingdom since the 1420s that eventually prevailed; in 1442, Alfonso V of Aragon was installed, favoured by the papacy over Angevin rivals.

There was another Italian prize over which the monarchy of France, or its ruling Valois dynasty, had in the late fourteenth century managed to gain an interest: the duchy of Milan. It was through the marriage of Giangaleazzo Visconti's daughter Valentina with Louis, Duke of Orleans, although this Orleanist claim to the Visconti inheritance remained dormant for over a century. Milan, under the control of Giangaleazzo Visconti from 1378, duke in 1395, had become the most formidable of Italian powers. Visconti ambitions under Giangaleazzo, only cut short by his sudden death in 1402, had threatened both the papacy and Florence; renewed under his son Filippo (duke from 1412 to 1447), they caused from the 1420s to the 1440s a new series of wars involving Florence, Venice and the papacy.

If one were to pause and contemplate the condition of Italy in about 1450, however, it would be clear that a degree of stability had been restored; indeed, the next forty years or so would come to be regarded by sixteenth-century writers as almost a golden age. There was a single papacy, and even the alternative idea of a General Council of the Church, the body which at least had ended the Great Schism in 1417, was discredited, since the Council of Basel in the 1430s became too radical. The kingdom of Naples was stable under the able rule of the Aragonese Alfonso I, succeeded by his bastard son Ferrante in 1458; Milan, after a brief republican interlude, passed in 1450 into the hands of Francesco Sforza, the military captain who had married Filippo Visconti's daughter, and the ducal regime (sanctioned, but not much more, by the emperor) continued there until 1499. Venice was advancing as a mainland power in north-east Italy, having acquired not only Verona and Padua but, in the wars against Filippo Visconti, Brescia, Bergamo, Crema and Ravenna. The republic of Florence, which had expanded within Tuscany, annexing Arezzo and Pisa, was now informally controlled by the hyper-rich banker, and main financier of the papacy, Cosimo de' Medici, succeeded by his son Piero 'the Gouty' in 1464 and his grandson Lorenzo, known as 'il Magnifico', in 1469. The main Italian powers had even attempted in 1455 to set up a system of arbitration to monitor future conflicts and preserve peace. It did not work, but at least it was an attempt to put diplomacy before force. The various minor states were still carrying on with civic regimes dominated by princes – for these former mercenary captains, city bosses and landed proprietors were assuming an increasingly princely style. Mantua, in most respects a satellite of Sforza Milan, continued to be ruled by the Gonzaga family, most notable of whom was the highly cultivated *condottiere* Ludovico Gonzaga (marquis, 1444–78); Ferrara, since 1471 a papal dukedom, was still ruled by the d'Este, as were Reggio and – an imperial dukedom – Modena; Federico di Montefeltro of Urbino likewise became a papal duke in 1474.

Admittedly, several internal Italian wars and some sensational assassinations disturbed the relative stability of the political balance which lasted to 1494. The murder of Duke Galeazzo Maria Sforza of Milan in 1476 led to the dominance of his brother Ludovico 'il Moro'; the young heir to the dukedom, Giangaleazzo, died in 1494, and the ambitious Ludovico obtained this title. The attempted murder of Lorenzo de' Medici in 1478 (contrived by the Pazzi family, but with the support of the Pope's nephew Girolamo Riario and others) and successful killing of his brother Giuliano caused a war between Florence and the papacy, allied with its traditional standby, the King of Naples; it also led to a tightening of direct Medici control over Florence's politics. Two more wars broke out in 1482 and 1485–86, in both of which the papacy was drawn into the complete reversal of its traditional position, declaring war on the kingdom of Naples, its principal vassal and supposed protector. Soon after this, the assassination – partly an act of Florentine revenge – of Girolamo Riario in 1488, whose mini-princedom of Imola and Forlì had represented a new papal experiment in control of the Romagna, was another destabilising event. The Riario state within the papal state was nevertheless a precedent for the much more formidable princedom to be established by force by Pope Alexander VI's son Cesare Borgia in 1499–1503.

But it was the invasion or 'descent' (*calata*) of Charles VIII of France in 1494, urged on by Ludovico Sforza out of jealousy or fear of Ferrante, King of Naples, that shattered the system which had prevailed during the previous half-century. Once again the southern kingdom was the fulcrum of crisis. Charles professed to be representing the Angevin claim to the throne of Naples in his rapid advance down the west side of Italy. Alfonso, Duke of Calabria, the son and heir of King Ferrante, who had died early in 1494, proved less formidable as king than he had been as a military commander, and abdicated in the face of rebellion while Charles was still on his way; after the French arrived in Naples, Alfonso's son Ferrantino fled to Sicily. But the collapse of the southern kingdom and its Aragonese ruling dynasty was not the only upheaval in Italy. Piero de' Medici, Lorenzo's son who had succeeded to his father's role in 1492, had bargained unsuccessfully with Charles VIII on the latter's journey south through Tuscany in early November 1494, and was overthrown on his return to the city. Deeply influenced by the threatening sermons of the Dominican friar Girolamo Savonarola, the Florentines established a more constitutional republic that for the next twenty years remained steadily pro-French, largely in the vain and costly hope of reconquering its rebellious subject city, Pisa.

Charles VIII did not manage to stabilise his conquest of the southern kingdom, for which in any case he had failed to obtain papal sanction and investiture. In 1495 he returned to France pursued by an Italian coalition in which Ludovico il Moro of Milan and Venice were leading members. In Naples the dispossessed dynasty attempted a comeback with Spanish help; Ferrantino recovered Naples but died unexpectedly in October 1496; Alfonso's brother Federico briefly succeeded him. However, the entry upon the scene of the King of Spain, Ferdinand of Aragon, freed by his conquest of Granada (1492) to turn his attention to the wider world, proved fatal. An entirely new, Hispanic era for the south of Italy was beginning, deeply alarming also for the papacy. Ferdinand turned from providing military aid to his relative to accepting Federico's deposition by the French in 1501, on the grounds that he had appealed for help to the Turks, and claimed the crown for himself. He alternated between fighting the forces of Charles VIII's successor Louis XII, and cynically making secret agreements to divide the southern kingdom with him. Disastrous French defeats in battle in 1503 led eventually to renunciation of the ancient French claims, and an agreement whereby the widowed Ferdinand would marry Louis XII's niece, pay him a large sum of money, and incidentally obtain the papal investiture as king. The outcome was a new regime in both Naples and Sicily of government by Spanish viceroys. In the north, meanwhile, another French invasion in 1499 led by Louis XII, making good his inherited claim to Milan as Duke of Orleans, had been even more unsettling than the first *calata*. Allied with Venice, the French army succeeded in overthrowing the regime of Ludovico Sforza. Milan faced a French government of occupation, and meanwhile the Venetians advanced their domination of eastern Lombardy, annexing Cremona. The spread of the Venetian land empire had been alarming the rest of

Italy for a long time; the suspicion that Venice was aiming to dominate Italy seemed more and more justified, because the republic had also seized southern ports in Apulia and was to move into some of Cesare Borgia's conquests in Romagna after his fall in 1503. The climax came in 1509, when Julius II, Louis XII and the Emperor Maximilian declared war on Venice, and after the victory of Agnadello, on the river Adda, occupied much of its land empire. The republic soon, however, regained most of it, as the subsequent war turned into an Italian alliance, including Venice, against foreign forces. The republic of Florence was punished in 1512 for its support of the French, and had the Medici reimposed by force; henceforward the Medici, who also acquired the papacy the following year, ruled Florence in a blatantly princely manner.

As this Foreword began by stressing the vulnerability of Italy to invasion, so it might end on the same note, with reference to the Ottoman Turks. The great call to arms against the Seljuk Turks and for the liberation of Jerusalem at the end of the eleventh century was important in formulating ideas and practice about war in defence of the Church and against Islamic power, but the Ottoman Turks represented a more direct and formidable threat to Italy, Rome and the lands of the papacy. After becoming a naval as well as a land-based military power in the course of the fourteenth century, their encroachment upon what was left of the Byzantine empire proceeded rapidly. Its climax was the capture of Constantinople in 1453, and was followed at intervals by conquest of the rest of the Greek mainland and islands. It should be appreciated that the papacy felt very much at the front line of defending Christendom, particularly after mainland Italy was invaded and the civilian population of Otranto massacred in 1480; its coastline, meanwhile, was for long threatened by Muslim pirates. There was no lasting relief from this sense of imminent danger until the naval victory of Lepanto in 1571.

Second, a final word needs to be said about the long-lasting theme of French invasions and occupations of Italy, and the ascendancy of France, which from the later thirteenth century the papacy had tried to use for its own advantage and security. This came to an end in the early sixteenth century. For, in spite of renewed French military offensives under Louis XII and Francis I, Italy was not destined to fall under French domination so much as Spanish or imperial. This became the likely prospect after the election of the Habsburg Emperor Charles V in 1519, and the fairly inevitable outcome after imperial victories over the French in 1521 and 1525. Imperial or Spanish viceregal regimes governed both Milan and Naples, and Florence – after the fall in 1530 of the briefly revived republic – was restored to the Medici thanks to Charles V. Cosimo I became an imperial duke in 1537, and married Eleonora of Toledo, daughter of the imperial vicar of Naples. Siena came under his control in 1557, and in 1569 his title was raised to grand duke. The principal independent Italian powers left after the storm were Venice and the papacy, both of them to survive unharmed until the time of Napoleon.

It remains a debating point whether the papacy, which had invested so much military and financial effort into the recuperation and consolidation of its possessions in Italy, had contributed greatly to Italian political disunity and weakness, as the Florentine writer Niccolò Machiavelli (1464–1527) in one context suggested (*Discorsi*, I chap. 12). Perhaps, on the contrary, and since the empire had become so ineffective in the fourteenth and fifteenth centuries, the papacy was potentially quite a powerful force for stabilising Italy. Machiavelli also appreciated this possibility, and some of the popes of the later renaissance period, particularly Julius II, were among his model princes, along with Ferdinand of Aragon and Cesare Borgia, for their skills of deception, decisive resolution, and domination of fortune. But Machiavellian theories and paradoxes are not the issue in this book, which is concerned rather with why the Church, or its principal officers, were so inescapably involved in war.

# Prologue

'What monstrous new fashion is this, to wear the dress of a priest on top, while underneath it you are all bristling and clanking with blood-stained armour?'

Thus St Peter's famous greeting to Pope Julius II when he presented himself at the gates of heaven in 1513, according to the satirical dialogue 'Julius Exclusus',[1] most often attributed to Erasmus. Julius replies defiantly that, unless St Peter surrenders and opens the gate, he will return with reinforcements and throw him out.

This book will emphasise that, however monstrous, it was not a new fashion at all in the early sixteenth century for popes, let alone cardinals, to participate actively in war. And war sponsored and sometimes even conducted by themselves is intended here, war by the central government of the Catholic or Roman Church, rather than war declared by a secular power that enjoyed the Church's blessing. Even if the Gospels on the whole enjoin peace, the cause of defending the Church by force had plentiful sanctions, metaphorical or otherwise, in the Old Testament and was all too compatible with the idea of 'just war' formulated by St Augustine and developed by many later writers. Canon law forbade the clergy to shed blood, but was ambiguous on various other points (in addition to the fact that mortal harm can be inflicted in many ways without involving bloodshed). They were not banned from uttering exhortations to violence or accompanying, directing and granting absolution to its perpetrators. Only a fine line distinguished such permissive pugnacity from the prohibition addressed to all clergy, except those monkish knights in the military religious orders that arose in the twelfth century, from wielding weapons and slaughtering foes in combat.

Four or five centuries of war against Islam, whether hot Holy War or cold Holy War, further contributed to the militarisation of western

Christianity, but 'holy war' was not only to be fought in the east, in defence of the faith or (even more of a catch-all slogan) defence of the Church. It was also to be fought in the west, sometimes against heresy, schism or disobedience committed by secular rulers but more

'Julius Exclusus': anon. woodcut, ca. 1522–23 in a German version of the text, printer and place of printing unknown (Beinecke Rare Book and Manuscript Library, Yale University).

continuously in defence of jurisdictions and territorial rights in Italy – rights believed to be the papacy's by divine sanction as well as by legal prescription and long-established custom. There will be some concentration here upon the fifteenth and sixteenth centuries, the era conventionally labelled 'Renaissance', but stress will be laid that this period saw only the climax of a war process stretching back in time to the Lombard invasions of Italy in the sixth century and continuing, if rather less ferociously, right until the final collapse of the temporal power in 1870. The use of force, initiated by successive popes and – from the eleventh century – their close assistants, the cardinals and other higher clergy to whom power was delegated, lay behind the expansion of papal government and jurisdiction in Italy and Europe from the thirteenth century onwards. It persisted during the papacy's nadir in the fourteenth century and its recovery in the fifteenth century, perhaps reaching a climax during Julius II's reign as pope, but still continued thereafter, in spite of the diffusion of disapproval and dissent. In general, the point is the paradox that leaders of the Church, although their vocation was peaceful, in the course of many centuries contributed rather more to the process of war than to that of peace – and in some cases they did so with a surprising directness and brutality. No doubt they firmly believed that God and righteousness were on their side, but it is a truism that firm belief often underlines barbarous acts. In other branches of the Church a parallel story might be told, but the present enquiry is concerned with only the most highly organised and prominent institution of Christendom: the papal monarchy.

Julius II simply went a step further than most popes, particularly in his winter campaign of 1510–11 against the Duke of Ferrara and his allies, when he took personal command in an offensive military operation (the siege of Mirandola). Julius's direct participation in war, an episode central to the theme of this book, will be re-examined in detail, but it will be set comparatively within the widest possible span of time and presented as one episode of a complex and continuous theme in the history of the papacy.

# 1 'Dux et Pontifex': the medieval centuries

'Blessed are the peacemakers.' But blessed, too, have been the war-mongers throughout the Christian centuries. Among the many aspects of this paradox a particular problem arises: how far could papal authority and the clerical hierarchy go in supporting or even committing acts of war in defence of the Church? The question has never been resolved with precision. St Ambrose (ca. 340–97) proclaimed that – unlike Old Testament leaders, such as Joshua or David – Christian clerics should refrain from force: 'I cannot surrender the church, but I must not fight' 'pugnare non debeo'; 'Against weapons, soldiers, the Goths, tears are my arms, these are the defences of a priest.'[1] These precepts set the canonical line, but a fine distinction in culpability came to be admitted between inflicting violence directly and inciting others to acts of violence and bloodshed. It remained a matter of serious concern throughout the Middle Ages and beyond: how was the necessary defence of the Church to be defined and limited? Could the clergy, the officers of the Church, in conscience wholly avoid being involved in homicidal physical conflict, at least in self-defence? This opening chapter has to take the main story, which concerns the fifteenth and sixteenth centuries, a long way back in time, and cannot attempt much more than a skeletal outline.

In practice, when acute physical dangers threatened the Church, and its Roman power base in particular, active response must have seemed a matter of duty. The site of Rome, halfway down the 'leg' of Italy, was extremely vulnerable once the huge resources, military and naval strength, and well-maintained road system of the empire had gone.

Successive hordes of invaders attacked or threatened the Roman bishopric's sanctuaries and scattered estates, as well as overrunning other provinces of Italy. In the summer of 452 Pope Leo I reputedly stopped the Huns in their tracks only thanks to a miraculous if terrifying overflight of St Peter and St Paul, but Pope Gregory the Great (590–604) confronted the Lombards with military leadership. He exhorted his military captains to strive for glory, and provisioned and directed troops in defence of Rome.[2] Two centuries later the recurrent invaders were Muslim Arabs or Moors from North Africa. Leo IV (pope 847–55) accompanied the Roman army that fought victoriously against Muslim pirates at the mouth of the Tiber, and was responsible for building fortified walls to protect the Borgo Leonino, the district near St Peter's.[3] John VIII (pope 872–82) in 877 commanded a galley in a joint naval campaign with Amalfitan and Greek forces against the Muslims. Maybe the scale of the victory was exaggerated, but the nineteenth-century historian Ferdinand Gregorovius felt justified in writing 'this is the first time in history that a Pope made war as an admiral'. He quoted a letter allegedly from the Pope himself, claiming that 'eighteen ships were captured, many Saracens were slain and almost 600 slaves liberated'.[4] In 915 John X (pope 914–28) was present at another victory against Muslims on the river Garigliano in 915, and wrote to the Archbishop of Cologne boasting that he had bared his own chest to the enemy ('se ipsum corpusque suum opponendo') and twice joined battle.[5] It is arguable that the papal resistance was largely responsible for saving the mainland of Italy from the Muslim domination that befell Sicily and much of Spain.

A very different challenge was presented by the northern ascendancy of the Frankish monarchy in the eight and ninth centuries. Its professed role was to protect the papacy, and this included large-scale 'donations' of territory in Italy, by Pepin (754), Charlemagne (774) and Louis the Pious (817).[6] These confirmed at least some of the items in the forged 'donation' of Constantine, according to which the recently converted Emperor Constantine I, who moved his capital to Byzantium (henceforth Constantinople) in 330, transferred to the Pope extensive rights and possessions in the west. Not until the ninth century, however, did the boundaries of these claims begin to become at all geographically precise, including much of Umbria and extending north of the Appenines to parts of Emilia.

The Frankish kings' protective, military role was graphically expressed by Charlemagne in a famous letter congratulating Leo III (pope 795–816) on his accession. In this he declared that, while his own task was to defend the Church by arms, the Pope would simply need to raise his arms to God, like Moses did to ensure victory over the Amalikites (Exodus XVII, 8–13).[7] The other side of the bargain was that the Pope should perform coronation of his protector as emperor, the revived title duly conferred on Charlemagne in Rome on Christmas Day 800. As the imperial office also carried an aura of divinity, this protective role would eventually lead to trouble, a challenge over primacy of jurisdiction, but meanwhile it helped to preserve the papacy's dignity. Another Germanic dynasty subsequently rescued it from the scandalous if obscure confusion that prevailed in Rome during the first half of the tenth century. During that period the local nobility, and even two unscrupulous matriarchs, Theodora and her daughter Marozia, determined the appointment and even perhaps the deposition of several popes. After 960, however, three Saxon emperors, all named Otto, began to repair the situation. Early in 962 Otto I was crowned by Marozia's son, John XII (pope since 957), who had appealed for his protection, but in December 962 John was deposed by Otto.[8] According to Liudprand, Bishop of Cremona, who acted as Otto's interpreter and is therefore fairly credible as a source, this was in response to collective denunciations by senior Roman clergy. Among the alleged offences of John XII were fornication, drunkenness, arson and playing at dice, but a special emphasis seems to have been placed on publicly bearing arms. Ultimately he had turned against his imperial protector and advanced with troops against Otto's army 'equipped with shield, sword, helmet and cuirass'. Otto allegedly declared, 'There are as many witnesses to that as there are fighting men in our army.'[9]

Most successful in sharing or dominating the papacy's authority was Otto I's grandson Otto III. He resided in Rome once he had come of age in 996 and oversaw the appointments of his cousin Bruno of Carinthia (Gregory V, pope 996–99), who crowned him emperor, and the learned Gerbert of Aurillac (Silvester II, pope 999–1003). Both Otto I and Otto III also issued new 'donations', confirming the Frankish concessions of papal title to territories formerly occupied by Byzantine Greeks and Lombards. Much of central Italy, including Umbria, southern Tuscany and lands bordering the Adriatic roughly from the region of

Ravenna down to Ascoli, were redefined as potential lands of St Peter. Only 'potential', of course, because these claims under 'donation' would be hard to realise and enforce; centuries of effort, with many setbacks, lay ahead. After a relapse under local political forces in the early eleventh century, the papacy again came to be protected by a German royal dynasty. From 1046 to 1055, under the Salian Henry III, a succession of reputable popes were appointed, and to one of these, Victor II, Henry conceded rule over the March of Ancona, but seemingly as an imperial vassal.[10] For popes to have to admit the superiority or semi-parity of the emperor's office was a hard price to pay for security.

In the course of the eleventh century lofty ideas were advanced concerning both the nature of papal authority and – as an inevitable aspect of this – ecclesiastical sanctions of warfare. There were of course earlier pronouncements on the superior nature of papal power. Gelasius I (pope 492–96) is credited with introducing the idea of the Church as a principality set above all earthly princes and the pope as the vicar not only of St Peter but of Christ himself. Nicholas I (pope 858–67) pronounced that the papacy was the greater of the two lights set over the earth, that popes were princes over the whole world, and only with their sanction could the emperor use the sword; he even quoted St Peter's use of the physical sword against Malchus.[11] But it was not until the eleventh and twelfth centuries that scholars concerned with establishing the 'canon law' of the Church – pronouncements, rulings and precedents governing Church affairs laid down by successive popes and jurists – built up systematically, with the support of theologians, the 'hierocratic' theory of superior and universal papal power, including the power to depose unworthy rulers.[12]

These ideas, however strong in their implications for future wars, need not concern us at this point so much as two practical measures designed to ensure more effective papal authority, both of them the achievements of Nicholas II (pope 1059–61). One was the decree that laid down regular procedure in papal elections: that popes could only be elected by the 'cardinal' bishops, priests and deacons of Rome. As well as this constitutional provision aimed at stabilising the papal monarchy – though it failed for centuries to avert counter-elections of 'anti-popes' – in the same year 1059 a momentous step was taken to bring the southern half of Italy and Sicily under the legal lordship of the papacy. This was the grant of conditional rulership made to the Normans Robert

Guiscard and Robert of Capua, who had previously been regarded as the most troublesome and threatening of intruders in that region. The Treaty of Melfi created them dukes 'by the grace of God and St Peter', with a promise of the lordship of Sicily, conditional on its recapture from the Muslims. It decisively overruled or disregarded any surviving claims of Greeks, Lombards, Muslims or other *de facto* occupiers, and the inclusion of Sicily seems to have depended on the donation of Constantine rather than any later, more valid concessions. This turning of southern Italy into a papal fief, with obligations upon its ruler to owe the Pope military support, would have enormous consequences in the future.

Specifically on the issue of war, first, there was also a legalistic dimension that developed in the eleventh century. One of the earliest specialists in canon law, Burchard of Worms (ca. 965–1025), insisted 'the clergy cannot fight for both God and the World', but later canonists accepted that the problem was more complicated than this.[13] Second, there was also a spiritual dimension, investing war – in certain circumstances – with a positive value. This was an aspect of the monastically inspired reform movement in the Church. Leo IX (pope 1049–54), Bruno, the former Archbishop of Toul, was one of a group of serious reformers in Lorraine who combined austere religious standards with a warrior mentality, as did his colleague Wazo, Bishop of Liège, who was acclaimed by his biographer as a 'Judas Maccabeus' in his military exploits, praised for defending Liège and destroying the castles of his opponents. As archbishop Bruno had led a force in support of Emperor Henry III. As pope he waged war against his deposed predecessor Benedict IX and his partisans in 1049–50 and personally commanded an army of Swabians against the Normans in June 1053, suffering defeat at the Battle of Civitate, the disaster that made clear that the only way forward was to adopt the Normans as allies rather than enemies. Among Leo IX's recorded declarations was the precept 'Those who do not fear spiritual sanction should be smitten by the sword', though it was intended mainly against bandits and pagans.[14]

Penetrated by both monastic reforming zeal and by canon law experts who insisted on a universal, ultimate pontifical authority over the emperor and all other secular powers, the later eleventh-century papacy was almost bound to accept that force could be sanctioned, that war and bloodshed in the right cause could even be sacred. Matters reached a head in the 1070s, with recurrent conflict between the Franconian Henry

IV, king, and the emperor-elect since 1056 and the former monk Hildebrand as Gregory VII (pope 1073–85). Even before he became pope, Hildebrand had been involved in the use of force. He may have served with Leo IX; certainly he was associated with Alexander II (Anselm I of Lucca) in 1061–63. He had been largely responsible for bringing the Normans into papal service, and for employing independent military figures such as Godfrey of Lorraine. They enabled Alexander to overcome the anti-pope Cadalus, Bishop of Parma ('Honorius II'), who for a while had controlled Rome.[15] Hildebrand, unlike so many of the medieval popes, was not born into the nobility or warrior caste, but scientific tests of his bones have shown at least that he was sturdily built and used to riding a horse.[16]

Soon after becoming pope, Gregory VII issued direct orders to the papacy's mercenary forces, notably the Normans under Robert Guiscard. On 7 December 1074 he wrote to Henry IV, claiming that thousands of volunteers were calling upon him to combine the roles of 'military commander and pontiff' ('si me possunt pro duce ac pontifice habere') and lead in person an army to aid eastern Christians against the Seljuk Turks.[17]

Gregory's conflict with Henry IV was at first a war of words rather than of arms. It was partly legalistic, over investiture to higher Church appointments and the need for clerical reforms, but even more over incompatible temperaments and claims of superior authority. The conflict blew hot and cold; in 1075, until the autumn, Gregory seemed on the point of agreeing to crown Henry emperor, but the following year he was excommunicated. Nevertheless in January 1077 he presented himself at Canossa as a penitent. In 1080 Gregory excommunicated Henry IV for the second time, whereupon the pro-imperial bishops at the Synod of Brixen elected Guibert, Archbishop of Ravenna, as anti-pope. Then Gregory announced that 'with the cooler weather in September' he would mount a military expedition against Ravenna to evict Guibert. He also had in mind a campaign to punish Alfonso II of Castile for his misdeeds, threatening him not just metaphorically: 'We shall be forced to unsheathe over you the sword of St Peter.'[18] While it would be hard to prove that Gregory VII ever wielded a material sword, and his frequent pronouncements invoking 'soldiers of Christ' or 'the war of Christ' may sometimes have been metaphorical rather than literal,[19] it is easy to see how his enemies – those serving Henry IV or Guibert of Ravenna – could present his combative character as bellicose on an almost satanic scale.

'What Christian ever caused so many wars or killed so many men?' wrote Guy of Ferrara, who insisted that Hildebrand had had a passion for arms since boyhood, and later on led a private army. Guibert, who wrote a biographical tract denouncing Hildebrand, made similar allegations.[20] Such criticism carried on where the militant reformer and preacher Peter Damiani (1007–72) had left off; although in many respects Damiani's views on what was wrong with the Church were compatible with Hildebrand's, he had insisted that ecclesiastical warfare was unacceptable: Christ had ordered St Peter to put up his sword; 'Holy men should not kill heretics and heathen...never should one take up the sword for the faith.'[21]

Further justifications of military force initiated and directed by popes had to be devised. Gregory's adviser and vicar in Lombardy from 1081 to 1085, Anselm II, Bishop of Lucca, made a collection of canon law precedents at his request. In this compilation Anselm proposed that the Church could lawfully exert punitive justice or physical coercion; indeed, that such a proper use of force was even a form of charity. 'The wounds of a friend are better than the kisses of an enemy,' he declared, and – echoing St Augustine – 'It is better to love with severity than to beguile with mildness.'[22] He invoked the Old Testament parallel, arguing that Moses did nothing cruel when at the Lord's command he slew certain men, perhaps alluding to the punitive slaughter authorised after the worship of the Golden Calf (Exodus XXXIII, 27–8) or to the earlier battle of Israel against the Amalekites, when the fortunes of war depended on the effort of Moses's keeping his arms in the air (the episode Charlemagne had quoted to Leo III). Anselm does not go so far as to recommend that popes and other clergy should personally inflict violence on erring Christians, but he allows that they could mastermind it; the rules might be even more relaxed in wars against non-Christians, including lapsed and excommunicated former members of the Catholic Church.

Few of Gregory VII's successors could equal that extraordinary pope's remorseless energy, but on their part there was no renouncing of coercion by force. Even Paschal II (pope 1099–1118), a sick and elderly monk, who submitted to the humiliation of imprisonment by the Emperor Henry V in 1111, spent much of his pontificate going from siege to siege in the region of Rome. In the year of his death he supervised the mounting of 'war machines' at Castel Sant'Angelo to overcome rebels occupying St Peter's.[23] Innocent II (1130–43) was engaged in war with a rival elected soon after himself – possibly by a larger number of the cardinals – who took the name Anacletus and for a while even controlled Rome itself. Both of them found strong backers. Anacletus persuaded the German king Lothar to bring military force against his rival; Innocent obtained the support of Roger II, the Norman ruler of Sicily. In July 1139 Innocent definitely had the worst of it when an army led by himself was ambushed at Galluccio, near the river Garigliano between Rome and Naples. He was taken prisoner and had to concede to Roger investiture as king of Sicily, which Anacletus had previously bestowed on him. This was a considerable upgrading of the title 'Apostolic Legate', which had been conferred on Roger's father and namesake in 1098 in recognition of the successful reconquest of Sicily from the Muslims. The grant of kingship was the culmination or reaffirmation of the policy intended to ensure a strong and loyal military defence for the papacy in the south. As a favoured relationship it had not worked altogether smoothly. One of its lowest points was Robert Guiscard's delay in coming to the help of Gregory VII in 1084, when he delivered Rome from its long siege by Henry IV, but caused a bloodbath; another low point was the war in the 1130s mentioned above. Yet another papal defeat by Norman forces, in spite of the concession of kingship to Roger II, befell Adrian IV at Benevento in 1156.[24] In all these military conflicts it cannot be proved that Paschal II, Innocent II, Anacletus or Adrian IV engaged physically in fighting, but in each case they accompanied armies and appear to have directed – or misdirected – field operations.

A formidable challenge arose in the middle of the twelfth century on the part of the empire, the very authority that was supposedly 'protecting' the papacy. In the hands of Frederick I 'Barbarossa', of the Swabian Staufer or Staufen family – generally but incorrectly called Hohenstaufen – the empire or its lawyers advanced its own claims to government of cities and lands in northern Italy, including the city of Rome, despite local civic aspirations. The English cardinal Breakspear, elected as Adrian IV (pope 1154–59), duly crowned Frederick in 1155, but his safe arrival at St Peter's had depended on his relative, Cardinal Octavian, securing it with armed force.[25] The imperial decrees issued at Roncaglia, near Piacenza, in 1158 made clear that Frederick had no greater respect for the judicial, fiscal and territorial claims of the papacy than he had for civic autonomy.[26] Adrian IV, under whose rule there had been a certain advance in papal control of central Italian castles and towns, protested vehemently to the emperor.[27] In practice, however, in his three invasions of Italy Frederick was more concerned with Lombardy and its rapidly growing and *de facto* independent mercantile cities, above all Milan, which as punishment for its defiance he devastated in 1162. Without seeking direct military confrontation, the astute Sienese jurist Cardinal Rolando Bandinelli, elected as Alexander III (pope 1159–81), gave financial and moral support to the Lombard cities. He had meanwhile to contend with a series of anti-popes elected by pro-imperial cardinals. After the Lombard League's famous victory against Frederick at Legnano in 1174 Alexander was able to play the role of mediator and peacemaker. Much of central Italy nevertheless was subjected in his time to imperial, not papal, jurisdiction and taxation, under the direction of men such as Christian of Mainz, whose administrative capital was Viterbo, and Conrad of Urslingen, who in 1177 became imperial Duke of Spoleto. In 1164 Frederick Barbarossa had even ordered Christian to move with an army to help install his anti-pope in Rome.[28] The reversal of this imperial heyday had to wait until after the deaths of Barbarossa (drowned on crusade in 1190) and his son Henry VI in 1197.

* * * * *

Since the end of the eleventh century, meanwhile, a vast extension of papally authorised warfare had developed, with the aim of aiding eastern Christians and capturing and holding Jerusalem and the Holy Land against Muslim forces. The military expeditions of the cross – crusades – instituted by Pope Urban II at Clermont in 1095, drew much of their appeal from the indulgence promising many privileges, including assurance of salvation to sworn-up participants. Recruitment was from the beginning mainly the business of the clergy, and often military operations were also under their control. Although Urban II did not himself accompany the First Crusade, he delegated authority to Adhémar, Bishop of Le Puy, reputedly the first person to make the vow at Clermont. Adhémar, as papal legate, showed rather more tactical skill and leadership than most of the lay warriors in the earlier stages of the expedition. At the siege of Nicaea he commanded the right flank of Raymond of St Gilles's army and supervised the undermining of one of the towers; he was responsible for the diversion that led to the capture of Dorylaeum and played an important role in fighting off the Saracen siege of Antioch.[29] Adhémar's death at Antioch prevented him from taking part in the capture of Jerusalem, or being held at all responsible for its horrendous sacking.

The new crusading warfare in the east must have done much to extend within Catholic Christendom the language and justification of sanctified violence, in addition to wars in the cause of imposing universal papal authority in the west. The notion that the ecclesiastical ruler was obliged to defend the Church by force was clarified by the severe Cistercian Bernard of Clairvaux (1090–1153), a staunch supporter of Innocent II and inspirer of Eugenius III (pope from 1145 to 1153). St Bernard, Abbot of Clairvaux since 1115, liked the imagery of the sword. The pope, he declared, possessed two swords to suppress evil, one spiritual, the other physical or material. The first was only his to use, but the second he could delegate to a secular ruler to use at papal bidding. 'The [material] sword also is yours and is to be drawn from its sheath at your command, though not by your own hand,' he wrote, in his famous book of advice, *De Consideratione*, addressed to Eugenius.[30]

Not even St Bernard, however, made entirely clear this subtle distinction between direct and vicarious use of force; only recently, in 1149, he had reproached Eugenius for using the sword, in the form of Sicilian troops and the papal militia – led rather improbably by a cardinal known as Guy the Maiden ('milicie prefecit cardinalem Guidonem cognomento Puellam') – to overcome the seditious Roman commune and regain control of the city.[31] It was permissible, however, for the material sword to be wielded on behalf of the Pope by members of the new religious Orders of Knights of the Hospital of St John and Knights Templar; the latter's rule St Bernard supposedly had drawn up and caused to be accepted in 1128. Even if, in the case of the Hospitallers, the fighting brethren were distinct from the numerous priestly brethren in the order, it is clear that the whole order was associated with 'holy violence'.[32]

While St Bernard's forceful teaching was based on spiritual inspiration, the compilers of canon law and commentaries upon it also dealt with the subject. The greatest of these, Gratian (d. by ca. 1179), a monk at Bologna, went to the heart of the matter in Causa 23, Questio 8 of his famous *Decretum* (ca. 1140). Gratian discussed at length the obligation of ecclesiastical rulers to defend the Church; clerics, he reiterated from St Ambrose, should not bear arms, but they could exhort others to attack the enemy. He justified this by historical examples, and, while insisting there should be no shedding of blood by clerics, was somewhat equivocal about their role in military operations.[33] Other contributors to the debate included Huguccio (d. 1210), who was adamant that clergy could not take any active part in fighting, and the writer of an anonymous *Summa*, who was, however, prepared to allow some participation, for instance in self-defence.[34]

Although for various reasons, including temporary weaknesses of the papal see, kings and other lay rulers took command of the Second and Third Crusades, popes generally came to prefer placing the management of 'holy wars' in the hands of senior clergy. In particular they favoured members of the College of Cardinals, those papal electors and advisers sometimes styled 'senators of the Church' or 'members of the Pope's body', whose formal powers had been growing since the mid-eleventh century.[35] The first example of a papal legate commissioned to raise and lead an army against heretics in a Christian land was Cardinal Henri de Marcy, who was sent against the Cathars of Languedoc in 1181; he succeeded in capturing the castle of Lavaur.[36] Only a few years later, after the loss of Jerusalem to Saladin in 1187, it was reported that all the cardinals had sworn to take the cross.[37] In fact none did so, and the management of the Third Crusade was assumed by the Emperor Frederick Barbarossa – persuaded into the job by the same Cardinal Henri de Marcy – together with Richard I of England and Philip II of France. But in August 1198, when planning began for a Fourth Crusade, that great administrator, Innocent III (pope 1198–1216), intended that it should be in the hands of four cardinals, two of whom, Cardinals Soffredo and Peter Capuano, should go ahead of the army to Palestine.[38] It need not concern us here that the original plan went wildly wrong, that Peter Capuano was snubbed after the management had passed to secular French and Burgundian barons and their Venetian creditors – leading to the famous diversions first to Zara and then to Constantinople (1202–4) – even if some collusion in these events by Innocent III himself has sometimes been suggested.[39]

Maybe it was partly because of the Fourth Crusade and its outcome that Innocent III and his successor Honorius III (pope 1216–27) tried to ensure that the next papally authorised 'holy wars' would be commanded by churchmen. This was demonstrated first in the campaign against the Cathar or Albigensian heresy in south-west France, which became a major extension of crusading warfare against enemies of the Church within Catholic Christendom. At first Innocent appointed various prelates as his special legates to try methods of persuasion, but the murder of one of them, Pierre de Castelnau (14 January 1208) – presumably by an agent of the Cathars' protector, Raymond VI of Toulouse – made repression by force all the more inevitable. The main crusading army was entrusted by Innocent to Cardinal Milo, but the Abbot of Cîteaux, Arnaud Amaury, soon took over the command. In his report to the Pope, Arnaud Amaury described with gusto the taking of Béziers (22 July 1209): 'Our men did not spare class, sex, or age; almost twenty thousand perished within an hour; and after this total slaughter of the enemy, the whole city was sacked and set on fire.'[40] Arnaud Amaury, explaining this as the effect of divine fury exerting revenge upon the heretics, may have exaggerated the numbers slain, and may have spilt no blood himself, but his report should disabuse one of any idea that clerical warriors were less bloodthirsty than laymen.

Similarly, Honorius arranged for the Fifth Crusade, which Innocent had been planning since 1215, to be launched in 1218 under the direction of two cardinals. Its aim was to regain the Holy Land by way of the Nile delta. Cardinal Robert of Courçon was spiritual director, but Cardinal Pelagius, a Spaniard, was in charge of military operations. Pelagius was too assured and forceful; his intransigence – acting against the advice of John of Brienne and other military laymen – wrecked the expedition. He rejected favourable peace terms offered by the sultan, which would have handed back Jerusalem, central Palestine and Galilee to Christian control, and although the successful taking of Damietta might seem to have vindicated his policy (Pelagius claimed it for direct rule by the papacy) little was done to rebuild and strengthen the city over the next year. In July 1221 the crusaders were surrounded, outnumbered and their camp flooded. Pelagius escaped, carrying with him food and medical supplies, and finally in August had to accept much less favourable terms than were previously offered. It is hardly surprising that Pelagius's shortcomings provoked criticism. 'When the clergy take on the function of leading knights to battle that is certainly against the law,' commented the author of a polemical poem (ca. 1226).[41] For a long while most of the initiative in launching crusades passed back to lay rulers and commanders – not that they obtained much greater success.

The failure of successive crusading expeditions in the east, above all the humiliating capture of Louis IX of France (St Louis) and surrender of Damietta early in 1250, provoked criticism, even a suspicion that perhaps such wars – not to mention the use of crusading ideas to attack disobedient Christians – incurred divine disfavour. Worse was yet to come, with the return of Constantinople to Greek hands in 1261 and the fall in 1291 of the Palestinian port of Acre, the last remnant of the crusader kingdom established in the early twelfth century. A new generation of scholars reviewed the whole contentious question of coercive papal power and military violence. The most famous of them, the Dominican theologian Thomas Aquinas (ca. 1227–74), taught that the clergy could be supportive, but active participation was a violation of decorum, of what was appropriate to their office.[42] A much more robust line was taken by the canon lawyer Henry of Susa (b. ca. 1200; d. ca. 1271), since 1261 Cardinal Bishop of Ostia (hence known as 'Hostiensis'): in his *Summa Aurea* he defended unequivocally papal warfare against recalcitrant Christian rulers. Hostiensis had even had some military experience, as papal legate in the north Italian war against Ezzelino da Romano in 1259.[43] Others were called in 1270 to advise the new pope, Gregory X, who had been in Palestine when elected and was strongly motivated as the would-be revivalist of eastern crusading. Among these commentators upon the prospects and the morale of western Christendom was the Dominican Humbert of Romans, who set out to refute all the objections of the pacifists. He dealt with Christ's injunction to St Peter to put up his sword by suggesting that Christ meant Peter only to refrain on that particular occasion.[44] Normally Peter had an obligation to defend himself as well as to defend the Lord, otherwise he would be conniving at both homicide and (by not defending himself) suicide. From this followed the strict obligation of Peter's apostolic successors to defend the Church and themselves by force. Humbert had to acknowledge the traditional canonical ruling that the clergy should not shed blood, but he left the ethics of clerical warmongering ambiguous and flexible. 'God approves of the sword,' he insisted: it was the duty of prelates to concern themselves with Holy War, and of the Pope to take charge of a crusade; he cited the Old Testament to sanction priests encouraging warriors before battle (Deuteronomy, XX, 2–3).[45]

\* \* \* \* \*

Italy, however, became the main theatre of papally led Holy War from the thirteenth century onwards. For a long while popes did not hesitate to sanctify these territorial Italian wars as crusades, extending to their participants the attraction and privilege of indulgences; such campaigns, although directed against fellow Christians, were after all in theory also about defending the endangered Church.[46] While the recurrent issue of universal jurisdiction in Christendom had much to do with this, of enforcing the papacy's authority over all other rulers including that of the emperor, in practice much of the conflict related to the more pragmatic, less ideological policy of extending and imposing papal lordship in the central part of the peninsula, east as well as west of the Appenines. Apart from some episcopal estates in the region of Rome – the original 'Patrimony of St Peter' – these territorial claims rested on the successive deeds or supposed deeds of donation to St Peter mentioned earlier, to which had been added, but then disputed and denied to the papacy, the vast bequests of Matilda Countess of Tuscany (d. 1115), including lands in the northern region of Emilia.[47] It was the lawyer pope, Innocent III, and his successor, Honorius III, who systematically proclaimed and tried to enforce the claims, not shrinking from coercion by means of war. Their policy, which was to last for centuries, appears to have started with Innocent III's campaign in the March of Ancona against Markward of Anweiler, henchman of the Emperor Henry VI, who was trying to retain control of that region.[48]

Gregory IX (pope 1227–41) and Innocent IV (pope 1243–54) followed the example of Innocent III by expressing their belligerence verbally rather than by taking part themselves in the fighting against the Staufen. Henry VI's son, the charismatic Frederick II (1194–1250), was crowned emperor in Rome in 1220 but soon was in violent conflict with the papacy. It was provocation enough that he made his power base in Italy, having inherited the southern kingdom from the Norman line through his mother Constance, but his court became notorious for profanity and intellectual licence, tolerance of heresy and employment of Muslims, and the image was diffused of Frederick as a Messianic figure, the last emperor and lord of the world. Gregory IX excommunicated him, however, for disobedience, after he started on a crusade in September 1227 only to abandon it, and then – without making penance or seeking

17

absolution – set off again the following year, reached Jerusalem and crowned himself king. The success of this extraordinary adventure was brief and had depended on good relations with Muslim potentates, but it made the failure of so much papal effort to regain the Holy Land look ridiculous. During Frederick's absence in 1228–29 Gregory sent an army to invade the kingdom, which may have been 'the first army to fight under the banner of St Peter'.[49] An uneasy peace was made after Frederick's return, but in the later 1230s open war between pope and emperor broke out again, in Lombardy.

Innocent III's system of direct and centrally controlled papal government, meanwhile, with delegation of regional powers to rectors or legates, was being continued by his successors. These officials, usually cardinals, were often engaged in military campaigns or confrontations; indeed, in the early thirteenth century we enter the great age of the warrior-cardinal, which lasted for the next three hundred years. Unfortunately, as a rule it is very difficult to enter the mental world of these martial prelates, and their consciences, needless to say, are a closed book to us. They wrote few personal letters that survive, no diaries or memoirs. Only during and after the fifteenth century will it be slightly easier to gain some conception of personality. But in the papal wars of the thirteenth century they had many prototypes and predecessors. It was a time when war was becoming steadily more complicated and expensive; the papacy, like other powers, had to rely increasingly upon mercenary troops, often non-Italian, though even those raised within the papal lands by customary obligation might also expect to be paid.[50] The scale of the Church's investment in war and defence was enormous, and always increasing; it accounts for much of the trouble concerning taxation and fund-raising that the papacy was continuously to encounter.

Innocent IV, who withdrew from Rome first to his native Genoa and then to Lyon, was more politician and jurist than man of war, but in his own commentary on the Decretals, completed in about 1245, he laid down a strong ruling about the obligation to use force in self-defence, particularly in the cause of recuperating lost lands from the infidel,[51] and although he did not appear on the battlefield himself, some of his cardinals did. Innocent summoned a General Council of the Church at Lyons in 1245 mainly to discuss the continuing conflict with Frederick II and depose him. It was allegedly at this council that broad-brimmed scarlet hats with tassels on strings were introduced for the cardinals, to remind them to be ready to shed their blood, not so much as martyrs for the faith as for their role as defenders of the liberty of the Church.[52] Soon after the Council of Lyons the emperor fulminated in a reform manifesto: 'Whence have our priests learned to bear arms against Christians?' in reply to scurrilous invectives against himself as the beast of the Apocalypse.[53] The tone of the invectives, attributed to Cardinal Ranier of Viterbo, was relentless: 'This Prince of Tyranny, this over-thrower of the Church's faith and worship... like Lucifer... Destroy the name and fame of this Babylonian... Cast him forth!'[54]

There seems to have been no lack of warrior-cardinals ready for appointment to the rectorships of different regions, sometimes to hold greatly extended authority for the duration of military campaigns. Cardinal Ranier of Viterbo, for example, who had organised the massacre of the imperial garrison at Viterbo in 1243, had then become the Pope's vicar in Tuscany and central Italy, as well as the master of invective against Frederick.[55] From 1249 Cardinal Pietro Capocci (ca. 1200–59), formerly a lay military commander who had led a force against the Romans in 1231, was made legate and rector throughout central Italy. Capocci was charged with directing the campaign against Frederick II and organising an invasion of the southern kingdom.[56] After initial victories in the March of Ancona, Capocci's campaigns went less well; he suffered heavy losses and had to fall back on defensive tactics and regrouping his army with troops drawn from civic militias. His nephew Giovanni retook Foligno, but Cardinal Capocci made little headway in provoking rebellion and carrying out an invasion of the southern kingdom after the death of Frederick II. He nevertheless earns a place of honour (if 'honour' be the appropriate word) among committed military cardinals.

Even more distinguished in that class was Cardinal Gregory of Montelungo, the legate of Lombardy since 1238, who masterminded the defeat of Frederick II's siege of Parma in 1247. Gregory was praised by Salimbene, the eccentric Franciscan chronicler of Parma, for his knowledge of war, both theoretical (he allegedly owned a book on the subject) and practical: 'He knew well how to order the line of battle... he knew when to lie quiet and when to overrun the enemy.' Cardinal Gregory succeeded in 1247 in capturing the emperor's new fortress of Victoria, and even appropriated Frederick's camp pavilions and 'special equipment pertaining to war' ('peculiaria que pertinebant ad bellum').[57] In a letter to the Greek emperor in 1250 Frederick ranted:

These priests of ours wear cuirasses instead of liturgical vestments, bear lances instead of a pastoral staff and, for a eucharistic reed, darts and sharp arrows... Holy cardinals and prelates... one gives orders to the troops, another organizes the cavalry, another exhorts men to war, some leading the army and bearing the battle standards.[58]

Two other militarised prelates were involved – but not very gloriously – in the continuing conflict between the papacy and the Staufen dynasty, represented since Frederick's death in 1250 by his son Manfred. The struggle over the southern kingdom continued. Innocent IV's nephew, Cardinal Guglielmo Fieschi, led a papal army against Manfred in September 1254, after the collapse of a precarious peace treaty.[59] Manfred's victory near Foggia, the papal army's dispersal for want of pay and the cardinal's own flight made this a rather inglorious instance of clerical military campaigning. Even more galling was the failed expedition in May 1255 of the Florentine Cardinal Ottaviano Ubaldini (a cardinal from 1244 to 1273), who had led an army of mercenaries, and others who had taken the cross, to attack Lucera, the Muslim stronghold and colony established by Frederick II in Apulia.[60] Ubaldini was forced to capitulate. Later he was immortalised by Dante as 'il Cardinale', characterised as an epicurean eternally entombed in the sixth circle of Hell (*Inferno*, X, 120).

A prelate more successful in war than Guglielmo Fieschi or Ottaviano Ubaldini was Filippo Fontana, Archbishop of Ravenna. Perhaps it is surprising that Fontana was never created a cardinal, but he distinguished himself as apostolic commissary sent in 1252–53 to pacify the Romagna and then to oppose the tyrannical Staufen protégé Ezzelino da Romano. In 1256 Fontana raised an army to recapture Padua from Ezzelino, calling up 'soldiers of Christ, St Peter and St Anthony'. He rode out 'in Christ's name with a silver cross preceding him and the banner of the cross raised above him'.[61] According to Salimbene, two Franciscan lay brothers gave extraordinary service to Fontana in the attack on Padua; one of them, acting as standard-bearer and leader of the army, shouted battle cries from Old Testament sources, and the other, who had formerly been Ezzelino's military engineer, constructed a battering engine that in front spouted fire and behind was full of armed men.[62]

In the 1260s papal authority finally destroyed the Staufen and their allies in Italy. The main strategy was the adoption by Urban IV (pope

1261–64) of Charles of Anjou, brother of Louis IX of France, as his vassal to rule over Naples and Sicily.[63] The hope was – as before – that the papacy would be able to depend on a grateful and loyal dynasty in the south, to protect and to fight for, the interests of St Peter. As ever, the danger was that the adopted dynasty might overreach itself.

Charles was crowned king in January 1266 by Urban's Provençal successor, Gui Faucoi, Clement IV (pope 1264–68), and lost no time in hastening further south to win his usurped throne by force with huge financial support from the papacy. Cardinals Riccardo Anibaldi and Ottaviano Ubaldini accompanied the Angevin troops and granted absolution; the latter, as papal legate, continued with them as far as the border of the kingdom, but no cardinal appears to have been present at the bloody Battle of Benevento at the end of February, where Manfred was slain. The Bishop of Cosenza, Bartolomeo Pignatelli, was allegedly sent afterwards by the pope to have Manfred's corpse exhumed from the (papal) soil of Benevento and deposited in a distant river. Charles wrote a coldly gleeful letter to Clement: 'I inform your Holiness of this great victory in order that you may thank the Almighty, who has granted it and who fights for the cause of the Church by my arm.' Some years later, the deplorable fate of the glamorous libertine Manfred was immortalised by Dante: 'Fair-haired he was, beautiful and noble in appearance' ('biondo era e bello e di gentile aspetto'); Dante lodged him outside Purgatory to delay his entry (but only for thirty years), on account of his contumacious defiance of the Church (*Purgatorio*, III, lines 103–45).

The final end of the Staufen came two years later, with the downfall of Manfred's young nephew Conradin, who had inspired surprisingly wide support in Italy, including the city of Rome. Cardinal Rodolfo of Albano preached the crusade in February 1268 against this tragically doomed adolescent, and against the Muslim military base at Lucera, which held out for another year,[64] but in August Charles of Anjou's army overcame Conradin's forces at the Battle of Tagliacozzo. After this victory, Charles of Anjou again wrote in triumph to the pope, to bring 'the happy tidings which have so long been desired by all the faithful of the world... We have slain such numbers of the enemy that the defeat of Benevento appears insignificant.' Conradin escaped from capture, only to be recaptured near Rome and surrendered by his partisans to the armed forces of Cardinal Giordano, cardinal legate of the Campagna. Taken back to the kingdom, the boy was publicly beheaded in Charles's presence at Naples on 29 October. Dante found only few words to express the ultimate outrage, listing it in the confession of Hugh Capet about the iniquity of his descendants (*Purgatorio*, XX line 66), but the nineteenth-century historian Ferdinand Gregorovius – a German Protestant and nationalist even more anti-papal, pro-imperial and anti-French than Dante – represented it as 'the sentence of history that Germany should no longer rule over Italy...though', he added more hopefully, 'the struggle of the Staufen was successfully continued in other processes for the deliverance of mankind from the despotism of the priesthood'. Clement IV, who died only a month later, may have been rather shocked, but presumably he convinced himself that Charles of Anjou's mission to destroy Satan's brood had been for the good and defence of the Church.

Another favourable arrangement, made later in 1275–78, was Rudolph of Habsburg's gift to the papacy of imperial rights in the Romagna; the papacy had for long claimed the Romagna in vain by virtue of the historic donations.[65] This development, however beneficial in appearance, like the adoption of the Angevin dynasty soon committed the papacy to even more warfare in Italy. In the first place, all prospects changed regarding the southern kingdom when a conspiracy and rebellion in Sicily against French domination broke out in Palermo on the eve of Easter 1282 (known as 'the Sicilian Vespers'). Supported by the forces of Peter of Aragon, sent to claim for him the Staufen inheritance, this insurgency turned into a war that dragged on for the next twenty years.

The Pope at this time of humiliation for the papal–Angevin design was Martin IV (pope 1281–85), the French cardinal Simon de Brie (created in 1261). Martin was berated by the Franciscan Salimbene for being 'a strong hunter before the Lord', but if he was obstinate in pursuing war to make good the concession of Romagna, thereby causing many lives to be lost, he achieved little in the cause of Charles I of Anjou, only squandering most of the enormous funds put aside for a crusade in the east.[66] Cardinal Gerardo Bianchi of Parma was sent to Sicily in June 1283 to obtain unconditional surrender, but failed to do more than put down the rebellion in Naples.[67] In these closing years of the century, papal military campaigns were more successful in the north, where cardinal legates continued to head punitive military operations. Cardinal Bernardo of Provence reduced the city of Forlì to obedience,[68] while Napoleone Orsini, as papal legate in the March of Ancona, had a similar commission against Gubbio in 1300.[69] This is not to forget the outbreak of violence south of Rome between the Gaetani and Colonna clans in 1297–99, a war over landed possessions provoked by the seizure of a consignment of money by the Colonna; it was essentially a family vendetta between Boniface VIII (Tommaso Gaetani) and Cardinals Jacobo and Pietro Colonna. The Pope tried to dignify his campaign by issuing crusading indulgences, and, although he did not participate himself in any military action, he specifically ordered the destruction of Palestrina and other inhabited castles, for which he was reviled by Dante (*Inferno*, XXVII, 102).[70] Having vanquished the Colonna, however, in the end Boniface – whose papacy expressed the zenith of the medieval papacy's aspirations to universal authority – did not persist with violence. He gave way to Guillaume de Nogaret, the legal henchman of Philip IV, King of France, without a fight; his arrest at Anagni in September 1303 was a notable display of non-resistance. But it came at the end of two and a half centuries of extraordinary aggression and bellicosity on the part of St Peter's successors and their principal agents in central Church government.

There is no simple explanation for all this bellicosity. In part, as we have seen, popes were driven by obligation and immediate danger to provide defence for the sacred places and associations of Rome, their seat of dignity and divine authority. But they also used the physical sword – not only delegating it to secular rulers and commanders but often retaining its administration under clerical, but seldom personal, control – for the wider purposes of defending Rome and the Church. From the late eleventh to the thirteenth century military force was even used in furtherance of the papal claim to universal authority. It was also used against Muslims and heretics. But its most habitual use was to defend or regain control of lands, titles and possessions in Italy over which the Church claimed legal rights. This was to continue and to increase during the next centuries, always at enormous financial cost, which may help to explain the papal loss of momentum over organising crusades in the east. The arrest of Boniface VIII by the agents of the King of France meanwhile seems a fitting end to this introductory chapter. For by 1300, just as the heroic age of the Crusades was past, the empire's prestige and authority were much reduced. France remained for several centuries the most formidable secular power to not only dispute the authority of the pope over the Church, but also to determine the papacy's status in Italy.

# 2 Relapse and Renaissance, 1305–1458

## BABYLONIAN CAPTIVITY

For over a century after the humiliation of Boniface VIII there was no steady resurgence of papal political authority and military power, only phases of apparent recovery – some striking displays of bellicose leadership by individual cardinals – and daunting setbacks. The first of these was the papacy's removal of its base from Italy to Provence, often known as the Babylonian Captivity, although it was not an involuntary exile, lasting from 1305 till 1367 and resumed from 1370 to 1377. The second was the split in the papacy itself from 1378 to 1417, during which time there were two and, later, even three separate papacies or 'obediences' in different sectors of western Christendom. The fourteenth-century papal court already saw some facets of what has come to be called the Renaissance, in relation to cultural patronage, the pursuit of literary texts and other relics of classical antiquity. But it is only after 1420, when Pope Martin V brought the reunited curia back to Rome, that this word can be applied to the papacy not only with cultural reference but also with a political and institutional relevance, which will be discussed later.

The Italian political context during this century and a half gives a bleak overall impression, characterised by the lack of settled peace and security, the vacuum of both papal and imperial or any other authority over much of the peninsula, and the catastrophic climatic conditions and mass epidemics of the middle of the fourteenth century. Nevertheless, in the north, autonomous urban civic life continued its astonishing development. Florence (traditionally Guelf or pro-papal) and Venice (virtually independent) were two of the most successful examples, and both of them were far more important on an international scale than any city within the papal state. They were strong and rich enough on different occasions – respectively in 1309 and 1375 – to face war with the papacy; so, from the 1320s onwards, did Milan, the metropolis of Lombardy, dominated by the aristocratic Visconti dynasty.

Under pressure from Philip IV of France, Pope Clement V (1305–14), formerly Bertrand Got, Archbishop of Bordeaux, had stayed in France – or rather in the papal enclave of Comtat Venaissin – after his election and coronation at Lyons. In March 1309 he established the papal court in Avignon. In spite of the papacy's prolonged absence from its proper setting in Rome and the lands of St Peter, its military commitment in Italy would continue. Already in 1309 Clement declared war on Venice, which disputed papal overlordship of Ferrara. Cardinal Arnaud de Pellegrue was placed in charge of the papal army, and advanced in May 1309 through Asti to Parma, Piacenza and Bologna, raising belligerent mobs to take the cross and follow him. When he reached Ferrara in August he commanded a much larger army than that of Venice; he was able to block navigation on the Po and besiege the enemy force at Castel Tedaldo. This fortress fell in September, and according to Venetian reports those captured were treated atrociously, many being blinded.[1] Clement did, however, manage to avoid headlong confrontation with the emperor, Henry VII of Luxembourg, who invaded Italy in 1310–13 in his determination to have a proper imperial coronation in Rome.[2] Even if 'the crafty Gascon', as Dante called Clement, at first encouraged Henry's expedition, he subsequently responded to pressure from France and supported the resistance, never sending the letters that were intended to ensure Henry's safe entry into Rome.

Violent conflict was to arise, however, between the successors of Clement and Henry. The election as emperor in 1314 of Lewis of Bavaria was challenged by a rival and both claimants were rejected by John XXII (pope 1316–34), who himself had been elected only after a two-year delay. Formerly Cardinal Jacques Duèse, a lawyer from Cahors and protégé of the Angevin monarchy of Naples, John XXII, despite being over seventy, proved an exceptionally combative pope as well as a fiscal genius. His categorical non-recognition of Lewis, and declaration that the empire was vacant and devolved to himself, was bound to inflame all Ghibelline Italy, not least when he appointed as his 'imperial vicar' King Robert I of Naples. Hostilities broke out in Lombardy and Emilia between pro-papal or Guelf forces and those claiming to favour imperial hegemony, principally the Visconti of Milan. A new conflict between the papacy and the empire – or its *de facto* pretender and those who backed him – was unavoidable after Lewis declared in 1323 that the papal war against the Visconti was unjust. One uncompromising theologian, Agostino da Ancona, better known as 'Augustinus Triumphus', restated more forcibly than ever the case for supreme papal authority, temporal as well as spiritual, including the necessity of using violence against tyrants and others.[3]

From the other side, a radically opposed position was laid out by Marsilio of Padua in his *Defensor Pacis* (ca. 1324). Marsilio – an eminent teacher in Paris, from where he soon had to flee – argued audaciously against the whole thesis of Petrine authority and the plenitude of papal power. He maintained that ultimate authority lay with all Christian believers;[4] he proposed (not in very clear detail) that this popular authority, expressed in a council, should appoint its own figurehead or legislator to bring about peace in the world. In the course of his demolition of the existing form of ecclesiastical authority, Marsilio pointed to its provocation of wars, alluding to John XXII as 'this bloody and deceitful man'. He protested that the Pope even 'chose a priest from among his brethren or accomplices (who are called cardinals) and sent him with a large body of cavalry and infantry into the province of Lombardy for the purpose of attacking and killing Christian believers'. Here Marsilio was referring to the Pope's nephew Cardinal Bertrand du Poujet, who had served as cardinal legate in Lombardy since 1319, and whose main assignment was to overcome Matteo Visconti of Milan and his Ghibelline or pro-imperial allies and to prepare the way for the papacy's return to Rome. Years later, in a letter of 1357, Petrarch declared that du Poujet had been delegated by the Pope on a 'senile priestly military expedition' by the Pope against Milan, 'not...as Peter but rather as a Hannibal sent to conquer Italy'.[5]

Aided by cavalry sent by Philip of Valois, brother of King Philip VI of France, du Poujet at first had various successes, and in November 1322 was able to set up his headquarters at Piacenza, which had accepted the authority of the Church. In his support, John XXII's attitude was unreservedly aggressive. During a session of the papal consistory in October 1323 he was reported saying that he would teach Lewis's followers the meaning of ferocity, and ridiculing those of the cardinals who expressed fear of German savagery (*furia teutonicorum*).[6] In spite of many reverses, Cardinal du Poujet captured Modena in June 1326 and in 1327 Bologna, where he began to construct the massive fortress of La Galliera, intended to be both a defensive citadel and a residence for John XXII should he succeed in bringing the papacy back to Italy – an unlikely event, all the more so because the pope was now almost ninety. Du Poujet failed, however, to hold up Lewis of Bavaria's advance and its sequel in 1328, his highly uncanonical coronation in Rome, a ceremony at which Guido Tarlati, Bishop of Arezzo, officiated: Tarlati was a Ghibelline or pro-imperial prelate with a ferocious military record in Tuscany, commemorated in the well-known relief sculpture on his tomb in Arezzo Cathedral. But du Poujet was concerned less with an ideological struggle against the emperor than about regaining and securing control of papal lands and cities in northern Italy; this task was shared after September 1326 by Cardinal Giovanni Orsini, who held a parallel legation south of Pisa, Perugia and the March of Ancona. Though short of troops and money, and deceived by promises of support from John of Bohemia, son of the Emperor Henry VII, du Poujet remained on the offensive. He extended the war to Ferrara in 1333, but in 1334 faced rebellion in Bologna, when he was himself besieged in La Galliera for ten days, after which the fortress was sacked.[7]

The Avignon papacy made occasional efforts to revive active crusading in the east. Clement V had installed in Rhodes the Hospitaller Order of St John in 1307, intending them to serve – more actively than they proved – as front-line defenders of Christendom, and, although the Italian trading cities were not always supportive, there were various joint ventures. Following the Italian priorities of John XXII and the rather more pacific pontificate of Benedict XII (1334–42), and in spite of the distractions of the Anglo-French war and continuing instability of Italy, Clement VI (pope 1342–52) was anxious to take the offensive. As Cardinal Pierre Roger, he had previously served as a legate in the east; as pope he supplied funds as well as galleys to a joint Venetian, Genoese and Cypriot fleet that captured Smyrna, or at least its harbour and lower fortress, in 1344. This was a tangible Christian victory, even if the papal legate Henry of Asti and other commanders were later slain during a celebratory mass, and the retention of Smyrna as a papal dependency proved a difficult burden until it was lost again in 1402. Clement's crusading league against the Turks otherwise failed, though his successor Innocent VI (pope 1352–62) supported some further campaigns overseas, the fanatical papal legate and Carmelite friar St Peter Thomas was largely responsible in 1359 for capturing a Turkish fortress in the Dardanelles and Satalia (Adalia) was also seized from the Turks in 1361;[8] finally, a new expedition in 1366 led by Peter I of Lusignan, king of Cyprus, achieved the spectacular capture and sacking of Alexandria. The major port of Mameluke Egypt, which might have been used as a bridgehead on the way to Jerusalem, nevertheless had to be abandoned for lack of sufficient forces to hold and defend it, in spite of the desperate exhortations of St Peter Thomas.[9] Innocent VI had given only limited backing since he had resumed from Avignon an energetic military policy in Italy, on which it has been reckoned he spent as much 45 per cent of the papacy's income.

At much the same point in the mid-fourteenth century when the poet Petrarch was deploring the universal prevalence of war and violence, a symbolic papal sanction of military force, which was to become customary every year, was first recorded (1357). This was the papal gift of a sword to a selected ruler; a cap usually accompanied the sword, signifying the protection of the Holy Spirit.[10] This symbol, expressing the promise of divine favour in warfare, was an addition or variant to the older custom of presenting a selected monarch with a papal banner bearing the keys of St Peter. That custom, which may go back to such distant events as Leo III's gift to Charlemagne and Alexander II's gift to Roger I of Sicily in 1063, became associated with the conferment of the title of *Gonfaloniere* (banner-bearer) of the Church, which by the early fourteenth century had grown into a rather formal or ceremonial honour. The parallel office of Captain General of the Church usually carried more specific obligations of military service, and was most often conferred on an Italian prince with a professional military reputation, later even on a papal relative.[11]

The execution of Innocent VI's new papal offensive in Italy was largely owing to Gil Albornoz, a distinguished clerical lawyer, grand chancellor of Alfonso XI of Castile and Archbishop of Toledo. Albornoz had seen earlier military service against Muslims in southern Spain, having distinguished himself as apostolic legate at the Battle of Taifa

(1340) and the siege of Algeciras (1344). By his own account, at Taifa he had acted as a dynamic commander in the field, mounted on horseback, wielding a sword (even if not using it to draw blood) surrounded by attendant priests.[12] Appointed a cardinal in 1350, three years later this clerical warrior was sent to Italy with a small military escort and full powers as papal legate and vicar, described in his letters of appointment from Innocent VI as the 'angel of peace' upon whose strong shoulders heavy burdens had been placed.[13] It was a peace to be imposed by force and ingenuity in dealing with the regional warlords and itinerant mercenary companies infesting central Italy, with the sanction of dubbing the Church's enemies heretics or tyrants and promising an indulgence for its armed proponents.

Any notion of the physical appearance and presence of Albornoz eludes us; there are no contemporary portraits, visual or written, but he obviously had sharp intellect, stamina and vision. His letters to Innocent VI express his punctilious application to detail and forward planning, and his intolerance of bad discipline. In July 1354 he was advising the pope of the need to build a fortress at Viterbo, and warning his sub-ordinate captains to be wary of the wells at Città Castellana in case they were poisoned. On 23 January 1359 he wrote to order clergy in Amelia (far away in southern Umbria) that if they continued to bear arms – this is noteworthy – they would be arrested and imprisoned.[14] Like many great military leaders, however, Albornoz was often desperate for lack of funds and supplies, or of consistent support from the government that employed him. Innocent VI let him down by shortfalls of money in the 1350s, though he sent him congratulations for 'stitching up the lacerations of the Church, the Lord's spouse', in, for instance, the recovery of the castle of Bertinoro in September 1357.[15] Urban V (1362–70) treated him worse, by succumbing to French pressure and diverting resources to an abortive new crusading project in the east, instead of giving top priority to the papal state and the containment of Bernabò Visconti of Milan.

Albornoz had to depend mainly on professional captains and mercenary forces; his attempts to use recruits levied from the Romagnol peasantry were not very successful; but again and again it is clear that the overall campaign planning and field orders were his own. His Italian campaigns fall into two phases, separated by a period of about a year in 1357–58, when he returned to Avignon. The first phase was in the region north of Rome, directed against Giovanni di Vico, and in Umbria and the Marche; the second phase was concentrated more to the north, in Romagna. The offensives began with Albornoz urging Giordano Orsini to be more ferocious and to emerge from Montefiascone; Toscanella then fell in an assault (April 1354), Orvieto surrendered to the Church and the systematic devastation of the regions of Viterbo and Spello quickly led to the fall of those towns. In the March of Ancona and Romagna the forces of resistance to the legate became personalised by three designated 'tyrants' – Giovanni da Mogliano, ruler of Fermo, Galeotto Malatesta of Rimini, and Francesco Ordelaffi of Forlì. A story circulated that Malatesta, approaching Recanati with superior forces, sent a defiant message to Cardinal Albornoz, who replied, 'Here I am on the battle field. I want a hand-to-hand encounter with him!' Galeotto was appalled by the idea, commenting that he would be the loser – the moral loser – even if he won, because Albornoz was an elderly prelate whose function was to be fatherly. Later, after Malatesta was defeated at Padermo near Ancona in June 1355 and most cities in the March capitulated, Albornoz made peace, lifted all the ecclesiastical censures imposed on Malatesta and subsequently made use of his services as a military commander, though he was less conciliatory with Giovanni da Mogliano and Francesco Ordelaffi, both of whom betrayed pacts he made with them.

Cardinal Albornoz's vengeance could be terrible. His campaigns against the Ordelaffi were among the more ruthless operations. They included the siege in 1357 of the citadel of Cesena, a particularly memorable occasion since Albornoz's will was pitted against that of Cia degli Ubaldini, the wife of Francesco Ordelaffi, who had taken refuge there with her family.[16] The beautiful 'Madonna Cia' has a place in a long tradition of courageous and warlike Romagnol women; wearing armour, she first defended the town on horseback, then retreated to the citadel, having ruthlessly punished five disloyal townsmen and burnt the bell tower of the cathedral. Equipped with hundreds of Hungarian archers, sappers and colossal catapults to hurl boulders and flaming missiles, Albornoz ordered the citadel to be bombarded and undermined; one tower collapsed and another was on the point of doing so before 'Madonna Cia' gave in. Albornoz treated her person with a degree of clemency, however, sending her under escort to Ancona, but remained implacably hostile to her husband. Francesco surrendered at Faenza in July 1359, but subsequently joined forces with Bernarbò Visconti and opposed Albornoz from

Forlimpopoli. Albornoz had that town razed flat; its bishopric was removed to Bertinoro and a castle called Salvaterra was built on the derelict site. In August 1360 the cardinal crushed a fresh rebellion in the March of Ancona; those to suffer most severely were the inhabitants of Corinaldo, all of whom were slain, allegedly, except for widows and children.[17]

Crucial to the success of Albornoz's military mission was the possession of Bologna. Its citizens had placed the city under his control in March 1360, but this was unacceptable to Bernabò Visconti, who rallied Francesco Ordelaffi and other opponents of Albornoz. The cardinal travelled from Ancona to supervise operations against the Visconti army encamped against Bologna at Casalecchio, using a deception to make the enemy suppose he had quarrelled with his Hungarian military captain (Albornoz favoured the military qualities of Hungarian mercenaries over others) and intended to withdraw. His other major success against Visconti was at the bastion of Solera outside Modena in May 1363, but by then Urban V's support for Albornoz was becoming ambiguous, leaving it to him to continue the war if he considered it 'necessary', which was hardly an instruction inspiring confidence. Even if Albornoz's pacification of Italy by force was curtailed and impermanent, his efforts were lastingly expressed by the law code issued at Fano in April 1357, expressing his great qualities as an administrator as well as a military leader, and by the many fortresses constructed to his orders, the first at Viterbo (1354), where supposedly he laid the foundation stone himself. Other castles were built at Assisi, Gualdo, Terni, Narni and Montefalco. Two were particularly famous and long-lasting. One was the huge Rocca di San Cataldo at Ancona, begun in 1355, which was intended to serve in the future as a papal residence; Albornoz also attempted to make Ancona a naval base, with a papal war fleet under the command of one Rafaelle Roverini, to patrol and control ports along the Adriatic coast. The other famous fortress was at Spoleto, designed by Matteo Gattaponi da Gubbio and begun in 1362,[18] a site of central strategic importance in the papal state.

Albornoz, who was relieved of most of his duties in 1365 and died at Viterbo in 1367, was the exemplary warrior-cardinal for all time. His success in regaining Bologna in 1360 inspired John of Legnano, a pro-papal jurist who taught there, to enunciate strong statements about the right and duty of the Church to make war. His book *On War* (originally titled *On the City of Bologna and War*) was dedicated to the cardinal.[19] In the preface Albornoz is not only called the brother of Jupiter – meaning the Pope – but also compared to Ahab, King of Israel, who reluctantly 'changed his raiment and entered into war' (I *Kings*, XXII, 30). John of Legnano distinguished 'heavenly spiritual war' (the war in heaven provoked by the revolt of Satan), human spiritual war – the sort of war that the papacy might wage, and obviously wars on behalf of the property and possessions of the Church were lawful – and universal corporeal war. He argued that Christ's injunction to St Peter to put up his sword was only intended for one particular occasion, and that in principle Peter was right to take defensive action on Christ's behalf; indeed, John cited texts in canon law that authorised clergy to act in self-defence rather than to offer no resistance (which would amount to suicide), and which justified bishops going to war to defend their rights or to encourage others in battle. The theoretical case for active bellicosity on the part of popes and cardinals could hardly be taken further; in practice, as we shall see, it would be vigorously carried on in the next century and beyond.

## DIVIDED COMMAND

'Up then, Father, don't sit still any longer...And take care, as you value your life, that you don't come with a human force, but with the Cross in your hand like a meek lamb;' 'Peace, peace...alas, my father, no more war... Let war be directed against the infidel, where it should be.' Thus St Catherine of Siena, in a series of letters, urged Gregory XI (pope 1370–78) when he was on the point of returning the papacy to Rome in 1376–77.[20] Instead of heeding her rather naive appeal to come unarmed, he came with a force of 2000 under Raymond of Turenne, and it seems unlikely that he would have been able to impress the population of Rome by other means. If there was one clear lesson from the last seventy years, it was that the papacy had been obliged to stay in a safe haven in southern France because it was not physically strong enough to prevail safely in Italy.

In spite of all that Cardinal Albornoz and other papal legates had achieved, the returned papacy was far from secure on Italian soil. In 1375 a serious rebellion throughout the papal state had been fostered by Florence, known as the War of the Eight Saints on account of the puritanical anti-papal stance of the eight elected members of the special war committee in Florence. Florentine propaganda accused the prelates of Avignon of greed and arrogance, and plans to expand over Tuscany. To punish the rebellion there were brutal acts of suppression by the mercenary forces in papal pay. Cesena, in spite of having remained loyal to the Church, suffered harsher punishment than most. This was after Galeotto Malatesta had surrendered the city to the cardinal legate Robert of Geneva. The people of Cesena, however, in their indignation at the indiscipline of Robert's Breton and English mercenaries led by Sir John Hawkwood, had killed a few of them; a pardon was granted by the legate, but then set aside. On 3 February 1377 the mercenaries entered the walls by stealth and massacred many of the inhabitants, including women and children. This atrocity inspired a rhetorical lamentation addressed to the rulers of Italy, apparently composed by a Florentine as anti-papal invective. A curious dialogue also circulated expressing the outrage and disgust felt by lay people, which has been attributed to a notary of Fabriano writing at Perugia. The betrayal of the people of Cesena by their overlord, the Church, is emphasised, and the cruelty of such a reward for their good faith. 'Have you heard,' one of the speakers asks of his fellow, 'what horrible things have been done in Romagna, absolutely barbarian savagery, with one of the cardinals of the Roman Church looking on and ordering the soldiers into action?' ('unum ex Romanae Ecclesiae Cardinales aspiciente et iubente ut milites agunt').[21]

After the death of Gregory XI in 1378 papal authority was shattered by the double election that brought about the Great Schism of the western Church. A number of cardinals, mostly those of French origin, who had not wanted to leave Avignon,[22] refused to accept as pope Bartolomeo Prignani, Archbishop of Bari, who was elected by the majority in Rome and took the name Urban VI. The dissident cardinals withdrew to Fondi, south of Rome, and elected none other than Robert of Geneva, who took the name Clement VII (anti-pope 1378–94). It soon became clear that both the rival popes were exceptionally bellicose characters. Clement VII did not delay waging war on his rival to try to get possession of Rome, but his Breton mercenaries were routed at Marino in April 1379 by Urban's Romagnol mercenary commander Alberico da Barbiano. Urban allegedly presented Alberico with a banner inscribed 'Italy free from the barbarians', and Clement fled first to Naples then back to Avignon. He later devised a new war plan, but it required an army provided by Charles V, King of France – his principal supporter – and there was a condition that the king's brother, Louis d'Anjou, should become ruler of most of the papal state, to be known as the kingdom of Adria. This was not very realistic, and too much time was lost without any initiative being taken. Legal opinion was dubious, in any case, about the 'hard line' (*via rigoris*) of military action to end the schism; as the prominent French theologian Pierre d'Ailly, later a cardinal, pointed out in 1381, even if there were scriptural texts that might seem relevant, there was little basis in canon law since heresy could not be alleged against the supporters of either pope.[23]

On the Roman side, Urban's irascible character ensured no lack of violent action, some of it quite psychopathic; certainly from his election onwards force was readily used not only in his cause as legitimate pope, but as the instrument of an increasingly erratic and adventurous policy. While his ferocious legate in the Patrimony of St Peter (territory mainly north of Rome), Cardinal Napoleone di Manopello Orsini, achieved some success against the Vico from his base at Orvieto,[24] Urbanite supporters in northern Europe also invoked force on his behalf. In July 1383 the 'crusade' against the Clementines headed by Henry Despenser, Bishop of Norwich, achieved little, however, beyond the sacking of Gravelines and an unsuccessful siege of Ypres, which anyhow was an Urbanist city; Despenser never moved south into Clementine territory in France.[25] But the most exciting and shocking action was in southern Italy, over repercussions in the kingdom of Naples; here Urban, himself a southerner, was most directly involved. Because Giovanna I of Naples, descendant in the direct line of the original Charles I of Anjou, recognised Clement VII as pope, Urban declared her deposed in April 1380 and sponsored instead Charles of Durazzo, from a cadet branch of the same family, negotiating a large appanage for a nephew of his own, Francesco or Butillio Prignani. In July 1381 Urban crowned Charles, who had successfully seized control of the kingdom and apparently arranged for Giovanna to be strangled a year later. Clement, meanwhile, had sponsored for the kingdom yet another Valois prince, Giovanna's chosen heir, Louis I d'Anjou, Count of Provence, who gathered a large army of invasion in 1382, but his death curtailed any hopes of victory.

In 1383, however, Urban broke with Charles of Durazzo, resentful that he was unwilling to oppose Clement actively and unwilling to confirm favours demanded for the papal nephew. Urban even declared a crusade against his former protégé in February 1385. The Pope set off with troops, but was besieged for six months in the castle of Nocera by Alberico da Barbiano, the mercenary leader now in Charles's service. Not content with calling down anathema upon the besieging army, Urban imprisoned a number of cardinals who opposed his policy, had them tortured – jerks on the rope and vinegar and quicklime poured up their nostrils were among the alleged torments – and later, when he escaped to Genoa, arranged for them to be drowned. After Charles's death abroad in Hungary in 1386, Urban resolved to use force to resume direct control of the kingdom, which he may have hoped to confer on his nephew. In 1388, clad in armour, he rode out of Perugia with his troops, bound for Naples. At Narni, however, some of Urban's soldiers deserted; near Tivoli he fell off his horse, and thereafter had to be carried on a litter. At Ferentino the enterprise was abandoned, as its prospects looked hopeless.[26] One of Urban's most faithful and serviceable supporters, Pileo da Prata (ca. 1330–1400, created a cardinal in 1378), who had been relatively successful in gaining adherents to the Roman cause in northern Europe, and even urged the Pope to declare war on the King of France, deserted him in exasperation over this Neapolitan fiasco. Pileo joined the rival Avignon papacy, and was commissioned to lead the war against Urban, though he had to flee with the Breton mercenaries under his command when opposed at Orvieto in September 1389.[27] Pileo da Prata was not the only warrior-cardinal to desert Urban; in May 1387 Cardinal Tomasso di Napoleone Orsini had given up his modestly successful campaigning on Urban's behalf because of a quarrel with him, and Urban even sent forces against Napoleone for exceeding his authority in Umbria.[28]

The second pope of the Roman 'obedience', Piero Tomacelli, who took the name Boniface IX (pope 1389–1404), was more reasonable than Urban, or at least more inclined to work through others with the aim of achieving some stability. He received – although perhaps barely earned – the Forlì chronicler's accolade of 'victorious'.[29] One of Boniface's most important early acts was to crown as King of Naples Charles of Durazzo's young son Ladislas in 1390. Cardinal Pileo da Prata reverted to the Roman cause, receiving a red hat for the third time in 1391 (he would hence be known as 'the cardinal of the three hats'), and as Boniface's legate led the Roman militia against Viterbo in May 1392.[30] But Boniface had now to contend with a new challenge from 1392 to 1395, a revival of the scheme for a 'kingdom of Adria' embracing most of the papal state, which the anti-pope Clement VII was meant to confer in exchange for recognition as the true pope, either upon Giangaleazzo Visconti or upon Louis, Duke of Orleans. This scheme was nurtured by the tireless freelance agent Niccolò Spinelli, who had in the 1360s been associated with Cardinal Albornoz and could claim from experience to know how costly, wasteful and harmful to the papacy's reputation – in hiring armies, waging wars, building and maintaining fortresses – the temporal power had proved. This scheme could not have been implemented without major conflict, and fortunately perhaps for all parties it collapsed on account of French mistrust.[31]

Meantime Boniface had attempted, making at first very limited progress, to regain some control over the papal state. In 1389 he employed the brutal Cardinal Tomasso di Napoleone Orsini to attack with bombards the fortress of Spoleto, but this mission was a failure and Tomasso had to flee.[32] One successful device of the Pope's was the use of his own brother Andrea Tomacelli, who was appointed rector or governor of the March of Ancona, and pursued a short-term policy of stabilisation through the granting of apostolic vicariates to dominant families such as the Malatesta at Rimini, Montefeltro at Urbino and Trinci at Foligno, a policy that later popes would expend much effort in overturning for the sake of more direct control. Tomacelli could be ruthless in his methods, such as inviting the mercenary captain Boldrino da Panicale to a feast at Macerata in 1391 only to have him murdered.[33] Boniface's former chamberlain, Baldassare Cossa, made a cardinal early in 1402, was another violent henchman. He was sent to the Romagna as legate in January 1403 with the special task of recovering Bologna from the Visconti. Cossa succeeded in this, with the help of Carlo Malatesta and other local warlords,[34] and also recovered Faenza from Astorre Manfredi in 1404, first compelling him to resign his inherited lordship to the Church, and a year later having him beheaded.[35] According to the short account of Cossa's life by Dietrich of Niem, a German working in the Curia throughout the Schism as an apostolic secretary, Cossa had been a pirate in his youth, a heavy drinker and debauchee;[36] whatever the truth of this, Cossa certainly had money, whether from piracy, abuse of power in the curia or favourable credit arrangements with Florentine bankers. His forceful character enabled him to govern the Romagna effectively if perhaps brutally, and his legation was renewed by Innocent VII in 1404. Gregory XII (pope 1406–17), whose authority Cossa refused to recognise, deprived him of his office and heaped condemnations upon him, but Alexander V, elected in June 1409 as a rival pope by the Council of Pisa, which Cossa himself had organised, restored Cossa to his legation.

Cossa succeeded Alexander as the Council of Pisa's pope, taking the name John XXIII, in May 1410. The strong policy of war he had sponsored as legate of Bologna he now pursued as pope, against allied warlords or *condottieri* pursuing their own interests in central Italy, not to mention the rival Italian pope, Gregory XII. Thus the preoccupations and expenses of both these so-called popes were directly governed by war. In the south John XXIII supported Louis II d'Anjou against Gregory's XII's protégé, Ladislas of Durazzo. Ladislas had no intention either of acting as protector of a schismatic pope or of being a cowed papal vassal; instead, in the course of his extraordinary career he attempted to turn the tables and even to subject Rome and the papal state to Naples. In 1409 not only Rome submitted to him, but also Perugia and most of Umbria. A peace treaty, negotiated in June 1412 by Cardinal Rinaldo Brancaccio, was broken; John XXIII fled to Bologna, and the defence of the papal state seemed a lost cause; in 1413 Ladislas even attacked and ransacked Rome. All was saved, however, by his death in the summer of 1414.[37] A number of prelates, in particular Cardinal Jacopo Isolani as principal legate for Italy, were delegated to restore order and direct military operations against the warlords, especially Braccio da Montone, who was now threatening to take over large areas of papal territory. John XXIII was meanwhile obliged to attend the general council of the Church assembling at Constance. This body, summoned under the aegis of Emperor Sigismund to end the Schism, deal with heresy and consider reform, finally deposed John XXIII in May 1415.[38] Although Cossa was later rehabilitated as a cardinal, the name he had used was erased from the list of legitimate popes, enabling it to be adopted in the twentieth century by an incumbent of very different character.

The ethics of papal warfare was not on the agenda of the Council of Constance, apart from a written proposal that a prelate on his own authority should not declare war on another prelate, which left it more or less open for popes to declare war. Two separate motions in reform tracts boldly laid down that popes should not be bellicose nor enrol armed men to shed blood, and that the whole income of the Church should not be spent on hiring soldiers instead of succouring the poor. These ideas seem to have made no progress.[39] Fortunately the Great Schism was eventually resolved by the Council through talking rather than by fighting, but it seems remarkable that the use of force in defence of the Church had not been more called in question, considering the many papal and anti-papal military campaigns and copious bloodshed during the half-century of schism; there seems to have been a consensus that much greater scandals needed to be resolved. Some military operations even continued in the name of the Council of Constance. Cardinal Isolani, who had been reappointed as legate in Italy in June 1415, two years later had to undergo being besieged in Rome by the *condottiere* Braccio.[40] There were no military restraints placed upon the restored papacy in 1417, when Martin V was elected by the Council. It had a virtual mandate to use force against those who threatened it, including secular adventurers or rebels in the Italian lands of the Church.

Meanwhile the second high priority of the Council, to extirpate heresy, inevitably led to the use of force. It is clear that there was an element of panic, at least on the part of Sigismund and the upper hierarchy of the German Church and German society, on account of the teachings of Jan Hus. The proto-Protestant preaching in Prague of Hus and his followers attacked traditional clerical privilege, invoking scriptural authority and insisting on communion in both kinds for the laity.[41] In 1412 a crisis arose over opposition to the indulgence for support of the papal war in Italy against Ladislas. Hus was excommunicated but moved his mission to the countryside and smaller towns. No time was lost at Constance. Hus agreed to come to the Council to expound his views, but in spite of his imperial safe conduct he was put on trial and condemned to the stake in July 1415, only two months after Cossa had been rather more mildly dealt with. The result in Bohemia of Hus's death was a national as well as confessional rebellion, with military resistance expertly organised by nobles and gentry. This provoked a whole series of papally blessed campaigns attempting repression of his followers over the next twenty years.

## RENAISSANCE: THE EARLY PHASE, 1420–58

After the resolution of the Great Schism and the return of the papacy to Rome in 1420 a distinctly new period in its history and character began, which was to last for roughly the next century and a half. The background to this of the wider political history of Italy must not be disregarded, though it may not always be easy to keep in focus. An attempt to sketch the contours is provided in the Foreword to this book but some familiarity with the scene will have to be taken for granted in what follows, or the main themes will be lost to view.

With respect to the papacy, the 'new period' of the opening sentence above may be defined in various ways, but Renaissance is as good as any overall label. Recent studies[42] have emphasised as the dominant aspect a more monarchical role for the pope, clearly evident by the mid-fifteenth century, particularly because of the gradual collapse of the conciliar alternative at Basel (1431–49), and further increasing in the sixteenth century. One symptom of this by the sixteenth century was the growth in numbers of the Sacred College, accompanied by the decline and fall of the 'corporate power' of the cardinals.[43] It is true that by then the Sacred College became larger than it had ever been before, but it may be questioned whether the disappearance of the cardinals' corporate power was an essential feature in the papacy's enhanced role; had this ever existed except during papal vacancies? In any case, popes continued as always to lean upon groups and individuals among the cardinals. But undeniably a main feature of the 'Renaissance papacy', emphasised by a number of ideologues, such as Cardinal Juan de Torquemada in his *Summa Ecclesiastica* (1449),[44] and Domenico de' Domenichi in his *De potestate papae* (1456), was the re-establishment of more effective papal authority, sometimes invoking as papal predecesssors or prototypes Moses and Aaron as well as St Peter. There was less emphasis on the old claims of universal supreme jurisdiction, which had provoked so much trouble from Gregory VII to Boniface VIII, and a greater flexibility in dealings with secular powers concerning Church appointments and taxation.

An immediate concern was the realisation of lawful temporal power and diplomatic weight in Italy, enabling defence of the rock of St Peter and western Christendom against infidels, heretics and other subversive forces. An additional priority was the cult of splendour, based in particular upon regeneration of the city of Rome as a world capital. Indeed, it has been suggested, Rome became in this period a prototype of the early modern European metropolis, the seat of a complex bureaucratic structure and hub of diplomacy.[45] Obviously all this could not be achieved without maximised revenues, particularly revenues from the papal state, since ecclesiastical revenues from all over Christendom were becoming greatly curtailed by concessions and concordats, not to mention rebellions. In order to survive, dominate and flourish, for better or worse, the papacy almost inevitably became in many respects more like other Italian principalities; within its own zone of control in Italy it could perhaps even justify the use of compelling force, since its role of jurisdiction there was instrinsically different from the nature of its authority in the rest of Christendom.[46] To be respected, feared and efficient, it needed a reputation for armed strength and readiness to use that strength; in campaigns against secular enemies and non-compliant vassals, this would usually be without even the pretence of waging a holy war supported by indulgences.[47]

The initiators of this drama were Martin V (pope 1417–31) and Eugenius IV (pope 1431–47), who between them ruled over the Church for nearly a third of the fifteenth century. Martin was Oddo Colonna, a scion of the notorious Roman baronial family; before his election he had served as vicar of the Patrimony in 1413 and had a warlike reputation, which his enemies, particularly supporters of the Aragonese claim to the kingdom of Sicily, stressed maliciously.[48] Eugenius, a Venetian patrician, had a very different family background, but in his earlier career as Cardinal Gabriele Condulmer he too had some quasi-military experience, in 1420–22 when he was legate of the March of Ancona and in 1423 when briefly legate of Bologna.[49] Like Martin, he proved willing to devote enormous attention and expense to redeeming the papacy's lands and temporal jurisdictions in Italy. Under Martin, two events in 1424, the defeat at Aquila and death of Braccio da Montone, the principal tyrant of Umbria, have been hailed as a turning point in this long struggle.[50] Under Eugenius, one of the main figures still to overcome or tame was Francesco Sforza, the son of Muzio Attendolo Sforza (who had also died in 1424), with his power base in the March of Ancona.

Both these popes were also energetic in committing force against erring Christians. The effect in Bohemia of Jan Hus's death in Constance, the betrayal of his safe conduct, had been the outbreak of revolution. Martin V launched a campaign against the Hussites in 1421, commanded by his legate to Bohemia, Cardinal Branda da Castiglione (ca. 1360–1443, a cardinal since 1411). Castiglione had to flee after the Hussites raised the siege of Zatec.[51] In July 1427 Cardinal Henry Beaufort, as legate to

Germany and Hungary, launched a campaign in support of German forces after reaching Nuremberg, but he too had to retreat after vainly planting the papal flag on a hill near Tachov, which had just fallen to the Hussites. For the next year and a half he planned a new crusade from England, and succeeded in importing bow staves from the Teutonic knights and money from Rome, but when his expedition eventually set off in 1429 it was diverted to fight the French, much to the fury of Charles VII.[52]

Finally, in March 1431, Giuliano Cesarini (ca. 1360–1443), a cardinal since 1427 and now papal legate to Hungary and Bohemia, launched yet another doomed campaign against the Hussites. He set off with a huge force of cavalry, but in July the army was outmanoeuvred and routed. According to the account of this war by the theologian John of Segovia (d. 1458), Cardinal Cesarini raged more than anyone in favour of war against the heretics, ('Julianus autem, qui circa expedicionem hereticorum, ut via belli reducerentur, plus quam toto estuabat'). He expected the army to capture the town of Tachov easily, but nothing had been achieved but burning and devastation when news came that Procop, the priest leading the Taborites, was on his way. Cardinal Cesarini himself saw from a hilltop the approach of the dreaded war wagons and other equipment. The army broke up; Cesarini fled from the scene, without his cardinal's paraphernalia, riding non-stop in disguise ('Julianus, habitu mutato... nullo sumptu cibo nec de equo descendens, egressus est'). John of Segovia included these details in the first book of his long history of the Council of Basel,[53] where he must have met Cesarini soon after these disastrous events in Bohemia. Both of them began as moderate conciliarists, but otherwise had rather little in common; Cesarini was reconciled to the Pope, but John, who was one of those made a 'cardinal' by the conciliar anti-pope Felix V, was not among the few allowed to retain that title. He wrote the *History* in his retirement and semi-disgrace in the 1450s and also made the first Latin translation of the Koran. His pacific approach compared to that of Cesarini is demonstrated by his treatise *On sending the spiritual sword among the Saracens* (*De gladio mittendo spiritus in Sarracenos*), proposing the conversion of Muslims rather than fighting them.[54]

Eugenius IV continued the intense employment of cardinals and other prelates in military operations. A papal letter dated 28 January 1432 recites some significant points in support of the practice. It is addressed to the Bishop of Camerino, Pandolfo Almiano, appointing him papal commissary and lieutenant to the papal army opposing enemies and rebels of the Church in the Patrimony of St Peter and various cities and other places near Rome. The Pope declares that it is particularly appropriate and useful to have in the army a prelate thoroughly loyal to himself and expert in the matters in hand, who will carry out his policy, advise and assist him and stay in close communication; all military captains and officers are obliged to take orders from him, and he is granted full powers to restrain, to order into battle, or to punish.[55]

During Eugenius's absence in Florence in the later 1430s and early 1440s, two cardinals were particularly associated with papal warfare. The first of these was Giovanni Vitelleschi (1396–1440), the Pope's special deputy in Rome and central Italy, who was a master of sackings, massacres and summary executions. In 1435–36 Vitelleschi was responsible for the destruction of the Colonna stronghold of Palestrina (April 1437) and a lightning campaign of forced marches and massacres against Alfonso of Aragon, pretender to the throne of Naples, whom he nearly captured.[56] His military achievements (and atrocities) by no means diminished after he became a cardinal in August 1437, when his enormous stipend of 400 ducats a month for military services to the papacy was raised to 500 ducats a month.[57] He seized Bologna from Niccolò Piccinino, the commander serving Filippo Maria Visconti of Milan, captured and sacked Zagarolo, another Colonna fortress near Rome, defeated and decapitated Corrardo Trinci, the ruling lord of Foligno in Umbria, seized Spoleto and put to death the governor of the citadel.[58] A vast territory north of Rome came under his control, and he commanded a private army several thousand strong in knights and infantry.

In spite of his notorious cruelties, many – including the inhabitants of Rome itself – acclaimed Cardinal Vitelleschi as a saviour, a 'Father of His Country' (Pater Patriae) who had prevented the total breakdown of order. One Roman chronicler emphasised his courage and total commitment to the Church of Rome, maintaining that his cruelty was necessary.[59] There was even a bronze statue of him projected in September 1436, with inscriptions equating him with Romulus and the Emperor Augustus. This monument to a warrior-cardinal would have been the first statue of a triumphant military hero to be erected in Rome

Artist's conception of the proposed equestrian statue of Cardinal Giovanni Vitelleschi. Detail of fresco (anon., seventeenth century) (Tarquinia, Palazzo Comunale).

since antiquity.[60] In the Palazzo Comunale of Tarquinia, formerly Corneto, the small city north-west of Rome that the Vitelleschi family dominated, there is a mural painting dated 1629 that includes the artist's version of the projected statue of the cardinal on horseback. He is shown fully robed and hatted, bearing his baton of command; the setting is supposed to represent a meeting of the Roman civic council that commissioned the sculpture. In the same palace there is also a seated 'portrait' of Cardinal Vitelleschi, of about the same date, which includes his baton of command and helmet. It has been suggested that this might be based on a copy of the destroyed portrait head that, according to Vasari, Piero della Francesca painted in Nicholas V's apartments in the Vatican.[61] If that seems rather implausible, at least both works suggest that in the seventeenth century citizens of Corneto still took pride in Vitelleschi's violent reputation, or were meant to do so; but it is unlikely that these later portraits bore any to resemblance to him. Perhaps the nearest we can get to Vitelleschi's appearance and far from straightforward

'Portrait' of Cardinal Giovanni Vitelleschi, with helmet and baton (anon., seventeenth century) (Tarquinia, Palazzo Comunale).

character is the description by Niccolò della Tuccia, the Viterbo chronicler. Niccolò recalled him as a tall, well-built man ('di persona grande e ben fatto'), pale and a bit sickly ('infirmiccio'); clever, high-spirited, pompous and avaricious, even in many matters just and reasonable, but 'once he got an idea in his head, the whole world could not make him change his mind'.[62]

'The patriarch', as Vitelleschi was commonly called – not as a variant on *Pater Patriae* but because, since February 1435, he was titular patriarch of Alexandria *in partibus infidelium* – fell from power in March 1440. This was owing to Antonio Rido, governor of Castel Sant'Angelo in Rome, who is portrayed in a detail of Filarete's bronze doors of St Peter's. Rido arrested 'the cardinal patriarch', allegedly on the Pope's orders, and quickly had him put to death.[63] Among the rumours was a story that Vitelleschi was planning to seize the castle and then the papacy for himself, something unheard of except perhaps in the darkest days of the tenth century, but that such a rumour could circulate at all shows the degree to which brute force or the fear of it dominated papal politics. According to a contemporary source, Cardinal Vitelleschi unsheathed his sword and vigorously resisted arrest, thus displaying his total contempt for the canonical precepts about clerical non-violence.[64]

Different rumours about Vitelleschi's downfall may have been circulated by his rival, the Apostolic Chamberlain Lodovico Trevisan (1401–65). Another man of war, though he originated from an obscure non-military Paduan family, Trevisan was also a 'patriarch', with the title of Aquileia, in north-east Italy. Although not yet a cardinal, he had immediately succeeded to Vitelleschi's role and may even have engineered the latter's fall, for Antonio Rido was his man. Lodovico Trevisan's first job was to mop up the troops still loyal to Vitelleschi and reduce to obedience the regions of Viterbo and Civitavecchia.[65] Soon, however, he was directed to a bigger operation. Already on 4 June 1440 a special military standard was conferred on him, and together with a force of 3000 horsemen and 500 foot soldiers he proceeded to Tuscany to support Sforza and other *condottieri* in papal and Florentine service against Niccolò Piccinino; he was active in obtaining victory over Piccinino in the Battle of Anghiari on 29 June, commanding in person the right flank.[66] In recognition of his effectiveness, in July the red hat was conferred on him, a medal in his honour was designed by Cristoforo di Geremia to commemorate the event,[67] and a

Cristoforo di Geremia, medal of Cardinal Ludovico Trevisan, commemorating the Battle of Anghiari, 1440, obv. and rev. (British Museum, Department of Coins and Medals).

contemporary poem, which will be discussed later, praised his valour and leadership.[68]

In the early 1440s Trevisan was not only, therefore, the paymaster of Eugenius IV's forces, drawing on huge sums to buy troops, but, like Vitelleschi, if not quite so brutal, also a commander in the field. With a new commission in August 1440 as 'legate in Romagna with the army, with the aim of recovering the lands of the Church', he engaged for months in military operations with the general purpose of capturing Bologna. In spite of his large army, he had to call off the campaign in November, but in the following spring it was renewed with further huge expenditure from the papal Camera.[69] In August 1442, when Eugenius IV and Filippo Visconti turned against their protégé Francesco Sforza, Trevisan organised the campaign to recapture the March of Ancona for the papacy. He was described as an 'angel of peace', the same phrase that had been applied a century earlier to Cardinal Albornoz.[70]

Vitelleschi and Lodovico Trevisan were both men of strong physique and violent character, and one may assume that military operations were relatively congenial to them, or fitted them by nature. There were, undoubtedly, some rather more peaceable characters in the College of Cardinals or among aspirants to the papacy in this period, yet it is difficult to find a single pope or cardinal who consistently opposed war on principle. One exception – though only in part an exception – was Eugenius's successor Tommaso Parentucelli, Nicholas V (pope 1447–55), who declared at the beginning of his pontificate that he wanted war with no one and that his only weapon would be the cross.[71] His biographer, Giannozzo Manetti, testifies that he was determined from the outset to end the long series of military campaigns launched by Eugenius IV.[72] The humanist Platina, in his history of the popes written in about 1470, recalled that he was a sincere lover of peace and quiet.[73] Even before Cardinal Parentucelli became pope he had had experience as a pacifying arbitrator between conflicting secular powers, first in 1422 in the service of his mentor and employer Cardinal Niccolò Albergati and then on his own account.[74] And he had probably been shocked when working in the Camera Apostolica in 1445 to find just what enormous sums he had to authorise being paid to military contractors,[75] money that he probably felt would be much better spent on books or buildings, for both of which he had a passion. The costs of defence, let alone of waging war, continued remorselessly to rise. They included keeping fortresses and fortifications in repair, as well as stocking munitions and hiring soldiers, usually in companies commanded by Italian mercenary captains who obtained high fees.

In fact, during his pontificate Nicholas was by stages forced away from the pacific view of his office with which he began, having had to accept its temporal claims and obligations. He probably spent more money on fortifications in central Italy than on any other sort of building: restoring city walls, reconstructing castles such as Nepi, Città Castellana and Spoleto, even turning the Vatican itself into a fortress.[76] He took advantage, nevertheless, of the new situation resulting from the death of Filippo Maria Visconti, Duke of Milan, in 1447, and welcomed Francesco Sforza's aspirations to succeed Visconti, his father-in-law, not least because as Duke of Milan he would no longer need his earlier power base in territories of the Church. After a brief republican interlude in Milan Sforza achieved his ambition. As matters turned out it was not the peacemaker Nicholas V but Duke Francesco Sforza, the Venetian Republic and Cosimo de' Medici of Florence who put most effort into contriving the Italian non-aggression treaty signed at Lodi in December 1454. Nicholas V, apprehensive of what Alfonso, King of Naples, would do, and constantly suspicious of sedition after the Porcari plot against himself early in 1453, dithered for months before ratifying it (February 1455), though he had eventually to muster enthusiasm, declaring, so his biographer Manetti records, that a general peace had always been his aim, and, if this were achieved, united Christian forces could at last deal with the Ottoman Turks.[77] Unfortunately, after Nicholas's death later in 1455, the aims within Italy of the Peace of Lodi came to be no more respected by the papacy than by the secular powers, in pursuit of their separate interests.

Meanwhile Ottoman aggressions in the eastern Mediterranean had reinvigorated the call to holy war or Crusade against Islam. This other martial obligation weighing upon the papacy accompanied if not outweighed the Italian area of ecclesiastical warfare in the Renaissance period. In both cases there was active involvement by popes and cardinals that went far beyond the non-violent roles of exhorting and absolving Christian combatants. From the reign of the first Venetian pope, Eugenius IV, the papacy was trying to revive something of the crusading initiative of the great mediaeval popes from Urban II to Innocent III. In this context, the term 'Renaissance papacy' has a special resonance, particularly in the mid–fifteenth century in 1471, from the time of Eugenius IV to the accession of Paul II in 1471.

Some cardinals were directly involved in military and naval action against the Turks. One of these, Giuliano Cesarini, whose narrow escape from a Hussite army in 1431 has already been mentioned, eventually lost his life on the battlefield. This was in the disastrous crusade of 1444, when the naval task force, accompanied by the Pope's nephew Cardinal Francesco Condulmer, failed to reach the Black Sea (Condulmer arrived back in Rome, however, in January 1446) and Cardinal Cesarini's overland expeditionary force was defeated at Varna in the Danube delta. Aeneas Sylvius Piccolomini (later Pope Pius II) wrote in 1444, on hearing the news that Cesarini was missing, that he had never had good fortune in war, no doubt alluding to the Hussite campaign of 1431, and was probably dead.[78] Aeneas later claimed to have more certain information about Cesarini's death at Varna, that he had been wounded by three arrows, and on his retreat fell from his horse in a marsh. There was some suspicion that he had got his deserts for encouraging Vladislas, King of Poland and Hungary, to break his word to the Turks, ratified in a recent treaty, and launch a new but ill-fated attack on them.[79]

The challenge became even more urgent upon the fall of Constantinople in 1453. Since the higher clergy of Spain were most prone to the military tradition of defending the faith against the infidel, it is not surprising that Nicholas's successor in 1455 was the Archbishop of Valencia, Cardinal Alfonso Borgia, Pope Calixtus III, to whom was attributed a few years later as axiomatic: 'The palm of glory grows nowhere but on the battlefield.'[80] Calixtus gave war against the Turks absolute priority.

Cardinal Juan Carvajal (1400–69, created a cardinal in 1446) was dispatched to Hungary to support John Hunyadi and the Franciscan preacher Giovanni da Capestrano against the expected Turkish land offensive, which culminated the following July in the siege of Belgrade. The Christian forces, however, triumphed at Belgrade, repelling the invaders, who had hoped to advance up the Danube to Buda. Cardinal Carvajal himself played an active role in this operation, and sent a detailed account of it to Francesco Sforza, for whose help he had been appealing.[81] A naval campaign against the Ottomans was also planned by Calixtus. In this, Cardinal Lodovico Trevisan, who continued in office as Apostolic Chamberlain or chief finance officer of the Church, was to play the most important role; in December 1455 he was not only responsible for the construction of a papal fleet, but appointed to be 'the apostolic legate, governor general, captain and general *condottiere*' in charge of it.[82] By the end of May 1456 ten galleys were ready, and the cardinal joined them some weeks later, though it was not until early August that they left Naples for the Aegean. Mitilene and other islands, including Samothrace and Naxos, were liberated by the end of the year, and the fleet's base was established at Rhodes. There are no detailed sources for the campaign but Cardinal Trevisan apparently defeated a Turkish assault on Mitilene in August 1457 and captured many Turkish vessels. Calixtus expressed full confidence in his command and urged him to attempt to defend Cyprus.[83] The cardinal's portrait by Andrea Mantegna (Gemäldegalerie, Berlin; reproduced on the dust jacket of this book) shows a tough-looking character in late middle age, with a dark jowl, broad shoulders and a determined expression in his eyes. It must have been painted fairly soon after his return to Italy in 1459. Trevisan attended the new pope's congress or war conference at Mantua, and the chronicler Andrea Schivenoglia described him on arrival there as 'aged sixty, a small, dark, hairy man, very proud' ('homo pizolo, negro, peloxo, com aìero molte superbo e schuro').[84]

Among the cardinals of this dangerous period perhaps the most determined to inflict vengeance upon the Turks was the one who had in person suffered the horrors of the siege and capture of Constantinople. This was the Greek Cardinal Isidore, Metropolitan of Kiev and All Russia, one of the Orthodox upper clergy who had accepted union with the Roman Church in 1439. He was sent as papal legate to the last Byzantine emperor in 1451, taking with him a company of 200 archers, raised at his own expense. Isidore was wounded in the fighting when the city was captured in 1453, but survived by changing clothes with a corpse (allegedly the cadaver was left wearing the cardinal's robes and hat) and eventually found his way to Venice.[85]

\* \* \* \* \*

What was the attitude of scholars, particularly of humanists, scholars of the ancient classical languages, to all this active belligerence of the Church? It would be hard to find a voice among them raised in protest against war with the infidel Turks, particularly after the fall of Constantinople in 1453. Many of them wrote exhortations to take arms and fight 'these barbarians'.[86] Papal war against the professedly Christian enemies of the Church in Italy was also acceptable to most of the growing but heterogeneous category of 'Renaissance' humanists; in general, war was a theme that gave them endless opportunities for employment, writing letters, orations, histories, treatises, poetic verses, eulogies and epitaphs. An example of a war poem, already mentioned, is the lengthy composition *Trophaeum Anglaricum* about the Battle of Anghiari and the inspired military leadership of Cardinal Lodovico Trevisan. The author, Leonardo Dati (1401–77), was a young Florentine humanist badly in need of a job; he dedicated the poem to the cardinal, who is of course given all the credit for the victory over Niccolò Piccinnino.[87] Lodovico's initial caution is praised as much as his impetuosity on the day of the battle, which was the feast of St Peter and St Paul. According to the poem, on the previous night he had had a vision of St Peter, who told him: 'Tomorrow you must fight, and I shall assist you.' Cardinal Lodovico is compared to the greatest captains of antiquity, from Alexander the Great to Hannibal, for encouraging his officers, haranguing the troops, rushing always to the most dangerous spots on the battlefield.[88] The historian Biondo of Forlì (1392–1463), from 1434 a papal secretary under Eugenius IV but previously Vitelleschi's chancellor in the March of Ancona, defended his former employer for his good service to the papal state as a military leader, even though he was a terrible priest. He compared him to Pope Leo IX, the victor of

Civitate in 1053.[89] Even Nicholas Cusanus (a cardinal since 1448), who was dismissive of the donation of Constantine and had presented his great work, *De Concordantia Catholica*, to the Council of Basel in 1434, argued that St Peter's successor was, at least figuratively, the captain of an army,[90] and he unfailingly supported later papal wars.

A few, however, of the humanists employed in the curia of Eugenius IV did not conform in approving its more bellicose aspects. The Florentine Poggio Bracciolini (1380–1459), another papal secretary under Pope Eugenius, ridiculed the military gravity of warrior-cardinals in a story he told about the great Albornoz. When engaged in a battle in the March of Ancona, Poggio recounts, 'the cardinal urged the soldiers into battle with many prayers ('hortatur milites ad pugnam pluribus verbis'), and assured them that those who were killed would dine with God and the angels, promising remission of all their sins. Albornoz then retired from the heat of combat, and one of the soldiers asked him: 'Why don't you come with us to this dinner?' The cardinal replied, 'I am not accustomed to eating at this time of day. I don't yet have an appetite, ('tempus prandii nondum est mihi, quoniam nondum esurio').[91] But Poggio took a more serious tone concerning Cardinal Vitelleschi in his book *De varietate fortunae*. In the original version he declared there was no man in his time more wicked ('Nihil iniquius hec etas conspexit'); he subsequently omitted this, but still castigated Cardinal Vitelleschi as a man contemptuous of peace and repose ('erat animus pacis atque otii impatiens'), pointing to the cardinal's fall from power as an example of fortune's just rewards.[92] Likewise Lorenzo Valla (d. 1457), though himself a Roman, did not share his fellow citizens' adulation of Vitelleschi, and described him as diabolical.

In spite of holding an office within the papal chancery, Lorenzo Valla fiercely criticised Eugenius IV's wars and the whole aggressive trend in papal politics. In a famous tract (completed ca. 1443–44) he denounced as a forgery on philological grounds the donation of Constantine to Pope Silvester I, the earliest of the papal 'title deeds' but a text that for centuries was known to have no real legal validity and in any case had been overtaken by later 'donations'. Valla used this academic exercise as a pretext for more general invective:

How barbaric the government of priests often is! If people were not aware of this before, now it is plain to see from that monster and portent, the cardinal and patriarch Vitelleschi, who soaked in blood the sword of St Peter which cut off Malchus's ear, and by which sword he himself has perished. Popes use war, not law, against peaceful cities and sow discord between cities and princes; they squander money taken from people of goodwill on hordes of cavalry and footsoldiers.[93]

Valla even fantasised that Pope Silvester I might have refused such a donation, had it really been on offer, bearing in mind the great problems that would arise about raising taxes, conserving funds and paying armies; he might have foreseen that he would be caught up inevitably in the violence of power politics, punishing offenders, waging wars, destroying cities, devastating regions with fire and iron.

Directly or indirectly, for better or for worse, the papacy had done much to advance the art and practice of warfare in the fourteenth and fifteenth centuries. Just as it is striking, to say the least, that the papal zone of government in Italy was precisely the area where many of the leading military captains of the day were to be found, and the best foot soldiers recruited,[94] so is it remarkable that military architecture in its dominions was so often innovatory and in the lead for its time. This has been noted in the case of Cardinal Albornoz's fortress building, but a century later would be even more evident. Leon Battista Alberti, the Florentine intellectual polymath employed as a scriptor in Eugenius IV's chancery, wrote in the 1440s that 'most victories are gained more by the skill of architects than by the conduct or *fortuna* of generals'.[95] Although it is difficult to prove that as an architect Alberti did much more for the papacy's defences than offer lofty opinions, such as an insistence on the angled rather than the vertical bastion, his precepts certainly seems to have been upheld by Nicholas V and successive popes and cardinals, whose heavy investment in military building will be further illustrated below, and which typified in an outward and visible way the reinvigorated papacy.

# 3 Pius II (1458–64): warmaker and historian of war

Aeneas Sylvius Piccolomini became Pope Pius II in September 1458 after only two years as a cardinal. This former imperial secretary, poet, orator and diplomat personified many of the qualities already noted as characteristic of 'humanist' learning, above all a fascination with antiquity, with verbal expression and the proper use of Latin, and the study and writing of history. Not very memorable in appearance – no one portrait of him, whether medal or sculpted bust, seems greatly to resemble another, though the most convincing are double-chinned and irritable-looking – he was an extraordinary figure to occupy the throne of St Peter. Warfare was not the least among his interests, whether waging war in the name of the Church or writing about it and the problems to which it gave rise. Pius's irascible and – in view of his more humane traits – rather surprising bellicosity and sense of military obligation as pope, almost in the style of Gregory VII as 'dux et pontifex', is the main justification for devoting a whole chapter here to his short, six-year pontificate. But, in addition, his aims and his intellectual interests make him in the widest sense the most characteristic of Renaissance popes, and, thanks to his self-revealing pen, more is knowable about his thoughts than about almost any other pope, of any period.

## PIUS AND THE IDEA OF WAR

Only a short while before his accession Aeneas had written a dialogue about the donation of Constantine and its implications. In it he accepted Valla's contention that the donation was a forgery, but argued that long acceptance in principle itself created validity and that it was much better for people to be ruled by a good priest than by a good layman; he justified, in other words, the papal state and the effort and expense of defending it. Aeneas conceded that waging war or enforcing judgement by bloodshed was forbidden to priests, but he maintained that they possessed power in such matters even if in practice it might be best

Marcantonio Raimondi, engraved profile of Pope Pius II (based on medal by Andrea Giacolati) (Warburg Institute).

delegated to professional military captains and provincial governors or magistrates.[1] He also compiled a series of *Lives of Famous Men*, in which he included several cardinals, among them Eugenius IV's nephew Francesco Condulmer, whom he praised for his naval enterprise in 1444, mentioned in the previous chapter. But Aeneas also wrote in praise of secular rulers; prominent among these was Alfonso V of Aragon, the papally approved King of Naples who died just before Aeneas's accession as pope. In the latter biography Aeneas mentioned Cardinal Giovanni Vitelleschi; though critical in some respects, he expressed admiration for Vitelleschi's military qualities and their outcome for the papal state.[2]

After he became pope, Aeneas Sylvius retained an exceptional measure of direct control in the several war projects to which he was committed: overseas against the Turks, and in Italy against disobedient vassals and to restore the integrity of the papal state. 'He undertook war,' wrote the humanist Platina, himself a former soldier, 'for the safeguarding of the Church, for the peace of Italy, for the defence of religion, for the safety of the whole of Europe.'[3] Platina was a very loyal biographer of Pius, being beholden to him for a sinecure in the papal chancery, and he provides a vivid pen portrait of the Pope: short in stature, prematurely white-haired, with delicate hands and rather small feet.[4]

In his autobiographical *Commentaries*, Aeneas reveals a fascination or even positive zest for war, although he sometimes attempted to deny it. There were war clouds already looming over the succession to the kingdom of Naples in the months before he was elected pope in 1458, since Calixtus III had refused to recognise Alfonso's son Ferrante as heir to the throne and declared that the kingdom had reverted to the papacy. Aeneas was convinced that Pope Calixtus was preparing an army to seize the kingdom by force and bestow it upon one of his Borgia nephews.[5] Calixtus's death put an end to this, and one of Pius's first acts as pope was to recognise Ferrante, so that he could claim to have begun his reign as a peacemaker, but in the summer of 1460 war nevertheless broke out between Ferrante and René d'Anjou, the rival claimant to the kingdom, who had French backing. Both sides could call upon various supporters in Italy, Ferrante being able to rely above all upon Pius and Francesco Sforza, Duke of Milan.

At the point in his *Commentaries* where Pius records the siege and sacking of a castle held by Savello Savelli, a pro-Angevin opponent of

King Ferrante and the papacy, Pius quotes from a speech he made to the cardinals, declaring,

> We do not love war nor do we of our own will take up arms, nor do we fight for a trifling cause… We are not the first who have taken up arms for the kingdom of Sicily which belongs to the Church. Almost all of you can remember Eugenius IV and Martin V. Your fathers have seen Clements and Bonifaces and Nicholases. Who of them did not involve himself in war? [...] When justice and necessity compel we are ready not only to fight but to risk our life.[6]

He had affirmed a few months earlier that he would be ready to face death, if need be, in retaking possession of Rome against rebellious gangs supported by the mercenary captain Jacopo Piccinino: 'To die for Rome and in Rome, to meet death for the Patrimony of St Peter is glorious.'[7] Similarly in 1463–64 he insisted that he intended to go east with the crusading fleet. This was the 'bellum necessarium' that from his accession Pius was always determined to wage, and had tried to launch in the congress or diet held at Mantua from June 1459 to January 1460. It had had to be postponed not only because of logistical problems but also owing to the outbreak of war in central and southern Italy.

In October 1463 Pius had the text read aloud in consistory of a bull containing his solemn commitment to accompany a task force against the Turks the following June, embarking at Ancona together with all able-bodied cardinals.[8] According to Pius's version of his speech to the cardinals announcing the operation, he had declared that, like Jesus Christ,

> We too will lay down our life for our flock… We will embark, old as we are and racked with sickness, and endure a voyage to Greece and Asia. But some one will say: 'And what will you do in war? [...] Will you go into battle? What good will an army clad in cassocks do in a fight? What good will the whole order of cardinals do in a camp? [quid togata valebit in pugna cohors? Quid sacer ordo Cardinalium prestabit in castris?] They will hardly endure drums and trumpets, not to speak of the bombards of the enemy.[9]

He then clarified that he would not himself engage in combat, he was not strong enough, though it is left unsaid whether younger and stronger prelates might not at least defend him and themselves from being hacked to death, crucified or impaled by the Turks. 'We do not go to fight in person, since we are physically weak and a priest, whom it does not befit to wield the sword. We shall imitate the holy Patriarch Moses, who, when Israel was warring against the Amalekites, stood praying on the mountainside.'[10] Fortunately Pius did not have to put this to the test (what if there had been no convenient mountain near the scene of battle to which he could retire, or what if his physical weakness prevented him from keeping his arms raised up, the detail about Moses's participation which he does not mention?). For Pius died at Ancona, the port of embarkation, and the whole expedition was called off.

Although Pius may have implied that even if his strength permitted he would not fight in person, there is a passage in the *Commentaries* about Dietrich von Mors, Bishop of Cologne, where he refrains from judgement about whether or not priests ought to bear arms. Dietrich, even at the age of seventy, 'could mount his horse without help and carried arms as lightly as a youth'. But then, Pius adds,

> the bishops of Germany don cuirasses, breastplates and helmets and at the need of their churches and sometimes at their own pleasure wage wars as kings do and take part in battles [induunt loricas ac thoraces et galeas episcopi Germaniae... pro sua libidine tanquam reges bella gerunt intersuntque preliis]. Whether this is becoming or not we do not say. Laws held sacred in one province are often condemned in another.[11]

Pius, therefore, took an ambiguous but generally approving stance about papal commitment to military violence. At the same time, and on the more literary and aesthetic plane, he expressed serious interest in military matters. As a humanist scholar he was extremely well read concerning the wars of Greek and Roman Antiquity recorded by classical authors; even the title he chose for his autobiography refers to Julius Caesar's *Commentaries* on war. There is a famous passage in it about his meeting at Tivoli in 1461 with Federico di Montefeltro, Count (later Duke) of Urbino. Pius raved about the beauty of the troops drawn up in battle formation, 'with the brightness of their arms and equipment of horses and men. For what fairer sight is there than troops in battle array?'[12] But this artistic zest barely concealed his commitment to reality. After a lively discussion as to whether in antiquity military captains were armed as effectively as in the present, in which the Pope insisted (against Federico's opinion) that the Trojan War was a major conflict, he coolly urged the people of Tivoli to submit to the building of a huge fortress, which it turned out would depend on the provision of their own unpaid labour.[13]

As a humanist historian Pius could hardly have avoided writing extensively about war, which according to classical tradition was the central event in human history, and a surprisingly large amount of space in his *Commentaries* is devoted to describing military campaigns. Indeed, in the thirteenth (unfinished) book, started in 1464, he muses about its becoming an account of the forthcoming war against the Turks, and about the difficulty facing a historian who writes about events still happening, unable to see their outcome and make judgements.[14] When welcoming Duke Francesco Sforza to the Diet of Mantua in 1459, his praise of Francesco's father Attendolo Sforza as 'a second Ajax in battle, a second Nestor in counsel; he feared no man but inspired fear in all' typifies his veneration of heroic warriors. Francesco, he added, even surpassed his father, because he had committed himself to fighting for the Church.[15] Pius wrote at greatest length (particularly in Books IX–XII of his *Commentaries*) about the war, already mentioned, over the Angevin succession claim to the kingdom of Naples and Sicily.

This war, which broke out early 1460, at first went badly for Ferrante, Pius and their allies, but Pius appreciated that his *condottiere* Simonetto had made a bad mistake by urging Ferrante to mount a sudden assault on the castle of Sarno, where he had penned up the Angevin forces, some distance north-east of Naples. The attacking army was mown down by the handguns (*schioppetti*) of foreign mercenaries who had previously deserted from Ferrante's army – Simonetto himself being among those killed – which caused Pius to digress about the significance of these weapons in contemporary war.[16] Lessons were learnt and the papal and Aragonese armies on the whole did better in the subsequent fierce campaigns in the Abruzzi and the March of Ancona. Their forces were pitted against the commander in René of Anjou's service, Jacopo Picccinino, and against Jacopo Savelli and other turbulent figures, above all the recalcitrant papal vassal Sigismondo Malatesta, Lord of Rimini, sworn enemy of King Ferrante and of Pius's favourite military captain, Federico di Montefeltro. There was a campaign nearer Rome, too, against Everso of Anguillara, who with his son-in-law Antonello re-occupied Viterbo in September 1460. These Italian campaigns – officially designated wars for the defence of the Church – needed to be won, so Pius insisted in a lengthy recapitulation, before he could turn his attention overseas.[17] He acknowledged no essential differences between the papacy's main enemies: 'We fought for Christ when we defended

Ferrante. We were attacking the Turks when we battered the land of Sigismondo.'

## PIUS AND HIS CARDINALS AT WAR IN ITALY

In his Italian campaigns Pius, like Eugenius IV, made use of senior bishops and the more energetic cardinals to serve as legates in the field or apostolic commissaries, liaison officers between himself and the professional captains, though he also made much use of a lay relative, his sister's son, Antonio Piccolomini. He not only made Antonio Captain General of the Church, with a salary of 2000 ducats a year, and castellan of Castel Sant'Angelo, but arranged with King Ferrante to set up Antonio in a hereditary principate as Duke of Amalfi; a suggestive precedent for later papal nephews.[18] Among the younger prelates Pius conspicuously entrusted with military responsibilities was the Ferrarese Bartolomeo Roverella, Archbishop of Ravenna, who was to become a cardinal in December 1461. Pius dispatched him in 1460 to the war in the south, with particular charge of the papal enclave of Benevento, that strategically important hill city north-east of Naples, situated between two rivers, the Calore and the Sabbato, and commanding road communications.

Surviving correspondence confirms that Pius kept closely in touch with his officers, both lay and clerical, for instance ordering the *condottiere* Simonetto in June 1460 to support Roverella with horsemen and infantry and in a series of letters he instructed Roverella, in whose prudence he repeatedly declared his confidence and hope, to do his utmost to defend Benevento.[19] Later Roverella was moved from the southern campaign and sent as legate against Everso of Anguillara; to this task, Pius recorded in the *Commentaries*, he applied himself promptly, 'having hastily collected an army'.[20] Another of Pius's protégés was the protonotary Bartolomeo Vitelleschi, Bishop of Corneto (the notorious former cardinal's nephew), whom he appointed on 23 March 1460 as 'governor and commissary in the army of Ourself and the Roman Church', using a phraseology similar to that of the letter of Eugenius IV in 1432, already quoted, which might have been intended to reinforce and justify practices that had only slight or no basis at all in canon law: 'It is considered right and proper ('condignum') that in the army of the Church an ecclesiastical person and prelate, prudent and expert in the matters being undertaken, should preside.'[21] Bartolomeo Vitelleschi was not Pius's most successful appointee; the site of Nidastore, where he had set up the papal army's camp at the end of June 1461, was attacked in the night by Sigismondo Malatesta; weapons and tents were seized, and among the prisoners taken was the bishop himself, but rather surprisingly his captor let him go; meanwhile, a letter was found in the carriage of Lodovico Malvezzi proving that Pius wanted to continue the offensive and to occupy Senigallia.[22] Pius suppressed most of this in his own account, but noted that he appointed, in place of Vitelleschi, Giacomo Feo, Bishop of Ventimiglia. Pius's nephew, Francesco Piccolomini, who became a cardinal in March 1460, was also used in military commissions. Early in 1460 he had replaced Cardinal Giovanni Castiglione as legate of the March of Ancona, who had had to confront the rebellious city of Ascoli and, in Pius's words, 'riding up and down the country in arms' defended it from the threatened attack by Jacopo Piccinino; the strain of all this, the Pope reflected, may have brought on Castiglione's death. Francesco subsequently invested Sassoferrato with a force of local troops he had mustered, forcing the surrender of the tyrant Luigi Atti.[23]

Another of Pius's young cardinals with military potential was Francesco Gonzaga, second son of the Marquis of Mantua. His elevation to the red hat in December 1461 at the age of seventeen was in part a token of gratitude from Pius II for the diet hosted in 1459–60 at Mantua, the grandly conceived but not very well supported congress intended to launch his crusade. Letters from Francesco and members of his household, during his first year of residence in the papal court, record their close interest in events of the papal wars in progress. When it was hinted that he might have spoken out more strongly against Sigismondo Malatesta, with whom he was suspected of sympathising because he was a distant relative, Francesco declared that, on the contrary, because Sigismondo had deprived his paternal grandmother (Paola Malatesta) of some of her dowry, he would like to see him burnt in the same manner as his effigy.[24] He was referring to the macabre ceremony carried out in Rome in late April 1462, when crude effigies of the Lord of Rimini were set alight outside St Peter's and also in the Campo dei Fiori; Francesco watched the former of the two bonfires from a secret viewing point, in the company of Cardinal Francesco Piccolomini, much to the Pope's approval.[25] Francesco Gonzaga was in character typical of his Mantuan family, a mixture of intelligent semi-refinement and earthy roughness; he was, after all, a professional soldier's son, a somewhat lusty youth, fond of hunting. He may therefore have had a more instinctive understanding of war than most of the higher clergy around him, though he did not underrate their enthusiasm for it. Writing about the fall of Senigallia in August 1462, and the rejoicing in the papal court, he remarked that it was usual there to extol a victory with exaggerated joy and even a minor defeat with despair, 'in the manner of priests, to tell you the truth'. On that occasion, Pius himself was making a great celebration and had wanted the army at once to advance on Rimini, but then thought better of it and left the decision to Federico di Montefeltro.[26]

But the most committed to war among Pius's cardinals was his friend Niccolò Forteguerri (1419–73), a figure more reminiscent of Albornoz, resolute, straightforward and well educated, than of, say, the brutal Cossa or Vitelleschi. Pius, who was distantly related to the Forteguerri family of Pistoia, had befriended Niccolò when the latter was studying law at Siena in the 1450s, and after becoming pope quickly found employment for him, particularly in military administration. He conferred the bishopric of Teano on Forteguerri in 1458 and the red hat on 5 March 1460, the same day on which he promoted Francesco Piccolomini. In July that year Forteguerri was sent as special commissary to the papal army in the March of Ancona, which was to engage with the Angevin forces operating in that area under the command of Jacopo Piccinino. His first job was to liaise with the lay commanders in papal service, Federico di Montefeltro and Alessandro Sforza; but he soon seems to have acquired remarkable freedom of movement and initiative. In a letter of 6 August 1460, the Pope instructed his nephew, the cardinal legate in the March, Francesco Piccolomini, to do whatever Forteguerri proposed, even though he did not have the title and status of legate.[27] Forteguerri was, however, soon promoted to be legate to the army, and the Pope relied on him as his main informant, go-between, paymaster and executor of policy.[28]

Pius wrote to Cardinal Forteguerri in a frankly military, not at all sanctimonious, tone. In a letter of 22 October he warned him of Piccinino's reputation for cunning and deception, and ordered various exploratory movements against strongholds of Savelli and Malatesta; on 5 November he absolved the cardinal of any blame for cruelties suffered by the inhabitants of Sarno, on the grounds that worse things could have happened: 'We know what an infuriated army is capable of doing...not even Alexander, Hannibal or Julius Caesar could always restrain their troops;' on 25 November he instructed Forteguerri to wage war on Sigismondo Malatesta 'in all ways you can'; on 12 December he demanded pursuit of Piccinino's forces, however tired and terrified the horses might be ('the enemy's will be even more so'). Pius required the infliction of maximum damage by fire and sword to Jacopo Savelli's lands, before the papal army suspended operations and retired to winter quarters.[29]

Cardinal Forteguerri played a particularly powerful role in the renewed campaigns against Jacopo Savelli, Sigismondo Malatesta and other pro-Angevin allies. During the military operations in 1461–63 his activity and movements can be recorded from a variety of sources besides Pius II's somewhat rambling *Commentaries*, not least from the surviving correspondence of officers and observers in the war zone, writing to the Duke of Milan, Francesco Sforza or to the Marquis of Mantua, Ludovico Gonzaga and his wife. Forteguerri himself informed Sforza about the campaigns in progress. In early August 1461, for example, he explained to him that he was expecting to capture Avezzano and other castles very shortly, and that Federico di Montefeltro and himself were putting the inhabitants of Aquila severely to the test, having seized innumerable cattle and men (for ransom) from the surrounding country.[30] A month later he wrote from Albe that this strong fortress had been taken: 'The evil breed of Braccio's followers has been eradicated.'[31] He announced that, instead of following Alessandro Sforza with a detachment of the army into Apulia, he and Federico di Montefeltro were going to strike camp and proceed into the lands of the Duke of Sora. In late October he reported that they were encamped at Castellucio by the river Garigliano, within firing distance of the enemy, and within a few weeks he announced that they had forced the enemy to retreat and had taken Castellucio by assault.[32]

Meanwhile the war against Malatesta proceeded. By Forteguerri's initiative even the republic of San Marino was persuaded to help the papal forces in September 1462,[33] and a month later he had an assistant, Angelo Geraldini, Bishop of Sessa, appointed as special commissary to organise troops and supplies.[34] Later in November Forteguerri urged the Duke of Milan, not for the first time, to commit himself more strongly to the war against Malatesta, in which his brother Alessandro was already serving.[35] The war reached its climax in 1463, by which time Forteguerri had been appointed cardinal legate in Romagna. He shared with Federico di Montefeltro responsibility for the campaign's success by land and sea, involving the decisive siege in September of the port of Fano, though Federico's eulogistic biographer later tried to deny this and traduced Forteguerri.[36]

Subsequently, in the winter of 1463–64, Pius planned to dispatch Forteguerri, with the lay military captain Napoleone Orsini and Lorenzo Roverella, Bishop of Ferrara, to deal with Everso of Anguillara, his persistently subversive and destructive vassal to the north of Rome. This second campaign against the Anguillara clan had to be postponed, however, Forteguerri pointing out that it was too risky to carry out in winter;[37] in any case, priority had to be given to the forthcoming war against the Turks (in which he would again be cast in a commanding role). Forteguerri's career as a cardinal, particularly in the period of Pius II, was thus exceptionally focussed on his military services: these were even proclaimed in a Latin inscription on his tomb, designed by Mino da Fiesole, in the Roman church of S. Cecilia in Trastevere. Platina summarised these achievements in his first biography of Pius II: 'Fano successfully attacked, Flaminia overcome [perhaps meaning the Malatesta dominions in general, since they flanked the Via Flaminia], the Sabine [presumably the Savelli lands in the Abruzzi] and Eversan enemies of the Church conquered.'[38]

In addition to Pius II's literary and historical interest in war, his political commitment to its necessity and his judgement in the selection of clerical as well as professional lay commanders, a notable trait of the Piccolomini Pope was his fascination for technological developments in weaponry. He recorded in his *Commentaries* that he had specially commissioned three bombards – primitive heavy artillery designed by Agostino da Piacenza. They were named respectively after himself and his parents, Aeneas, Sylvius and Victoria; the wall-shattering roar of Victoria was even the subject of a few poetic lines by one of Pius's secretaries.[39] There was evidently a gun foundry within the walls of the Vatican, and the papal account-books under Pius record various payments to the experts producing munitions, among them in May 1461 not only the forenamed Agostino son of Niccolò di Piacenza, described as 'engineer of the sacred palace and master of the bombardeers', but also the sculptors Paolo Romano and Isaia da Pisa, who provided stone cannon balls.[40] The bombards Aeneas and Sylvius, the Pope declared, were each capable of discharging a stone weighing 200 pounds, but Victoria could use stones weighing 300 pounds and even shatter a wall 20 feet thick. The date of their production is made clear from letters of the Mantuan ambassador in Rome, Bartolomeo Bonatti. He wrote on 20 April 1461 that Pius was anxious to test the new bombard[41] and, although a week later he reported that 'this second bombard cast by maestro Agostino has not succeeded',[42] on 1 May it appears that a successful test was carried out in Rome 'at the twentieth hour' – i.e. four hours before sunset – with the bombard named Silvio (Bonatti also mentions that the first two bombards had been 'baptised' Silvio and Vittoria in honour of the Pope's parents). Bonatti further records that Pius had himself carried to Castel Sant'Angelo to witness the test-firing, and that a group of cardinals and almost the whole city witnessed it.[43] He does not state how well Silvio performed under trial, though he had been informed that it could discharge a projectile 230 pounds in weight for a distance of three miles. 'I think that the Savelli will be the first to feel these bombards,' he wrote on 20 May; indeed, both instruments had been sent 'in the name of God' to the war zone on the previous day.[44] He

Mino da Fiesole, detail of tomb of Cardinal Niccolò Forteguerri (Santa Cecilia, Rome).

added, 'As the cardinal [Forteguerri] is in the camp, I think something will be started soon.'

It was probably thanks to the efficiency of Cardinal Forteguerri in organising transport that the bombards arrived on the scene so promptly. One of them, Bonatti learnt, had been sent to each of the papal commanders, to Federico di Montefeltro, Count of Urbino, who was attacking Forano, and the other to Alessandro Sforza at Crotona,[45] who three days later began the bombardment of Palombara.[46] There were reports of heavy damage by the new weapon, but also of some essential part having been lost in transit, rendering it almost useless, of bombardeers being killed in action and stores of cannon balls, heaped by the banks of the river, being seized at night by enemy raiding parties and dumped in the water.[47] Whatever the truth, news reached Rome by 3 June that Savelli had sent a message to Cardinal Forteguerri offering terms of peace;[48] in spite of his overtures, Alesssandro Sforza's forces sacked and burnt the castle of Crotona a few days later.[49] Pius in his *Commentaries* insisted that the bombard had been crucial in the attack on Palombara.[50] 'For the first time,' he wrote, 'they learnt in Roman territory what bombards could do;' at Palombara a newly made mangonel (a sort of huge catapult) was also in action.[51] Pius described with satisfaction how Savelli 'followed the Cardinal of Teano [Forteguerri] through Rome like a captain led in triumph', referring to his submission in Rome a month later.[52] Pius's campaigns may well have reinforced the general trend in contemporary warfare of employing ever more violent firepower.

The war in general went well for Pius in the autumn of 1462, even if the technology of the new bombards was not always faultless. After the fall of Mondavio, Pius wrote, 'The legate [Forteguerri] decided to cross into Romagna and encamp in the territory of Rimini and besiege Montefiore.' He records, rather briskly, that 'engines were moved up and a tower was battered with stones from bombards'. They also 'undermined part of the mountain'. But then it was decided to use a quicker method, and so 'the citadel was surrendered to the Legate by treachery'.[53] Francesco Sforza was advised, however, that matters had gone rather less smoothly at Montefiore; on the first day of the attack, the rear section of one of the finest bombards had blown up in more than ten pieces. This was evidently not one of the Pope's machines, but belonged to Federico di Montefeltro, who at once sent to Urbino for equipment to repair it, but meanwhile the defenders gained time to repair the previous damage; Sforza was therefore asked for the loan of two bombards held at Pesaro. After a week the attack was still held up, although the bombards from Pesaro were on their way. Another bombard, called Ferlina, had proved defective, and taking Montefiore was judged to be a tough assignment, it was so strong.[54]

Episodes illustrating the physical power of the Church greatly appealed to Pius. He cherished a story about Niccolò Piccinino, who at the time of his defeat by the Florentine army at Anghiari (1440) allegedly declared that he abandoned in terror all hope of victory ('terrorem omnemque victorie spem adimisse') at the sight of the standards of the Church emblazoned with the keys of St Peter.[55] At Aquila, where Federico di Montefeltro and Cardinal Forteguerri laid waste the plain and Jacopo Piccinino's garrison was driven out, the citizens now realised what the Church was capable of doing ('sensere quid posset Ecclesia'): 'Previously they had despised it, but now they had seen papal forces ravage the fields and loot the countryside under their very eyes.'[56] Pius seldom expresses any wish for clemency or feelings of compassion for civilian victims: his approval of the plunder and devastation in 1463 by Napoleone Orsini's forces of the territory of the Duke of Sora, 'long hostile to Pius', is another example of his attitude.[57] He relates a rather similar anecdote concerning the attack on Castelluccio in October 1461 in the Neapolitan war. Antonio Petrucci, employed to defend the castle for the Duke of Sora, called out: 'Do you see the army of the Church? [...] Let them come on. We shall be fighting with women... What do you fear? Do you think that the Keys of the Church are stronger than our swords?' While he was shouting such words, a stone from a bronze engine of war smashed part of the rampart nearby and silenced him. Federico di Montefeltro finally stormed and sacked the town.[58]

Pius's personal capacity for belligerence was expressed most harshly in the punitive campaign in 1463 against Sigismondo Malatesta, Lord of Rimini since 1432. Sigismondo was much respected as a military commander, but his desertion of Alfonso of Naples and enmity towards the Montefeltro had made him a political enemy of the papacy, and the celebration of his mistress and other supposed profanities in his famous temple in Rimini, in progress from 1447 to 1461 but never finished, also helped to blacken his reputation. Already condemned in December 1460, the sentence upon Sigismondo included confiscation of his lands and titles and canonisation to hell; as has been mentioned already, effigies of him were publicly burnt in Rome in April 1462. What perhaps stirred Pius most to anger was Sigismondo's imperviousness to these terrible threats, his refusal to fear the power of the Church if both of the two swords were unsheathed against him. Sigismondo wrote to Francesco Sforza in March 1462 protesting that he would fight to the death against the Pope, who had even composed verses to his dishonour; he thought that the papal office had been much more tarnished by this indignity than he had been.[59]

Sigismondo Malatesta's victory at Nidastore (2 July 1461), mentioned earlier, had shocked Pius into temporary uncertainty whether God could be approving his efforts, and may have aroused a momentary suspicion that military operations might best be left to the lay professionals; the clergy, however effective as cheerleaders or strategists, might be unreliable when left in charge on their own. Such had been the unfortunate lot of Cardinal Francesco Piccolomini, who, convinced they were outnumbered, had ridden up and down vainly encouraging the troops that reinforcements were at hand, while Jacopo Ammannati, Bishop of Pavia, shortly to become a cardinal, worried about borrowing money to pay their wages. It was Jacopo, a close friend and admirer of the Pope, who reported that

> the army was strong enough to repel the enemy's assaults but had no general capable of leading it. Armed horsemen despise bishops in cassocks [armatos equites presbyteros togatos contemnere]. They might consult priests about waging wars or making peace but when there was need of action and swords were already in men's hands the priest's authority was over.[60]

It is evident from his *Commentaries* that Pius was not altogether convinced by this; he certainly believed in his own military inspiration, in spite of his high priesthood, and he followed and commented upon operations in close detail. In the following year, the papal campaigns against Sigismondo Malatesta were more successful. Senigallia fell in June 1463, owing to Sigismondo's last-minute withdrawal; at the end of September, when the fortress of Mondavio was besieged by Federico di Montefeltro for twelve days, the bombards worked effectively and the main tower fell. Francesco Sforza's agent on the spot wrote to the duke that it was unlikely the castellan of Mondavio could hold out for more than a few days against bombardment, as there were too few defenders inside, and anyway the castle was small and rather low.[61] In view of this it is rather surprising that Pius congratulated himself for proving that Francesco Sforza's advice that Mondavio would be too difficult to capture had been wrong; Pius declared, 'Although he put Francesco's judgement in regard to warfare above his own, there could be no certainty about future events of the war and it was cheaper and less dangerous to carry it into Sigismondo's territory.' He adds that Cardinal Forteguerri was sent with a large sum of money to reward the troops.[62] This may suggest that one of the advantages in the use of clerical officers in military operations was perhaps the greater security their status afforded them in carrying large amounts of cash; habitually, too, they were the mouthpieces of the Pope in negotiating terms of surrender.

Forteguerri meanwhile was beginning to plan an onslaught by sea as well as land against Sigismondo Malatesta. He wanted to requisition various boats (*fustarelle*) at Pesaro, since the Bishop of Ventimiglia had reported that galleys available at Ancona were in a bad state and repairs would take a month.[63] In the land campaign he and Federico di Montefeltro meanwhile sacked the port of Cesenatico and shortly afterwards took Verucchio, which they had judged to be very strong and well equipped, by a trick;[64] Archangelo and other places were bombarded, then ruthlessly sacked in the name of the Church. The Pope wanted to attack Rimini itself, Sigismondo's capital, but was dissuaded by Federico di Montefeltro, on the grounds that the papal forces were insufficient. In spite of this disappointment, Pius continued his memoir of the campaign in his habitually victorious tone, recording that 'places believed impregnable...were taken by us in a short time... Mighty is the vengeance of God!'[65] Meanwhile the war in support of King Ferrante continued to go well in the Abruzzi, directed by Napoleone Orsini as commander with Lorenzo Roverella, Bishop of Ferrara, as papal legate to the camp; Pius recorded with satisfaction the successful taking of fortresses such as Casale, Sora, Arpino and Mondragone and the plunder permitted.[66] But the most spectacular event of the summer of 1463, the endgame in the campaign against Malatesta, was Cardinal Forteguerri's blockade and siege of the port of Fano. He wrote from there in the middle of June 1463 that Sigismondo was in a very bad way; the port was closed to supplies, and by sea there was a papal war galley and two lighter boats on patrol; by land they were placing bombards in position. 'We hope to take Fano within a few days,' he added rather optimistically.[67]

Pius recorded the successful counter-attack, when a number of Venetian grain ships tried to break through the blockade, though he neglects to mention that the Venetians – cursed by Forteguerri as 'maladetti veneziani' – had so far been quite successful in getting supplies into Fano.[68] 'The Church's fleet,' he wrote, 'attacked with bombards, javelins and every kind of engine. There happened to be present a spirited priest, fitter for armed than sacred warfare, who suddenly hurled a brand which set the sails of the larger ship on fire. The Church's men boarded the ship on ladders and won a speedy victory.'[69] According to a correspondent of the Duke of Milan, Forteguerri turned down a special appeal from Sigismondo not to use a super-bombard against Fano by night, a machine reputed capable of hurling lumps of stone weighing 500 pounds to a great height, which on falling penetrated deep into the ground.[70] It was therefore an even more terrible machine than Pius II's Victoria. Fano was battered continuously for two whole days, and eventually surrendered on 25 September, as the Cardinal reported in a triumphant letter, mentioning that he had refused to accept a first offer of surrender on terms.[71] This was perhaps the zenith, if not yet the end, of his papal war service.

## ANTICLIMAX: PIUS'S CRUSADE

In the last year of his life, Pius was at last able to pay attention to the great 'bellum necessarium' against the infidel, to wage which he had from the first dedicated himself and of which he never lost sight. Perhaps this is the place to mention the curious fact that he even established briefly a papal fortress or colony on the southern coast of Greece, taking Monemvasia under direct rule in response to an appeal from the inhabitants after their ruler fled in 1460, and appointing a military governor early in 1461.[72] Even his donations to secular rulers of the ceremonial sword were intended as explicit encouragements to fight – in particular to fight Turks – rather than as symbols of the struggle against evil. Thus the sword blessed at Christmas 1460 went to Philip Duke of Burgundy in anticipation of his support for the crusade declared at Mantua, and a year later the sword sent to Louis XI even had an inscription exhorting him to use it against Turks to avenge Greek blood-shed. Subsequently swords were sent to the Doge of Venice, Cristoforo

Moro, and to Matthias Corvinus, King of Hungary, who – so Pius himself reports – promised specifically to wield this papal gift against the Turks.[73]

Probably only a minority of the cardinals shared Pius's eagerness for the Turkish war, either at the time of the Diet of Mantua in 1459–60 or when the fleet finally assembled at Ancona in 1464. The objection was not so much on principle as about practicality. The French cardinal Guillaume d'Estouteville, even at the time of the Diet of Mantua, had ridiculed it as 'the maddest enterprise ever seen or heard'.[74] The cardinals, or the sixteen more able-bodied of them who set forth, may have complied out of shame or obedience, but the majority's lack of enthusiasm helps to account for their quickness to abandon it when Pius died. Without doubt the most eager for action had been Cardinal Isidore, titular patriarch of Constantinople. A Mantuan customs register of 1459 reveals that, while nearly all the other cardinals were importing large quantities of wine from Verona and Brescia for consumption during the papacy's sojourn at Mantua, Cardinal Isidore was importing arms and armour – Brescia being the leading centre of arms production in Italy. Between October and December 1459 he had acquired bombards, spingards or military catapults, battleaxes and other items,[75] and went on to Ancona to equip a small flotilla of his own. On 31 May 1460 he wrote from there to the Marquis of Mantua reporting that only the danger to shipping from Genoese and Catalan pirates in the Ionian Sea was delaying his departure; illness, probably a stroke, later intervened, followed by long incapacity and death[76] in Rome in April 1463, his hopes disappointed. For a cardinal to stockpile arms was not altogether unusual: Martin V's nephew, Cardinal Prospero Colonna, for instance, imported in 1461 eight cannons, twenty-five smaller firearms, and 4000 arrowheads, as well as shields and helmets.[77] These might conceivably have been intended for use on the crusade, but were more probably meant for routine defence of his palace in Rome or family fortresses in the vicinity. In any case, Prospero, like Isidore, died in 1463, so there is no question of his arms being loaded up in 1464 for the Turkish campaign.

As papal legate, appointed on 3 May, Forteguerri was in overall charge of the papal fleet of war galleys, which was meant to be assembling at Porto Pisano and from there or from Ostia to sail round the coast of Italy to Ancona, for the official departure and rendezvous with the Venetian fleet. At the beginning of July it still was not ready, and several of

Forteguerri's own galley crew had died of plague; he himself hastened overland to join and reassure the Pope that all would be well.[78]

Cardinal Francesco Gonzaga, exceptionally, commissioned his own war galley at Venice and travelled from Mantua down the Po to embark on it in July 1464. He had shown himself to be one of the most eager supporters of the Pope's plans, and when he left Rome for home the previous autumn Pius had encouraged him to 'Go and be a St George'.[79] Back in Mantua, he was even measured for a suit of armour in the winter of 1463–64, and Andrea Mantegna's famous mural painting in the Castello San Giorgio might conceivably relate to Francesco's ambition to serve Pius II in holy war.[80] In the first weeks after his return, he could only meet his father in the countryside, because plague quarantine rules applied; when they met in December, his father presented him with warhorses, and a horse shown in the fresco bears Pius II's family emblem on its trappings. All this would have been quite a recent memory when Mantegna started work in this room in 1465, and much more recent than Francesco's return to Mantua from Pavia in January 1462 upon hearing that he had been made a cardinal, with which this scene has been more often connected. In spite of Cardinal Francesco's efforts to equip himself for war, a letter in late July 1464 tells us that by an oversight he had left his helmet behind at Mantua, and that his stablemaster bungled the arrangement to send the horses overland to meet him at Ancona.[81]

If only a minority of the cardinals (mostly the younger and more robust) were actively or enthusiastically engaged in Pius II's war projects, it does not seem that any of them tried to distance themselves from the policy of using force against declared enemies of the Church either in Italy or overseas. The occurrence of wars and rumours of wars was accepted as more or less inevitable; nobody could seriously entertain a long-term peace process, meaning conciliation or appeasement. This would be equivalent to a betrayal of Christ. The supposed Letter of Pius II to Mohammed the Conqueror, suggesting that if the sultan converted to Christianity he would be acceptable as emperor in the west,[82] was as unrelated to the real world as were Cardinal Nicholas Cusanus's speculations about the intellectual compatibility of Islam with Christianity, from which Pius borrowed some ideas. Even contemplative and scholarly cardinals seem to have had no inhibitions about supporting a war for the defence of Christendom.

## SEQUEL: PAUL II AND WAR, 1464–71

A postscript is owing here to Pius II's immediate successor, the Venetian cardinal Pietro Barbo, elected as Paul II (pope 1464–71). As the Ferrarese ambassador, Jacobo Trotto, wrote, the new pope was not warlike by nature ('non è di natura bellicosa').[83] Ceremonious, secretive and cautious, Paul's idiosyncrasies of character need not trouble us in the present context, but there was a certain continuity with Pius's policies, and those cardinals with previous experience of war remained powerful in the papal court, even if Cardinal Ludovico Trevisan – that military and naval champion, but no friend to Pietro Barbo – had died in the first year of the new pontificate. It has recently been argued that Paul was as determined as, or even more determined than, his predecessors to regain direct control over the lands and cities of the Church, and cherished in particular his 'design of the Romagna', appreciating the crucial importance of that region and its vulnerability not only to penetration by Milanese and Florentine interests, but also to the ambitions there of Venice, his own homeland.[84]

In the summer of 1465 Paul launched the punitive campaign against the Anguillara clan that Pius had had to postpone. Pius's old friend Cardinal Forteguerri was again called upon, and in June was appointed legate to accompany the army. From his base at Viterbo Forteguerri recruited troops and issued a proclamation promising that first occupiers of enemy property would be entitled to possession; he furiously rejected a placatory letter from Everso, and demanded his immediate and total submission, or else an attack by soldiers supported by frightful bombards and other war machines.[85] Forteguerri thereupon joined the *condottieri* Napoleone Orsini and Federico di Montefeltro in a lightning campaign, which lasted only twelve days.[86] The humanist poet Lodrisio Crivelli wrote and dedicated to Paul a long poem entitled 'The Kingdom of the Church' ('Regnum Ecclesiae'), in which he acclaimed the victory over the Anguillara and hailed Paul's papacy as a reign of peace.[87] Pius's literary protégé, Cardinal Ammannati, wrote of the Pope's satisfaction in having succeeded where his predecessors had failed; he acknowledged in various letters that Paul showed skill in military policy by using deception in the troop movements he ordered,[88] and went on to write in two versions his own triumphal account of the campaign, as a way of praising Paul II for attending to Pius II's unfinished business against the Anguillara.[89] Ammannati reveals in his writings not only, like Pius, a fascination about the details of military campaigns, but also the usual ambiguity. In his long letter of 1465 to Cardinal Francesco Gonzaga, laying down the duties and obligations of a cardinal, he declared that '[n]othing is less fitting than the business of war', but after Cardinal Forteguerri's death in 1474 he wrote a long appreciation in which he stressed the latter's skill as a military commander in successive wars of the Church.[90]

But Paul still had other military operations to undertake. There remained troubles – inherited from Pius – in the borderlands of the kingdom of Naples and in Romagna. King Ferrante threatened to recover possession of Sora by force, a dispute which was finally resolved by Cardinal Roverella, but the challenge led Paul to raise a large force of infantry in the autumn of 1468 to defend the region.[91] More seriously, the Pope was drawn back to armed conflict over Malatesta territory. He had succeeded in regaining Cesena by legal negotiation after the death of Malatesta Novello in December 1465,[92] but over Rimini war broke out after the death of Sigismondo Malatesta. In 1468 Sigismondo's son Roberto attempted to go back on the terms of submission of 1463 and keep control of the city.[93] In June 1469 a papal army laid siege to it, a major operation which Pius had not even attempted, but he would no doubt have approved that the army of the Church was newly equipped with light as well as heavy arms, having a company of seventy-seven handgun-men led by a German commander.[94] Although Venice had promised co-operation in this case (elsewhere in Romagna the republic was obstructive to Paul's great 'design') reinforcements did not materialise and eventually the campaign was abandoned.

Very much in the spirit of Pius II, incidentally, was the treatise on the militia written by the Vicentine Chieregino Chiericati, *revisore generale*, or inspector general, of the papal army, who set out to demonstrate the decline of arms since Antiquity. Chiericati dedicated it to Trevisan's successor as Apostolic Chamberlain Cardinal Latino Orsini, since his family was of such long-standing military distinction, and because, Chiericati declared, he had come to appreciate, in the course of many conversations, the cardinal's excellent and wise understanding of the profession of arms.[95]

Paul may, like Nicholas V, have been a genuine seeker for peace who found that obligations nevertheless dragged him inevitably into war.

Between his campaign against the Anguillara and the renewed Malatesta war, there was a period in 1467–68 when he made a sustained effort to prevent Florentine exiles, backed by Venice and forces commanded by Bartolomeo Colleoni, from exploiting the situation after the death of Piero de' Medici, the son and successor of Cosimo de' Medici as informal manager of the Florentine republic and papal banker. These enemies of the Medici system of political management planned a change of regime in Florence, thus risking the stability of Italy. Paul's plans for a general pacification – the so-called Pax Paolina, officially proclaimed on Ascension Day, 26 May 1468 – seem to have been what the humanist Bartolomeo Platina had in mind when he wrote, in prison, a humanistic laudation of peace, hoping that it would help to gain Paul's favour and forgiveness and earn his release. Rather more interesting, perhaps, is the companion piece – they were meant to be read in conjunction as though two sides of a disputation – by his gaoler, Rodrigo Sánchez de Arévalo. Sánchez, formerly a protégé of Calixtus III, was another learned protagonist of strong papal authority and military initiatives; he had accompanied Pius II to Ancona before becoming castellan of Castel Sant' Angelo in 1464.[96] His rebuttal of Platina consisted of a scholastic treatise on the necessity or inevitability of war, containing strong echoes of John of Legnano in its analysis of the nature of human conflict and the different levels of war, and in its fourth chapter emphasising that the Church blessed war, but citing mainly Old Testament precedents.[97]

Finally, even if Pius's death had put an end to his extraordinary plan for an anti-Turkish war led by the Pope and cardinals in person, events soon restored the policy of armed crusade to the utmost priority.[98] During the last year of Paul's pontificate, after the fall of the Venetian island of Negroponte in July 1470, war against the Turks again dominated papal policy. Paul took the loss of Negroponte very much to heart. Although he expressed no wish to imitate Pius by leading a vengeful Christian task force into battle, he even contemplated having to flee Italy and return the papacy to Avignon.[99]

# 4 God's work or the Devil's? Papal wars 1471–1503

## INTRODUCTION: THE MIDDLE AGE OF THE RENAISSANCE PAPACY

It may come as no surprise after the previous chapter, about Pius II's deeds and writings concerning war, to find that another humanist of the papal curia, Sigismondo de' Conti (1432–1512), opened with the word 'Bellum' his *History of His Own Times*, a long work that begins fourteen years after Pius's death. For Sigismondo, as for Pius, war was the nerve of history, even papal war and even if (as he wrote) the devil was the sower of war.[1] Sigismondo had become an apostolic scriptor in 1476 and a papal secretary in 1481, but he had a special attachment to Sixtus IV's nephew, Giuliano della Rovere, who was appointed a cardinal in December 1471, aged about twenty-seven. Sigismondo accompanied him on his legation to Burgundian Flanders in 1481, and was made his domestic secretary in 1504, a year after Giuliano became Julius II, the figure who inevitably dominates the whole theme of papal belligerence. In Melozzo du Forli's painting of the appointment of Platina as the Vatican's librarian in 1475 (Pinacoteca Vaticana), Giuliano is the tall, handsome figure with dark hair standing beside the chair on which his elderly uncle, Sixtus IV, is sitting. Later portraits, whether engraved on medals or painted, illustrate the same strong jaw and beetling brows; written descriptions in chronicles and letters illustrate his personal aggressiveness, explosive impatience and, latterly, his reckless use of oaths and foul language.

Sigismondo de' Conti started his book as an account of the papal war in 1478–80 against the Florence of Lorenzo de' Medici, 'il Magnifico'. More will be said below concerning this war, and something needs to be said at this point about Lorenzo. From the age of nineteen he had dominated the republic of Florence as his father and grandfather had done, not by holding any title to do so, but by clever political management. He also dominated Italian diplomacy for over twenty years (1469–92); some would say he did most to ensure that in this period the various independent but interdependent states of Italy flourished in liberty from foreign interference. To some he was also a paragon, the charismatic figure who best represents the cultural values of the Italian Renaissance. But Sigismondo de' Conti, who came from Foligno in Umbria, was not primarily concerned with Florentine affairs or Florentine culture, and in any case accepted the war against Lorenzo's regime was justified. Most of his narrative is based on the succession of papally sponsored wars, which continued almost to the date of his own death. In spite of his emphasis on war, Sigismondo assured the reader that of the three popes immediately preceding Julius II, all of whom he knew at first hand, two were personally not bellicose in character,[2] which is paradoxical in view of their policies. Sixtus IV (pope from 1471 to 1484), formerly Francesco della Rovere, a distinguished theologian and general of the Franciscan Order, was 'far from under-standing anything about arms...the mildest of men'; Innocent VIII (pope from 1484 to 1492), formerly the Genoese Giambattista Cibo, was a man 'of sweet and good character'. Alexander VI (pope from 1492 to 1503), the Catalan Rodrigo Borgia, could hardly be described by any such anodyne phrases, but Sigismondo simply characterises the man who, as Vice-Chancellor of the Church since 1457, had been his own head of department, as very changeable ('virum versatissimum').[3] This seems a rather mild assessment of that plump-cheeked, smooth-tongued voluptuary. The shrewd Mantuan chronicler Schivenoglia had observed Rodrigo at the Diet of Mantua back in 1459, when he was only twenty-five, and described him then as having 'a look of being capable of any evil' ('uno aspeto de fare ogni malo').[4] In spite of the three popes' alleged peace-loving qualities, the military dimensions of the papacy, already long established and fostered in the mid-fifteenth century, grew still more conspicuous in this period of over thirty years, aided by the services of their cardinals and other senior prelates. This was the background against which, or in the midst of which, the future Julius II matured.

In papal history the period under review in this chapter (1471–1503), roughly the early middle age of the Renaissance, has long had a certain unity imposed on it, with emphasis generally upon the papacy's Italian politicisation, increasingly princely style, financial corruption, family favouritism and luxury. Contemporaries themselves promoted the idea of the degenerate Renaissance papacy: among them the head of the Augustinian Order, Egidio of Viterbo (1469–1532), who became a cardinal in 1517; he dated the decadence from Sixtus IV's time, but prophesied a great regeneration was imminent.[5] To some contemporaries it might have seemed that warmongering was not the worst of the papacy's faults, and that, in an imperfect world, pacific inclinations had to be overruled in order to preserve the rights and dignity of the Holy See in Italy and to protect Italy and Christendom from the continuing threat of Ottoman expansion.

Even if the former of these two commitments usually prevailed, the defence of Christendom against the ambitions of Mehmed the Conqueror and his son Bajazet was not neglected by the three popes of the later fifteenth century. Sixtus IV inherited Paul II's pledge to avenge the fall of Negroponte, and had at his disposal the huge funds bequeathed by his predecessor. In May 1472 he blessed a fleet of galleys setting off down the Tiber under the command of Cardinal Oliviero Carafa (1430–1511; cardinal since 1467).[6] Together with a Venetian naval force, the cardinal's armada attacked Satalia (Adalia) and Smyrna in August and September, returning in January with twenty-five captive Turks and twelve camels, together with a section of the harbour chains of Satalia.[7] Said initially to have been displayed over the main threshold of St Peter's,[8] these pieces of chain still exist, and adorn the cardinal's tomb in Santa Chiara at Naples, immortalising his war service.

By 1480 it was not even possible to separate the Turkish from the Italian dangers of the Church, for there was well-grounded fear of Turkish landings in Italy, fulfilled in August 1480 when an expeditionary force captured Otranto and carried out a ferocious massacre. Cardinal Marco Barbo, a bibliophile without military inclinations, was sent on a tour of coastal defences in the region of Ancona, about which he submitted a report in September 1480.[9] A papal war fleet to avenge the outrage at Otranto was assembled at Genoa by Cardinal Giambattista Savelli. It eventually set sail under the command of Cardinal Paolo Fregoso, whose record included spells of piracy as well as the dogeship of Genoa, making him one of the most bizarre of all fighting cardinals; he had received the red hat from Sixtus in May 1480. After a call at the mouth of the Tiber to receive papal blessing, this fleet joined the army commanded by Alfonso, Duke of Calabria, which had for many months been besieging Otranto. Their recapture of Otranto in September 1481 caused frantic celebrations of joy and relief in Rome and all Italy. It was expressed by two medals designed by Cristoforo di Geremia, one to honour Sixtus IV, the other to honour Alfonso, but both with the same reverse design, not (it might be thought) one wholly appropriate in the case of the Pope. It depicted the nude female figure of Constancy in front of a wrecked naval fleet, with the Virgilian quotation 'To spare those who have been oppressed and to destroy the proud' ('Parcere subiectis et debellare superbos').[10] Cardinal Fregoso's contribution to the victory was not acknowledged; perhaps because he had returned to Italy in defiance of the Pope's order that he should continue across the Adriatic to attack Valona in Albania. He explained, perhaps not very courageously, that disease, discontent and the need for repairs in his fleet made this second offensive impossible, though one of the Genoese patrons of the fleet declared that Alfonso had opposed its revictualling.[11] The opportunity for a more sustained counter-attack was therefore lost, though Innocent VIII and Alexander VI continued to raise funds and promote plans for it. But, like Sixtus and so many of their predecessors, they constantly faced distractions in Italy, real or supposed dangers to the Church and

Medal of Sixtus IV commemorating the recapture of Otranto, 1481 obv. and rev., (Warburg Institute).

to the dignity of the Holy See, which consumed the resources they might otherwise have directed overseas.

## SIXTUS IV'S ITALIAN WARS

The involvement of Sixtus IV's own relatives in papal government lent a special feature to the military and almost secular role the papacy had come to play in Italian politics. Precedents were set which would be followed by many of his successors well into the next century and beyond. There seems to be no evidence that Sixtus suffered any crisis of conscience in associating the advancement of his relatives with the interests of the Church – maybe he at least started out in good faith, or maybe he was always weak in resisting strong family pressures. The earliest and most notorious example was his sister's son Pietro Riario, who was created a cardinal at the same time as his cousin Giuliano, in December 1471. Pietro set new standards of conspicuously lavish display; it has recently been argued, however, that behind this voluptuous façade the young cardinal was trying to impose a serious policy of conciliation and pacification, as demonstrated by the good relations he cultivated with Duke Galeazzo Maria Sforza of Milan and by his service as legate to Umbria in 1473.[12] Pietro's early death in 1474 brought to the fore his ambitious secular brother Girolamo, for whose benefit Pietro had negotiated the purchase of Imola and a political marriage with Caterina Sforza. It also left in a stronger position the della Rovere family, offspring of the Pope's brother. Cardinal Giuliano della Rovere, for whom force was in general a more effective instrument than conciliation, was the senior nephew, and the one with whom we are most concerned, but the career of the layman Giovanni is also relevant. Giovanni (d. 1501) was educated at the court of Federico di Montefeltro, whose daughter Giovanna he married in 1474. In the following year he succeeded his deceased brother Leonardo as Prefect of Rome, which was essentially a military appointment. As a *condottiere* and lord (*signore*) – Senigallia and Mondavio in the March of Ancona were conferred on him – Giovanni came to personify the dynastic and military ambition of the della Rovere. Giuliano always supported him and sometimes gave Giovanni's interests priority over his own.[13]

In the summer of 1474, nearly forty years before his exploits in the siege of Mirandola, Giuliano – the future Julius II – then aged about thirty, was sent on a punitive campaign in Umbria. This started well – he entered the rebellious city of Todi unopposed with his 3500 infantry – but at Spoleto he lost control of his men, who joined with exiles and other partisans in sacking the city. Subsequently at Città di Castello, seat of the disaffected *condottiere* Niccolò Vitelli, successive assaults failed.[14] From there, according to Cardinal Francesco Gonzaga, writing from Rome on 9 July, Giuliano had appealed to the Pope for fresh infantry and bombards, declaring that if he left the job unfinished he could never return to Rome, such would be the shame to himself and to the Pope; in response, bombards and troops were hastily dispatched.[15] By the end of the month Giuliano had twenty-eight cavalry squadrons and 2000 'good infantry', also bombards, but these at first achieved little against the walls and the morale of Città di Castello.[16] Three weeks later, however, Cardinal Gonzaga reported that within twelve days the legate would be able to capture the town. Two things are certain, he wrote: one, that 'the bombards have done much damage to houses within the city and have killed many people; the other is that the citizens are not entirely united… now the Pope is said to be resolved to capture it'.[17] In spite of this assessment, the arrival of Federico di Montefeltro, since 1474 Duke of Urbino, seems to have done more to bring about Vitelli's capitulation than the cardinal's bombards, but Giuliano was nevertheless acclaimed as a conquering hero on his journey back to Rome in early September.

Girolamo Riario was an even more bellicose influence upon Sixtus than Cardinal Giuliano. He built up a principality in the Romagna based upon Imola, to which was added Forlì in 1480. Girolamo's implacable hatred towards Lorenzo de' Medici, who had formerly tried to obtain Imola, was one of the several causes of the unsuccessful Pazzi Conspiracy of April 1478, which was intended to replace the Medici regime in Florence by a government dominated by the rival Pazzi family. This murky affair involving various outside powers seems to have had the implicit approval of Sixtus IV himself, according to the confession of one of the main executants, Giovan Battista, Count of Montesecco, a military captain previously in papal service.[18] Montesecco declared that Sixtus said to him repeatedly that he wanted to see a change of regime in Florence, but that it must be without bloodshed, which was a typical affirmation of the old ambiguities about permissive force: a prayer for getting the best of both worlds and an order almost certainly impossible to achieve. As events turned out, only Lorenzo's brother Giuliano was murdered in the cathedral, and Lorenzo himself escaped unhurt. This drew the papacy, supported by the kingdom of Naples, into war against Florence, on the grounds of its sacrilegious overreaction to the conspiracy, including the public execution of Francesco Salviati, Archbishop of Pisa, who had for his own reasons been implicated in the plot from its beginning. Between Girolamo Riario and Cardinal Giuliano della Rovere there was, meanwhile, a hatred festering that contributed to the extraordinary climax of violence in Sistine Rome in the last year or so of the Pope's life (1483–84).

Beginning, then, with the hostilities in 1478–80 against Florence, the papacy under Sixtus engaged in a series of offensive wars. In vain did Lorenzo's friend and humanist mentor Marsilio Ficino, translator of Plato's works from Greek into Latin and teacher of Neoplatonic ideas, compose letters in 1478–79 begging Sixtus to desist. In the first, of which three versions survive, he remonstrated, 'Remember that you are the vicar of Christ…forget injury…your victory rests not in war but peace;' in one of the subsequent letters his denunciation of this papal war against an Italian power was even more emphatic, protesting on Christ's behalf: 'Take your ferocious arms of war away from my flock at once. Turn yourselves upon the barbarian wolves.'[19] It may be questioned whether in fact Ficino had dared to send off any of these letters to the Pope, but they were available in print as early as 1495, with the implication that he had done so.

Although the military operations of this campaign were supervised by King Ferrante of Naples and his military commanders and allies rather than the Pope, Cardinal Francesco Gonzaga, legate at Bologna, allegedly wrote that Sixtus was considering descending in person upon the battlefield ('E scrive ancho el legato di Bologna / che'l pappa viene in campo esso in persona').[20] Whether or not Sixtus ever had this intention, and the allegation depends only upon a literary source which is full of invective against the Church's belligerence, with its bloodstained banners in place of the cross ('in loco della croce / sono I Standardi insanguinati e rossi'), Cardinal Francesco convinced himself that the Pope was right to go to war. He even set aside personal loyalty to his brother Marquis Federico Gonzaga, who was commanding the Milanese army in support of Florence. He promised Federico that he would still pay taxes owing on his Mantuan lands but not taxes on his person; he was bound to support the papacy against Florence and its allies; a few weeks later he expressed the hope that all good cardinals would respect the same priorities as himself.[21] Writing to the Mantuan ambassador in Milan, the cardinal insisted that his devotion to the Sforza regime was unchanged, but the war was a just one; Sixtus IV could not put up with such ignominy. The matter had to be settled by war 'to save the dignity of the Apostolic See'; he could testify that Sixtus had only made the decision reluctantly.[22]

The main theatre of war was Tuscany, which was invaded by forces of the kingdom of Naples, led by Alfonso, Duke of Calabria, son of King Ferrante. It was a minor war of skirmishes and ambushes, apart from the one pitched battle at Poggio Imperiale near Siena in September 1479, where Alfonso was victorious. Cardinal Gonzaga wrote to congratulate him, but with reservations, expressing concern about his brother, Rodolfo, who was said to have been wounded.[23] After Lorenzo de' Medici made a separate peace in March 1480 in the course of an audacious private visit to Naples, the papacy was not in a strong position to carry on, and had eventually to ratify the agreement.

A renewal or extension of the conflict developed in May 1482, in the War of Ferrara.[24] This was again a papal initiative, contrived by Girolamo Riario, arising from alliance with Venice against King Ferrante of Naples, who had to be punished for his recent support of Florence. Venice was (in theory) to be rewarded by the Pope with lordship over Ferrara. This was the first of two wars which the papacy declared against its vassal and protector the King of Naples. Action began in the south, with Ferrante marching troops into papal territory in April, but the counter-offensive led to an important papal victory. Sixtus and some of his cardinals watched from a window in the Vatican Palace a military parade on 15 August 1482, when the commander, Roberto Malatesta, led an army of 9000 foot soldiers and three huge bombards were dragged past the spectators.[25] Following Roberto's victory at the Battle of Campomorto there was another parade in Rome, with prisoners marched through the city by Girolamo Riario.[26] After a treaty had been signed in November, Sixtus rededicated the small church of S. Maria delle Virtù, with its miraculous image, as Santa Maria della Pace (the Madonna of Peace), even though he himself and Girolamo Riario had instigated the war.[27] He honoured Roberto Malatesta, who had died of marsh fever soon after his victory,[28] with a monument depicting him on horseback in armour, which was placed in the presbytery, the most sacred part of St Peter's. It was therefore one of the first monuments to be moved when Bramante started work on the new basilica in 1506; reassembled in the atrium, a century later it was moved again to the Borghese collection, and finally ended up in the Louvre.[29]

War was resumed later in the same year following an opportunistic switch of policy on the part of Sixtus IV and his nephew, abandoning their alliance with Venice and reverting to the side of King Ferrante. The papacy, supported by Naples, Milan and Florence, was now bent on defending its vassal state, Ferrara, against Venetian expansion, and the action was in the northern plain, along the lower course of the river Po. Sixtus was anxious to launch not only a land attack against Venice, but also to equip two armed fleets, one of which he put in the charge of a senior prelate, Branda Castiglione, Bishop of Como. He meanwhile appointed Cardinal Francesco Gonzaga legate to the papal and allied army commanded by Alfonso, Duke of Calabria, which was intended to prevent the Venetians from cutting off Ferrara by land and river. Francesco Gonzaga therefore re-enters the scene as potentially one of the papacy's most active warrior-cardinals. Disappointed by the collapse of Pius II's crusade, he could claim no military distinction under Paul II, except for the honour of being elected Cardinal Protector of the Teutonic knights in 1465.[30] But, as cardinal legate of Bologna from 1471 till his death in 1483, he had not only a local role to play that could involve force – as demonstrated by the firm suppression of an armed rising at Cento in August 1479, after the suffragan bishop had been murdered[31] – but a wider diplomatic and military role in Italian affairs. For Bologna was a city of crucial importance in relation to Girolamo Riario's possessions and ambitions, and likewise in relation to Sixtus IV's later wars.

Cardinal Gonzaga's role early in 1483 in the defence of Ferrara against the Venetians can be reconstructed from an unusually large amount of surviving correspondence, including his official letter register for the first four months of the year, giving an unequalled picture of a cardinal legate's military commitment.[32] There is no doubt that he participated very fully in the strategic planning and logistics of the campaign, including problems of supply, and was expected to prepare himself for direct physical encounter with enemy forces. Marquis Federico Gonzaga, who kept closely in touch (fortunately he was now on the same side as his brother), even advised the cardinal that he should procure some armour. In a letter to Federico of 25 January 1483 Francesco wrote that he was very eager to charge out into the country and engage the enemy as boldly as necessary, and was ordering various pieces of body armour from a leading master armourer ('Nui ne fariamo tanto animosi su questa impresa, che hormai pensiamo de uscire a la campagna et afrontare li inimici gagliardamente quando bisogni. E pur per andarvi più securi ne pare de ordinare alcune armature...').[33] The impression received is of ardour and would-be vigilance, perhaps the very qualities evoked on the cardinal's enigmatic portrait medal commissioned from Sperandio Savelli at about this time; its reverse shows a lynx, pyramid and martial paraphernalia.[34] The inventory drawn up after the cardinal's death (October 1483) confirms that he was indeed equipped with various items of body armour, including a cuirass and a helmet with a varnished plume.[35]

The Mantuan cardinal, who had arrived in Ferrara on 5 January to a rapturous welcome from Duke Ercole d'Este, wrote about the prospects and progress of the war not only to his brother but also to the Pope and to Girolamo Riario, and to the master of his household

Tomb sculpture (anon.), Roberto Malatesta, papal commander (d. 1482) (Museé du Louvre).

in Rome, Francesco Maffei, and to the various *condottieri*, Francesco da Tolentino, Roberto Sanseverino and Gianfrancesco Di Bagno. He reported in detail the positions and probable strategies of both the allied forces and – so far as they could be perceived – of the Venetians, though the most recurrent subject of his letters is the need for money, fodder and reinforcements. No campaign could begin until the arrival of Alfonso of Calabria, but this did not deter the cardinal from making his own tour of inspection of Ferrarese defences and of the enemy's encampment north of the city, once the weather had slightly improved, five days after his arrival. He wrote to Maffei about this tour, informing him that they had caught sight of the enemy, a great number of them according to the scouts, in woods beyond the walls of the park or hunting reserve ('vedevamo li inimici acosto ad un boscho verso lo muro del barcho, e le spie nostre referevano che erano grossi...'). 'Do not imagine that we were at all afraid, mounted on a mule; rather, seeing it with our soldiers, we assumed the spirit of a Hector' ('non pensare che havessimo paura cum tutto che fussimo suso una mula, anti vedendone cum quelli nostri soldati, metessimo un animo de Hectore').[36] After getting a good view of the land, including the house occupied by Roberto Sanseverino (the Venetian commander), beyond Ponte Lagoscuro, the party had returned home in safety; meanwhile the cardinal promised to gather more detailed information every day, which he would forward, and for this purpose he had had a map made with distances marked ('un designo di luochi cum le distantie annotate'). He also wrote to tell Girolamo Riario about his tour of the defence works with the various military captains,[37] and to Giangiacomo Trivulzio requesting that the hundred pioneers or sappers whom he had himself supplied from Bolognese territory should not be put to work where they would be in danger of enemy bombards or gunfire or other attacks; best would be the bastion of Bondeno on the Po.[38]

Duke Alfonso of Calabria arrived on 14 January, and Cardinal Gonzaga reported that a council of war was held the following evening, before he and the duke made an inspection of their army.[39] The cardinal feared that the Venetians might advance closer to the city, establishing – as he suggested in another letter to Girolamo Riario – a new headquarters for Sanseverino in the ducal park, and turning into a camp the monastic compound and buildings of the Certosa and the church of Santa Maria degli Angeli. These churches, in a virtual no man's land north of the city, were so vulnerable that both of them and all the houses in the area would have been pulled down if military advisers had had their way; Cardinal Gonzaga took a notably non-ecclesiastical view of the problem. Warned by Alfonso of Calabria of Duke Ercole's unwillingness to consent to this demolition, he had acknowledged Ferrarese reverence for both places, but, the case for it being so necessary, he had already tried to browbeat the duke. Failing in this, 'to save his honour' the cardinal had declared that every day Sanseverino did not move forward was a day gained ('per salvare l'honor mio quando altro ne avenisse, fara ben di protesti mei del parere mio, concludendo che ugni dì qual lo Signor Roberto non se faceva inanti o pigliare questi luochi, li pareva guadagnato').[40]

Certainly the Venetians were eager to take the offensive. As well as a surprise attack with scaling ladders on the fortress of Argenta in the last week of January, fully reported by Cardinal Gonzaga,[41] at the beginning of February there was an enemy sortie against Ferrara itself. The cardinal and the Duke of Calabria were in the cathedral hearing morning Mass when the news arrived that the Venetians were advancing on the gate of San Marco. 'We ourselves,' the cardinal wrote, 'bearing the office of Moses or perhaps of Judas Maccabbeus (should it be necessary) set off towards the noise' ('Nui anche per fare l'offitio de Moise, e forse non mancho quello de Iuda Macchabeo quando fusse bisognato, ne aviammo al rumore'). By the time he reached the scene, however, the invaders had fled.[42]

More often, however, the cardinal's letters were not about action, but administration. He complained to Girolamo Riario on 4 February that the constables and infantry were suffering for want of pay: '[T]hey say that the mess hall is too far from the kitchen' ('dicono loro essere la sala troppo lontana da la cocina'),[43] a graphic metaphor to emphasise the distance of the camp outside Ferrara from the money chests of the Camera Apostolica in Rome. He had already proposed to the Pope a vast extension of his own authority, so that his legation should apply to the whole of Italy: this, he declared, would add to the renown of the present campaign and to the glory of the Holy See.[44] But his most recurrent message was the need for more troops, money and food supplies before any major attack could be launched.

New offensive plans were discussed at the allied congress held at Cremona in late February–early March 1483,[45] though there was also some attempt to bring the war to an end by negotiation. But Sixtus's mediator, the aged Portuguese cardinal Costa, who prided himself on being straightforward and plain-speaking, unlike the Italian majority in the Sacred College, was mistrusted by both Girolamo Riario and the Venetians, and the talks broke down.[46] Costa himself walked out on them and returned to Rome; according to a Venetian report, he warned Sixtus that his soul was endangered by his responsibility for the war: the Pope might die at any minute and would have to answer to God for so much fire, slaughter, sacrilege and other evils, because the war was provoked by him.[47]

Back in Ferrara Cardinal Gonzaga found the situation much the same or worse than it had been in January. He wrote on 18 March, 'We see with the evidence of our own eyes, and in the course of heated discussions in our presence, that this campaign is in great danger should the enemy move, either to seize the Certosa, or the Angeli, from which vantage points, by bombardment, they would gain great advantage in order to seize and flatten our embankments, or else to camp at the bastion of Ponta, or to cut the dyke against Argenta. Any of these three schemes, and let us hope not all of them, might succeed, because of the smallness of our forces.'[48] His constant fear was that the Venetians would start a wider river and land offensive, bringing war even to the Gonzaga dominion, as he warned his brother in April and May.[49]

Cardinal Gonzaga was no longer taking any part in field operations, nor was he in a fit state of health by the time the stalemate was broken. The theatre of war was indeed extended to the borders of Mantua, so that even his own castles in its territory had to be put in a state of readiness with large supplies of gunpowder.[50] He died in October 1483, so he was not to see the outcome, the agreement that the Duke of Milan brokered at Bagnolo in August 1484, in which Venice came off best with the retention of Rovigo and the Polesine (the fertile area near Rovigo, north of Ferrara), an outcome which Sixtus IV and his nephew regarded as a disastrous humiliation for the Church.[51]

This final year of Sixtus's pontificate saw that aged Franciscan still more identified with armed force. It included his ruthless campaign against the Colonna family, who, as King Ferrante's allies, had again become the papacy's most insubordinate and detested vassals, almost as in the days of Boniface VIII, and in striking contrast to their direct control of the papacy under Martin V. On 23 June 1484 Sixtus ordered a parade of the bombards intended for attacking the Colonna fortress of Marino, on which massive weapons the della Rovere family emblem of the oak had been inscribed. 'After uttering many words, he [the Pope] raised his eyes upwards to God and lifted his arms to heaven, blessing the said bombards and making the sign of the cross over them. He prayed to God that wherever they were brought they would put to flight the Church's and his enemies,' recorded the Roman chronicler Stefano Infessura,[52] adding his own outraged comment: 'Whereas in other times the four Holy Apostles [i.e. Evangelists] intended that people should be won to the Faith and Christian worship by miracles and sermons and the sign of the holy cross, now they are to be won by the blasts of bombards.' On 2 July, Infessura records, Count Girolamo and the whole army of the Church, many bowmen and footsoldiers, with twelve huge carts bearing bombards, set off to destroy the Colonna: '[A]nd our Supreme Pontiff sent a message that, even if a thousand men should die at the setting up of the bombards and two or three thousand at the taking of Cave, they should capture it as soon as possible;'[53] in a subsequent order he insisted that it should be done on a Saturday – 'the day of the Virgin Mary'. Girolamo Riario's bombardeers did not even spare churches, and on 23 July the Pope sent twenty cartloads of cannon balls, made from the stones of an ancient Roman bridge. Cave at last surrendered, four days later, after enduring, allegedly, 577 direct hits from the papal bombards.[54] Infessura adds that this horrendous attack on a small fortress town had even inspired an (unidentified) Roman artist to make a painting of it, which at first pleased Sixtus, until he perceived that it portrayed the Church's forces in a bad light and as the losers; the unfortunate painter was summarily condemned to ten drops on the rope, followed by hanging, though the death sentence was not carried out.[55]

As a local inhabitant and civic official Infessura was prejudiced against Sixtus, but his stress upon the aggressiveness of papal policy and the appallingly violent conditions of life in Rome in the early 1480s was not unjust nor greatly exaggerated. Infessura reported that the citizens of Rome resolved to petition the cardinals to disarm; their houses were so stacked full of weaponry that they were more like barracks.[56] The squalid state of affairs in the last months of Sixtus's life was fittingly expressed by the atrocious persecution of the protonotary Lorenzo Colonna in June 1484,[57] and the demolition by papal forces led by

Girolamo Riario of property belonging to the Colonna and their partisans. Another Roman chronicler, Paolo dello Mastro, concluded summarily that Sixtus was 'a bad pope who always kept us in war and famine'.[58] But a generation later Niccolò Machiavelli, in spite of being a Florentine, owned to a grudging admiration for Sixtus: at least he was spirited ('animoso'), even if neither the vagaries of fortune nor his political understanding sufficed to overcome the problem of a seditious baronage, exploited by outside powers.[59]

## INNOCENT VIII (1484–92): THE NEAPOLITAN BARONS' WAR AND OSIMO

Innocent VIII was first drawn into more war in 1485–86 on account of the southern kingdom, yet again a problem after nearly five centuries of its being made a feudal dependency of the papacy. King Ferrante was unwilling to play the role of obedient vassal and defender of the Pope. He wanted to be invested with the three papal cities that since Norman times formed enclaves within the boundaries of his kingdom (Benevento, Pontecorvo and Terracina), and also to be perpetually excused payments of tribute money, which Sixtus IV had temporarily commuted.[60] In addition, the Pope's support as sovereign overlord was sought by leading barons of the kingdom,[61] who were on the point of open rebellion against Ferrante for depriving them of rights of jurisdiction and imposing penal tax demands; one of them, the Count of Montorio, had been arbitrarily seized, much to the fear and anger of the rest. Innocent's sympathy with their cause was in part engineered by Cardinal Giuliano della Rovere, who was motivated to defend his brother Giovanni's connections and interests in the region.[62]

It may be that Innocent was convinced that Ferrante, under the influence of his ruthless son Alfonso, Duke of Calabria, had treated the barons with injustice; also that he may have been interested by their proposals in late August that he might make them individual vassals of the Church, like the lords or so-called papal vicars in Romagna and elsewhere, with the obligation to pay tribute to the papacy and to fight under a banner of the keys of St Peter. Moreover, if he did not heed them, he was quoted as saying, they would appeal to the King of Spain or to France, to Venice or even to the Turks.[63] Innocent was still unmoved when Ferrante sent his younger son Cardinal Giovanni d'Aragona to dissuade him from war; on 1 September the Genoese Pope, in defiance of his 'sweet and good character', was said to be vehement ('focoso') and vigorous in calling for action to punish Ferrante and the Duke of Calabria; on the following day he refused even to receive the cardinal, who was intending to make a final appeal.[64] On 8 September the Florentine ambassador reported that Innocent was in high spirits, impatient for military action and confident of victory.[65] Barely a week after Cardinal Giovanni's untimely death from plague on 16 October, war was declared. On the morning of 24 October the Pope ordered his official letter announcing and justifying this to be posted for two hours on the main doors of St Peter's. No ambassador was given a copy, but the Mantuan Arrivabene managed to report the gist of it; apparently it cited at great length the 'insupportable exactions, injustices and oppression' suffered by the barons since the time of Sixtus IV, which had emboldened them to appeal to the Pope as supreme overlord ('supreme Signore') of the kingdom.[66]

Soon after hostilities began, Alfonso of Calabria and his ally Virginio Orsini, with financial backing from Florence, were threatening Rome itself. The newly appointed Gonfaloniere of the Church, Roberto Sanseverino, was slow to arrive from Romagna, and Cardinal Giuliano della Rovere was feverishly inspecting the state of Rome's walls in December 1485. Although the town of Aquila expelled the Neapolitan garrison and declared its allegiance to the Church, this was almost the only good news.[67]

From this dark hour of papal war-making, there survives an instructive letter to Innocent VIII written by Angelo Geraldini, Bishop of Sessa, dated 15 April 1486.[68] Angelo, it will be remembered, had served in the 1460s under Cardinal Forteguerri as military commissary in Pius II's war against Sigismondo Malatesta; more recently, he had been serving as Innocent's commissary against Ferrante, and was specially valued by the Pope for his 'robustness' ('robustum et vigentem et in huiusmodi rebus exercitatum novimus').[69] Angelo was in no doubt about the need of the Church to express its strength with all its forces. 'You have not castigated your enemies with spiritual censures as you should have done to defend the state of the Church. Things will go from bad to worse unless you take certain measures. If the temporal goes badly, so will the spiritual.' He underlined some of the stronger points in the papacy's present position, and some measures that in his view it needed urgently to adopt. 'You have gained Aquila and much territory; you have a famous captain [Roberto Sanseverino], and many men under arms who, if you deal with them quickly, will not only suffice for defence but also to obtain victory.' He stressed that the Orsini were once strong and now were very weak, and this advantage should be exploited; that special provision should be made for the population of the Patrimony (the lands of St Peter in the immediate neighbourhood of Rome), which had suffered so much damage from the enemy; but above all it was essential that Roberto Sanseverino should remain content. Angelo suggested that making his son a cardinal would help (a proposal that caused Innocent much agony, which will be discussed later). According to Angelo Gherardini, everything depended on Roberto Sanseverino and a strengthened army.

Interesting above all is Angelo's insistence that the papal army should be led by a cardinal, and that a mere bishop like himself would be much less effective. 'The army will gain enormously in reputation if a cardinal is appointed as legate; the Lord [God] will be more highly honoured than by a bishop; the men at arms will hold him in greater veneration, the people will be more devout towards him and the enemy more afraid.' One could hardly hope to find a better formulation than this to explain or justify the use of cardinals in papal warfare from the twelfth century onwards. Angelo goes on: 'I do not say this in order to refuse a hard and dangerous job. I would take it on willingly for your sake. Nor do I say this because I myself want to be a cardinal and legate (I have no mind to demand such a grand thing).' The cardinal appointed, he finally adds, 'should strive to equal Cardinal Giles of Spain ['Egidio da Hispagna', i.e. Gil Albornoz], the Patriarch Vitelleschi and the Patriarch of Aquileia [Lodovico Trevisan], who brought triumph and great exaltation to the Church'.[70] In the outcome, no such red-blooded, red-hatted hero was found for the job. The Venetian cardinal Giovanni Michiel, who was appointed legate 'over the armed forces of the Holy Roman Church' ('super gentes armorum Sancte Romanae ecclesie'),[71] was not at all of the right calibre. The war continued to go badly for Innocent and the Neapolitan barons, with a serious defeat by Alfonso, Duke of Calabria, at Montorio on 8 May.[72] The terms of peace negotiated by Cardinal Michiel were cynically disregarded by Ferrante and Alfonso, who were expected to resume paying tribute to the papacy, including all arrears, and to grant and respect a total amnesty for the barons.[73] Altogether, the so-called Barons' War seems to have been a conspicuous demonstration of divine disfavour towards the military commitments of the Church.

Innocent's other major involvement in warfare was in response to the seizure of Osimo (near Ancona) by the local warlord Boccalino di Guzzone, who threatened to call in the Turks in his support. Cardinal Giuliano della Rovere was appointed legate of the March of Ancona to deal with this matter on 2 March 1487, and surviving letters he wrote to the Pope over the next three months from Montefano, from where he was supposed to be directing the siege of Osimo, illustrate his partial application to the job, but also a singular lack of the success with which his protégé, the historian Sigismondo de' Conti, blatantly credits him.[74] Again and again he demanded reinforcements and money; in a letter of 5 May, for example, he reproached Innocent for exhorting him to attack and attempt to take Osimo without sufficient forces. The town was finally recaptured thanks to the Milanese commander Giangiacomo Trivulzio, who arrived with infantry and bombards. Branda Castiglione, Bishop of Como, reported to the Duke of Milan that Trivulzio wanted Cardinal Giuliano to be recalled because of his resentment ('umbrezza'), and Sixtus agreed to send a less eminent prelate; Giuliano was duly recalled to Rome and replaced.[75]

It is striking perhaps that Innocent did not launch his son Franceschetto Cibo on a career like that of Antonio Piccolomini or Girolamo Riario; perhaps Franceschetto's limitations of character discouraged this, though the Pope seems to have dallied with the idea of installing him in Forlì and Imola even before the assassination of Girolamo Riario in April 1488. After that event the same possibility was considered by Lorenzo de' Medici, Franceschetto's future father-in-law, but Lorenzo remained non-committal or ambiguous about it. In fact, Innocent's immediate resolve after the assassination was to resume direct control of Forlì by force. The papal governor of Cesena promptly arrived with bombards to intimidate Caterina Sforza, Girolamo's widow, and the governor's relative Cardinal Giambattista Savelli promised to send a powerful contingent from Rome.[76] But papal resources were too scant in the aftermath of the Neapolitan Barons' War to sustain a campaign in the Romagna, and instead Caterina remained in control under the protection of her Sforza relatives in Milan. Franceschetto

Cibo, meanwhile, was compensated by his father with various castles confiscated from the Anguillara family, but his main usefulness in the last phase of Innocent's pontificate was as a diplomatic and dynastic pawn. The marriage negotiated for him with Maddalena de' Medici was unconventional in that it was a gesture of peacemaking on the part of a pope (though perhaps more credit for the scheme should go to Lorenzo), but it seemed briefly to restore the papal–Florentine–Milanese concord with which Nicholas V had secured the stability of Italy. Unfortunately, the deaths of Innocent and Lorenzo in 1492 and Milanese intrigues to encourage French claims to the kingdom of Naples nullified hopes for a lasting peace.

## ALEXANDER VI (1492–1503): FRENCH INVASION AND CESARE BORGIA'S CAMPAIGNS

Rodrigo Borgia, elected Alexander VI in August 1492, had not had much practical experience of war during his long career as a cardinal (since 1456) and as Vice-Chancellor of the Church (since 1458), which office he had traded to Ascanio Sforza in order to gain his support in the conclave. Though his uncle Calixtus III had first made him legate of the March of Ancona, the voluptuous Rodrigo had not been available for, or particularly suited to, arduous military legations. He had, of course, long experience as an observer of papal policies. He had lived through Pius's II's and Sixtus IV's wars and Paul II's 'great design'; he would have been well aware of his uncle Calixtus III's ambitions (possibly meant to include the throne of Naples) for his elder brother, Pedro Luis, who had died in 1458, of Pius II's promotion of his nephew Antonio Piccolomini, and of Sixtus IV's exaltation of Girolamo Riario. He was probably less impressed by Innocent VIII's involvement in the Barons' War and use of Franceschetto Cibo as a marital pawn. If Alexander's pontificate was notorious for aggressive military campaigns in Italy, much of the impetus came from plans to follow his predecessors on a grander scale and to make use of his sons in the aggrandisement of the Church.

Alexander's eldest son had died; his second and most intellectually gifted son, Cesare, was to be a cardinal, so it was the third son, Juan, Duke of Gandia, who was first intended to be the new Girolamo Riario.

Juan arrived in Rome from Spain only in 1496; arrogant and hedonistic,[77] he was not well cast for the role, and there is little doubt he was resented by his much more forceful elder brother, though whether it was – as suspected – Cesare who contrived his murder in 1497 has never been established. Cesare, reputedly a brilliant law student in his time at the University of Pisa, had been made a cardinal in September 1493. A year after the Duke of Gandia's death, Cesare's career changed dramatically when he was allowed to renounce his red hat, to marry, and become a secular military and political leader: a unique case of such a total about-turn on the part of a cardinal. But, as Sigismondo de' Conti commented, Cesare was always more suited to be a man of war than a cardinal.[78] Even during the first five years of his pontificate Alexander may have consulted Cesare on military matters, about which he had to take many decisions. In the autumn of 1493, soon after the Pope made his son a cardinal and governor of Orvieto, they went together on an inspection of papal fortresses north of Rome and visited the captain-general Niccolò Orsini at Pitigliano.[79]

The initial war crisis facing Alexander VI was the threat of Charles VIII, King of France, to make good the Valois claim to the throne of Naples, based on the Angevin succession of rulers from 1266, and still being fought for in Pius II's time. In planning to invade Italy he was encouraged not only by Ludovico Sforza of Milan but also by Cardinal Giuliano della Rovere, whose detestation of the Borgia regime was such that he had left Rome for his castle at Ostia in early January 1493, and in April fled to France.[80] The impending invasion raised urgent questions about the defences of the papal state, through which the invading army would need to pass. After King Ferrante's death in January 1494, Alexander appeared to stand firmly by the Aragonese dynasty. He recognised Alfonso, Duke of Calabria, as successor to the kingdom, and Alfonso's coronation in Naples was celebrated by the papal nephew Cardinal Juan Borgia in May 1494. As Charles VIII's forces prepared to advance towards Italy, Cardinal Ascanio Sforza, in active support of his brother's schemes, slipped out of Rome and assembled a private army of about 2000 men – including heavy cavalry, mounted bowmen and foot soldiers – in Colonna territory, to threaten the borders of the kingdom and prepare a clear passage for the French.[81] These were extraordinary developments, highly placed curia cardinals taking up positions hostile to the papacy's official policy. Ascanio's move obliged

Alfonso of Calabria to take the inland or Adriatic route rather than the more direct road past Rome and Siena in planning to attack Milan and the invading French army. Alexander met Alfonso in person at Vicovaro on 12 July to co-ordinate strategy, against Cardinal Ascanio and his allies as well as against Charles VIII; the two Borgia cardinals Cesare and Juan were among those who accompanied the Pope.[82]

By the time Charles VIII and his army reached Rome in late December 1494, accompanied by Giuliano della Rovere and several French cardinals, Ascanio Sforza was supposedly reconciled and readmitted to papal favour. Even so, after Ascanio had been sent to meet and escort Charles, he and two other Milanese cardinals who were French partisans, Bernardino Lonati (Ascanio's former secretary, promoted in 1493) and Federico Sanseverino, were temporarily imprisoned in Castel Sant' Angelo. Alexander VI played a cautious but masterly hand in dealing with Charles VIII and the tense situation of a military occupation of Rome. He refused absolutely to hand over Castel Sant'Angelo, to which he retreated, though he conceded to the French the naval port of Civitavecchia. He allowed (he could hardly have prevented) the passage of the huge French army through papal territory, and approved the expedition as the supposed preliminary to a crusade. But in their face-to-face meeting in the Vatican on 16 January, and two days later, when the formal terms of agreement were ratified, Charles promising faithfully to fight the Pope's enemies, Alexander avoided granting Charles papal investiture as King of Naples. Without this Charles would have no valid title to present himself to the world as successor to the Norman kings and to Charles I of Anjou and as military protector of the Holy See. In fact Alexander conceded almost nothing to him except a free passage and the red hat for Guillaume Briçonnet, Archbishop of St Malo.[83] Cesare Borgia was appointed cardinal legate to accompany the French army south, more as a hostage than a mediator,[84] but he absconded even before they reached Velletri. Cesare made his way to Spoleto or possibly straight back to Rome: one of the first acts of inspired deception that were to make his career so famous. He was present at talks in the Vatican in March 1495 to promote with Venice, Spain (very significantly), Milan and other powers a new anti-French alliance or 'Holy League'. Signed on the last day of the month, the news of it presumably played a large part in Charles VIII's decision to withdraw from Naples with half of his army.[85]

The Pope reacted passively to the prospect of Charles VIII's return, withdrawing to Orvieto and then Perugia with most of the cardinals. Their number of course excluded Cardinal Giuliano della Rovere, who was with the retreating French army, though he left it to try (unsuccessfully) to stir up a rebellion in Genoa, with troops provided by the King.[86] The army of the Holy League, which awaited Charles VIII on the other side of the Appenines, was commanded by Gianfrancesco Gonzaga, Marquis of Mantua. He attacked the French army on the descent towards Parma, and at the Battle of Fornovo on 6 July claimed to have won (though this was disputable) a famous victory. It is surprising perhaps that no cardinal had been appointed papal legate to the Holy League army, who might at this point have claimed its victory as a sign of divine favour to the Church, rather than leaving Gonzaga free to personalise it for his own glory; presumably this lack of an appointee was because the Pope had chosen to be evasive. Meanwhile, Ludovico il Moro had tried in vain to have a papal legate appointed to direct the war against the French occupation in Lombardy. Resigned to the Pope's unwillingness to let Ascanio Sforza play such a role, he several times proposed Cardinal Lonati, but the latter was instead appointed in the autumn of 1495 to preside over the resistance to the remaining French forces of occupation in the south.[87] On the Feast of the Annunciation 1497, when the Marquis of Mantua came to Rome in his capacity of commander of the allied forces, and talks were held in the Vatican Palace, it was noted that the Marquis conversed only with the cardinals of Valencia and Milan (Cesare Borgia and Bernardino Lonati), two members of the Sacred College with the greatest interest in military matters.[88]

Giuliano della Rovere, meanwhile, had slipped into semi-obscurity since 1495, spending much of the time in his diocese of Avignon, but trying hard in 1496 to persuade Charles VIII to return to Italy. At the same time he invested his own money and energy in a further attempt to provoke a pro-French uprising in Genoa, which he claimed he could easily achieve with the aid of about 2000 Swiss infantry; he even led a Swiss force on his home town of Savona in January 1497 but had to withdraw. In 1499 he accompanied Louis XII and his army when the new King of France, allied with Venice, attacked Milan and overthrew the Sforza regime.[89] Giuliano's record of disobedience and belligerence during the eleven-year pontificate of Alexander VI seems to reflect his ambition to be pope in his place, and his vain hope of seeing Borgia deposed by a French-sponsored Council. Since his military activities as a cardinal were not carried out on the orders or on behalf of the reigning pope, it is difficult to see how he could have possibly justified them in the light of canon law or customary standards, but perhaps (if he did consult his conscience on the matter) he could somehow have convinced himself and his confessor that he was acting in the longer-term interests of the Church.

Meanwhile, having seen off Charles VIII on his withdrawal north-wards in 1495, Alexander reverted to one of the prevalent problems of his predecessors and resolved on war against turbulent Roman barons and other 'tyrants'. This started with a campaign against the Orsini in the autumn of 1496. It was here that Juan, Duke of Gandia, proved to be rather a disappointment. On 26 October he had received in St Peter's the staff of captain general and, together with Guidobaldo di Montefeltro, Duke of Urbino, the banners of the Church; Cardinal Lonati was appointed to accompany the expedition, with the remarkable title of legate de latere 'to assist the attack by storm' ('expugnationem') of the Orsini lords.[90] At first all went well, most fortresses offering little resistance, but assaults on Bracciano, the huge castle of Napoleone Orsini (Pius II's former general), failed. Orsini reinforcements, including troops led by Vitellozzo Vitelli subsidised with French money, caused a withdrawal, and then a pitched battle at Soriano in which the Duke of Gandia was wounded and discredited, and Guidobaldo captured.[91]

The Duke of Gandia's slightly greater success on his father's account was an artillery bombardment in March 1497 against the French garrison remaining in the castle of Ostia at the mouth of the Tiber, supported by the Spanish infantry of Gonzalvo da Cordova. Overshadowing this operation, however, is a sinister allegation about the ethics of papal warfare made by the French, or rather Basque, commander Menaut Aguerre. It depends on a document bearing a problematic date (over a year later, August 1498), which is the supposed confession of a certain Francesco, commissary of the salt works. This man had been acting suspiciously, and when arrested confessed to Menaut and the master of the ordnance that the Pope and Giambattista Ferreri, datary and later cardinal, had ordered the use of poisonous flames and fumes to kill the French garrison, 'en feu ardant et fumee empoisonnant': Menaut commented that this would be a death much more shameful and abominable than death by the sword. Thrown onto bonfires, certain chemicals supplied by an apothecary were said to produce a toxic infection of the air, though it seems that the plan (even assuming that the deposition is a valid document) was forestalled.[92]

The debate whether Alexander VI dominated or was dominated by Cesare Borgia cannot be discussed here in detail. Alexander's purpose resembled that of his predecessors: to maximise the extension of papal control within central Italy, over Umbria, Romagna and the March of Ancona and, around the district of Rome, to suppress overmighty barons. In general and, most of all, initially, Cesare was the instrument of papal war aims, and the equipment of his armies in all three of his campaigns was at the expense of the Apostolic Camera. The first campaign, launched in November 1499 against the former vicariate of Girolamo Riario in Imola and Forlì – still governed by his widow Caterina Sforza – was straightforwardly a papal military operation. Cesare was even accompanied by a cardinal legate, his cousin Cardinal Juan Borgia-Lanzol (son of Alexander's sister Juana); it was the cardinal, moreover, not Cesare, who formally received the obedience of the citizens of Imola.[93] In the second campaign, lasting from October 1500 to April 1501, against Pesaro, Rimini and Faenza, Cesare operated with less semblance of ecclesiastical control, but was only out of step with his father over his delay in conquering Faenza, having retired for the winter of 1500–1 to organise his government at Cesena. A more serious breach resulted from Cesare's decision to return to Rome only after a diversion in May and June 1501 through Tuscany, to intimidate Florence and attack Piombino. This sequel certainly went against Alexander's instructions. Indeed, Cesare's capture of the seaport and duchy of Piombino had no justification as part of a campaign in defence of Church lands, and the main purpose seems to have been to acquire a base for his future aggrandisement in Tuscany. After this, from June to September 1501, he returned south and assisted his father and French forces against Federico, the last Aragonese King of Naples, and his allies the Colonna, whose fortresses south of Rome the Pope confiscated and planned to extend and fortify more strongly.[94]

But in Cesare's third campaign (June–July 1502), directed against the remaining semi-independent rulers in the March of Ancona and first against Giulio Cesare Varano of Camerino, he reverted to taking initiatives of his own. It may be that he had even not consulted his father at all about making a treacherous attack on Guidobaldo, Duke of Urbino, before dealing with Camerino, though Alexander seems to have recovered quickly from any qualms he felt about this, to judge by the delight he openly expressed at the fall of Camerino. The Venetian ambassador in Rome, Antonio Giustinian, reported on 22 July that bonfires and peals of church bells were ordered in Rome, and that Alexander had declared that 'we have had many victories, but none has brought us such joy as this one'; he was still so elated a few days later that, when recounting it to the cardinals in consistory, he forgot to mention news about Turkish reverses received from the legate in Hungary.[95] Cesare's plans to establish himself in a new central Italian principality were beginning to mature in the winter of 1502–3 when he contrived the deception and murder at Senigallia of various *condottieri* whom he mistrusted; shortly before his father's sudden death in August 1503, it seems that Maximilian, the emperor-elect, may have been willing to cede to Cesare the lordship over Pisa and perhaps also over Siena and Lucca.

That Alexander was mainly concerned for Cesare to be the instrument of papal power rather than a new prince in his own right is shown by his insistence that Cesare should put other plans aside in the winter of 1502–3 and turn his attention against the Orsini. Alexander cursed him for his inactivity (he had retired again to Cesena in December): 'Son of a whore, bastard!' he declared in a loud voice for all to hear, according to Antonio Giustinian.[96] He may well have become alarmed by Cesare's ambitions and complained that his later operations cost far too much money.[97] The Apostolic Camera had indeed been paying out huge sums on Cesare Borgia's behalf: vast acquisitions of artillery and other equipment; for example, just in May and June 1502 it had paid for over 83,000 pounds of gunpowder.[98]

No doubt Alexander's paternal pride enhanced his admiration, widely shared, at Cesare's *fortuna* and lightning successes, but it is also striking how interested he himself had become in fortification and military matters. For example, father and son had gone on another tour of inspection together early in 1502, taking in Civitavecchia, Corneto and Cesare's new conquest of Piombino.[99] Alexander believed that strength lay in a network of fortresses, to be commanded by his relatives or Spanish cronies, and authorised the spending of large sums on improvements, particularly to Castel Sant'Angelo, Città Castellana (north of Rome) and other castles in the neighbourhood, including the Colonna fortress of Genazzano captured early in 1502.[100] In October the same year he was reported to have spent a whole day inspecting the ordnance and other weaponry in Castel Sant'Angelo as though, commented the Venetian ambassador, he was expecting imminent battle.[101] In the anti-Orsini campaign of 1503 the Pope took a close interest in the siege of Ceri, which, in spite of Cesare's doubts about its feasibility, began in early March; it fell eventually, after intensive bombardment, and the Pope is said himself to have supervised the destruction of its cistern and the cutting of steps up the precipitous cliff face.[102]

Meanwhile, the idea of an inevitable great war against the Turks, which it was his duty to plan and launch, was a serious preoccupation of Alexander's, just as it had been the fixed idea of his uncle Calixtus III and a major concern of subsequent popes. Even supposing Alexander had a few scruples of conscience about Cesare's campaigns, at least (he might have reassured himself) his ruthless and terrifying son had delivered, providentially, a rapid solution to the perennial problem of controlling the March of Ancona and Romagna, now even more of a risk to the papacy with their vulnerable Adriatic coastline open to Turkish invasion. In fact, Alexander's implementation of a crusade project coincided in time with Cesare's earlier triumphs. After commissioning a special report on the prospects of an expedition to the east, in June 1500 he published a crusading bull in which, like Pius II, he announced his intention to take part in a crusade, to face death if necessary, accompanied by the cardinals. A few months later, the fall of Modon and other Venetian fortresses in southern Greece strengthened his determination to raise funds by all means possible: extraordinary taxation of the clergy (including the cardinals), appropriation of rich bequests and sale of indulgences. In the spring of 1502, a Venetian war fleet commanded by Benedetto Pesaro sailed together with thirteen papal war galleys under the latter's cousin Jacopo Pesaro, Bishop of Paphos. They won a spectacular success at the end of August, capturing the island of Levkas or Santa Maura from the Turks, although the Venetians had soon to hand it back, on account of their treaty obligations.[103] This naval victory is commemorated in the votive painting that Jacopo Pesaro commissioned from the youthful Titian, thought to have been painted in 1506 (Koninklijk Museum voor Schöne Kunsten, Antwerp).[104] Here Alexander, wearing a bland expression of pride in the clerical commander's achievement, presents Jacopo Pesaro, bearing the banner with the crossed keys, to St Peter: a clear statement of the Pope's commitment to armed struggle against enemies of the Church and the defence of his own authority.

## CONCLUSION

The increasing militarisation of the papacy, which has been a theme of this and the previous chapter, found expression not only in the waging of war and leadership in campaigns by cardinals and lay or clerical papal relatives but also – particularly in the case of Pius II – the praise and celebration of war at the highest level of ecclesiastical authority.

It also continued to be expressed, on a growing scale, by military building. By the end of the fifteenth century the papal state, that large wedge bisecting the Italian peninsula, had become one of the most formidably defended zones of Europe. It has even been claimed that it

Titian, Pope Alexander VI presenting a papal banner and Jacopo Pesaro to St Peter (Koninklijk Museum voor Schöne Kunsten, Antwerp).

had its own arms industry at Spoleto, producing crossbow bolts, shields and lances, though this may not have been projected until a later date.[105] The main centres for the manufacture of armour, guns and other metal equipment were in northern Italy, particularly at or near Brescia and Milan; but the papacy under Sixtus IV and his successors was certainly supporting speculative ventures in mining for iron and other minerals.[106] Following the precedents in massive fortress construction, associated particularly with Cardinal Albornoz and Nicholas V, Sixtus IV and his successors were responsive to the improved technology of firepower and pioneered the construction of low, sharp-angled bastions and rounded defensive walls rather than vertical buildings. One of Sixtus's engineers, Baccio Pontelli (1450–92/4), should be mentioned in particular, for the new castle he designed in the early 1480s, at Ostia near the mouth of the Tiber, which has been called 'the most advanced fortress of its time'.[107] It was the stronghold of Cardinal Giuliano della Rovere, who brazenly assured Innocent VIII, who visited him there in November 1489, that he had had it built only 'for the benefit of Mother Church and the Pope's own security' ('ha fatto fare questa fortezza a beneficio dell Sancta matre chiesa e a conservatione de la Sanctità Vostra').[108] That it was perfectly appropriate for cardinals to act as governors of fortresses seems to have been generally accepted. Among members of the reform commission of 1497, set up by Alexander VI when stricken with grief for the Duke of Gandia, only the Portuguese cardinal Costa voted against the practice, and even he in 1503 – when well over ninety – was put in charge of Ostia, on behalf of Giuliano della Rovere.[109] Baccio Pontelli has also been credited with many castles in the March of Ancona and Romagna: Senigallia (slightly earlier than Ostia), Cesena, Forlì, Fano, Offida, Osimo, and Iesi; also the fortified pilgrimage church of Loreto and the defensive walls of the monastery of Grottaferrata.[110] Antonio da Sangallo the elder (ca. 1453–1534) continued as the leading building engineer under Alexander VI; among his works were the walls at Nepi and the towers at the corners of Castel Sant'Angelo.[111] Both these men were Florentines, and innovatory military building by Florence – not least as a consequence of war either allied with or opposed to the papacy – must at the same time be acknowledged; nevertheless, the military architecture sponsored by the papacy and its dependants was impressive in scale and quality.

Was this papal militarisation also expressed by new trends in the attitudes and modes of living of the cardinals and other senior prelates in Rome? Even without the specially dangerous circumstances of 1484, at the close of Sixtus's reign and beginning of Innocent's, it had become habitual, and long remained so, for most cardinals to keep – as did the Pope himself – a well-stocked armoury. This was not just for use in the event of being sent on a military legation or even a crusade, but also as defence against insurrection and looting at the time of a papal election, or just security against each other, or against baronial private armies. Meanwhile, war games had also become an accepted norm, which perhaps is hardly surprising in view of the numbers of underemployed knights and squires or other armed retainers in papal and cardinals' households. Jousts and mock battles were frequently held in papal Rome. Among many such events were the three-day-long tournament held in honour of the marriage of Girolamo Riario and Caterina Sforza in April 1476, the joust commemorating the conquest of Granada held in February 1492 at the expense of Cardinal Alessandro Farnese, and the one in August the same year to celebrate the election of Alexander VI.[112] More sinister than these elaborate games, the Borgia Pope adopted the practice of having a military escort when he moved around Rome. For example, at his first public appearance after the coronation, to attend

Fortress of Ostia, built for Cardinal Giuliano della Rovere.

a ceremony in Santa Maria Maggiore on 27 February 1493, the Pope was escorted by three squadrons of cavalry and a large troop of infantry, attended by the principal *condottieri* in his service, and followed by men at arms bearing long lances, equipped ready for battle, which according to the Florentine ambassador Filippo Valori was unprecedented, even in wartime ('drieto, due squadre di gente d'arme con lancie lunghe armate come se andassino a combattere, che questo *etiam tempore belli* li altri Pontifici mai hanno consueto fare').[113]

Potentially another militaristic symptom of the papal court in the second half of the fifteenth century was the advent of a new class of cardinal: the prince-cardinal, or son of an Italian ruler, whose character might derive more from a military and courtly than a religious up-bringing.[114] An example – virtually the first of the species – has been seen in Francesco Gonzaga, the protégé of Pius II, who continued to display his military capacity under Sixtus. Another, who had appeared on the scene at the end of Sixtus IV's pontificate, was Ascanio Sforza, sixth son of Duke Francesco Sforza of Milan, who has already been mentioned in the context of the French invasion in 1494. Ascanio, after repeated political pressure, had been admitted to the College of Cardinals in March 1484, soon after leading a Milanese army across the river Oglio against Brescia, in Venetian territory. On a previous occasion, when his candidacy for the red hat had failed, he was said to have declared that he would gladly abandon his robes (those of an apostolic protonotary, a title he had held from the age of ten) for a soldier's liveried surcoat, and serve the Sforza regime as a professional military captain.[115] As late as 1491 Innocent VIII complained that Ascanio was still new to the curia, implying perhaps that his presence was incongruous, and that he had been brought up among soldiers.[116] Throughout his extraordinary career Ascanio continued to raise, pay for and even lead armies. He had advanced money to support Charles VIII's army of invasion, out of solidarity with his brother's risky pro-French policy, and in June 1494 he enrolled troops – as was mentioned earlier – to block the northward route of the Neapolitan army.[117] In February 1495, when fortune was turning against Charles, Ascanio shamelessly declared, according to a Mantuan report, that since he was a priest – which in fact he was not, never advancing beyond deacon's orders – he did not wish to be involved in matters of war ('per essere lui sacerdote non vole impazare de guerra').[118] This did not inhibit him from financing Alexander VI's campaign against the Orsini in 1496 and persuading other cardinals to support it,[119] and true to his vocation he not only offered half of his income but actively assisted his brother Ludovico il Moro in trying to resist the French and Venetian invaders of Milan in 1499–1500. In the penultimate stage, when commanding a naval fleet with 2000 soldiers engaged against the French encampment by Lake Como, he was very nearly hit by a projectile.[120] Nor was he the only cardinal engaged in this defensive war; his youthful brother-in-law, Cardinal Ippolito d'Este, also took part, in spite of the attempt of his father, Ercole d'Este, Duke of Ferrara, to dissuade him, on the grounds, interestingly, of St Ambrose's ancient precept that 'the sole arms of a priest should be prayers'.[121] Their participation in this desperate attempt to save the Sforza regime was not quite the same thing as fighting on behalf for the Apostolic See, but it is particularly remarkable that Ascanio was commanding a military force in the field at the same time as holding the high office of Cardinal Vice-Chancellor of the Church. An elaborately wrought suit of armour, a warrior on horseback, supposedly wrought by Missaglia, the famous Milanese armourer, is associated with his name; it is preserved in the Reale Armeria at Turin, though most of it may be a nineteenth-century facsimile.[122]

One of the most blatant of warrior-cardinals in this period was Federico Sanseverino. Although Federico does not fit exactly into the category of prince, he was – like Francesco Gonzaga and Ascanio Sforza – the son of a famous military captain. Federico's father was Roberto Sanseverino, scion of a prominent baronial family of the kingdom of Naples, and to gratify him Innocent VIII had reluctantly included Federico on a shortlist of prospective cardinals in 1489 together with Lorenzo de' Medici's son Giovanni, both of them secret and strictly political nominees.[123] It will be remembered that Angelo Geraldini had urged the appointment of Roberto's son back in 1486, and Milanese political pressure eventually forced Innocent's hand to nominate him, in spite of his character. Cardinal Ascanio Sforza, who was largely responsible for the nomination, was quoted using the argument that office changes personality, citing himself as a parallel example, the son of a *condottiere* from a family that had never produced churchmen, who had turned out well in spite of expectations.[124] Innocent, however, was adamantly opposed to Federico, and refused subsequently to confirm the appointment.[125] Sanseverino's character was even worse than what was blameworthy in a soldier, so Pietro Alamanni, the Florentine ambassador, reported darkly to Lorenzo de' Medici on 18 May 1492.[126] The outcome was that Federico, who was described after his death in 1516 as 'a man of huge stature',[127] was only admitted to the Sacred College after Innocent's death in August 1492, when thanks to a small private army he gained admission to the conclave:[128] a remarkable instance of a cardinal actually taking up office by armed force.

It should be borne in mind, however, that some of the cardinals most active in war operations did not come from backgrounds at all princely or military, such as Ludovico Trevisan or Niccolò Forteguerri, or even Giuliano della Rovere. Likewise, some of the new generation of 'princely cardinals' such as Jaime of Portugal (1456), Teodoro di Monferrato (1467), Giovanni d'Aragona (1477) – or even Giovanni de' Medici (unofficially appointed 1489, admitted 1492) – had little or no aptitude for arms. Meanwhile, the phenomenon of prince-cardinals – and even the rogue warrior-cardinal Sanseverino – not to mention papal nephews and sons being made cardinals, provokes the question whether the Sacred College was changing overall in character and composition in the second half of the fifteenth century. No detailed analysis can be offered here; but numerically it seems to have been growing larger. Sixtus IV created thirty-four cardinals during his fourteen years in office; Alexander VI created forty-three in eleven years;[129] but the desirable maximum of twenty-four, after the 'four and twenty elders clothed in white raiment' (*Revelation*, IV, 4) that the cardinals themselves often imposed as a solemn obligation before papal elections, was never strictly respected. The rapid death rate of cardinals, owing more to average age than occupational hazards, makes it hazardous, however, to base judgements on the size of the college; in any case the 'princely' and political component was never very large in relation to the whole, and it seems doubtful whether its advent made much difference to the long-established tradition of readiness for active military service in the papal entourage. Not of much relevance either was the distinction between cardinal deacons and cardinal priests and bishops; the former category, since they had not been ordained priests, might have seemed a shade more suited to the battlefield than the other two holy orders, and it is true that junior 'princely' cardinals, such as Francesco Gonzaga, Ascanio Sforza or Giovanni de' Medici, were never promoted beyond the class of deacon. But, in practice, ever since the twelfth century cardinals in the higher orders had served irrespectively as military legates: Vitelleschi, Trevisan and Forteguerri are all examples of cardinal priests – the most numerous category of cardinals – from the 'Renaissance' period.

The character of members of the Sacred College, in both ideal and reality, was nevertheless a topic that excited contemporary interest. It was, for example, expressed in the form of letters by Pius II's protégé Cardinal Jacopo Ammannati, particularly by a short tract in the form of a letter addressed to Cardinal Francesco Gonzaga in the summer of 1468, advising him about the lofty moral role of a cardinal.[130] In another letter to Francesco, in October 1474, Ammannati struck a slightly

Armour supposedly made for Cardinal Ascanio Sforza (Armeria Reale, Turin).

different note, praising him as a princely cardinal with the special assets of noble birth, intelligence, authority, eloquence, grace.[131] In the long didactic letter of 1468 Ammannati's emphasis had been on dignity and usefulness ('utilitas') to the Church, the giving of counsel and performance of duty, stressing – against the monarchical trend, particularly displayed by Paul II – that the cardinals were a component of the papacy, members of one body. Ammannati praised as a paragon among contemporary cardinals the learned Greek Bessarion, and – in spite of his own devotion to the memory of Pius II – expressed distaste for war and any involvement in it. In another letter, however, addressed in January 1474 to Cardinal Berardo Eroli, which is a eulogy post-mortem of Cardinal Niccolò Forteguerri, he dwells on Forteguerri's skills as a military commander against Sigismondo Malatesta, Everso da Anguillara and other enemies of the Church: Forteguerri was strong in battles and siege warfare, sometimes fierce and vehement, but not cruel, Ammannati concluded.[132] 'Usefulness' was a broad criterion; it could justify military qualities or even munificence and a lavish style of living; though any suggestion of pomp was deplored by Ammannati in his letter of 1468, it was positively recommended in the exhaustive book about the office of cardinal compiled by an apostolic scriptor, Paolo Cortesi (1465–1510).

Cortesi's *De Cardinalatu*, dedicated to Julius II, was not published until 1510 but was conceived long before, thanks to a suggestion – so the Preface records – of Cardinal Ascanio Sforza. Cortesi places cardinals on the same moral and political high ground as Ammannati did in 1468, but includes a long section on the cardinal's economy and the quality of 'magnificence', of which Ascanio had certainly been one of the leading practitioners, at least until the downfall of Sforza Milan in 1499. Cortesi stressed that prince-cardinals were in a special category as 'benefactors', and therefore had less obligation to be learned or austere, but they were still bound by many requirements of prudent judgement, beneficence and so on, as were the other 'senators of the Church', of whom, incidentally, he considered the desirable total to be forty. Regarding the obligation to serve in war, Cortesi made no distinction between the duties of one category of cardinal or another. Under the heading of the moral virtue of 'Fortitude' he listed the various grounds on which a cardinal should be obliged to go to war, and elsewhere insisted on the necessity of self-defence, in maintaining an adequate bodyguard and armoury.[133] He suggested that scenes of victories of the Church would be appropriate for the main stairway in a cardinal's palace, and that it would help the cardinal to be mentally alert if he had an *exemplum* of military foresight painted in his bedroom, such as Francesco Sforza sharpening a spear.[134]

\* \* \* \* \*

In the course of a devious discussion about the prospects for Forlì and Imola after the death of Girolamo Riario, Lorenzo de' Medici made a famous remark to the Ferrarese ambassador in Florence that the time would come when the Church would be more dangerous to the rest of Italy than Venice.[135] The latter part of Innocent VIII's reign may not seem the best time for such a prophesy, although it is true that Innocent had wanted to reabsorb Girolamo's principality into the papal state rather than leave the way open for Milan or Venice or let in some minor figurehead (Lorenzo's preferred solution). But Lorenzo's warning was already being fulfilled under Alexander VI, or so Machiavelli reckoned in Chapter 11 of his book *Il Principe*, written in 1513–15. Machiavelli made clear that he himself was no partisan of clerical principalities, but maintained that the Borgia Pope, through his cruel but astute son Cesare, made papal forces really feared, whereas under his predecessors they had not been taken seriously.[136] Perhaps this was rather unfair to some of them, particularly Martin V, Eugenius IV and Pius II, but Machiavelli was not one for qualified judgements. A more staid Florentine political writer and historian, Francesco Guicciardini (1483–1540), in his *Storie Fiorentine*, written in 1508–9, made a similar assessment. Alexander VI, he reckoned, had demonstrated how great the power of a pope, was when he had a first-rate military commander on whom he could rely; he came to hold the balance in the war between France and Spain over southern Italy in 1501–3; all in all, he was both more wicked and more successful than perhaps any pope had been for centuries.[137]

# 5 The Julian trumpet, 1503–13

## ALARMS AND EXCURSIONS, 1503–9

It was of course Giuliano della Rovere, Julius II (pope from 1503 to 1513), who received the frank approval of Machiavelli as the pope who best understood the use of force,[1] and the slightly more measured judgement of Guicciardini in his magisterial *Storia d'Italia*, written in the 1530s, that 'Julius's concern and intention was to exalt the temporal greatness of the Church with the arts of war'.[2] Giuliano's record as a warrior-cardinal has already been noted in the previous chapter: how he served his uncle Sixtus IV as military legate in Umbria, built the fortress of Ostia, directed Innocent VIII's policy – without notable success – in the Neapolitan Barons' War and against Boccolino at Osimo. Subsequently, so disaffected from Alexander VI was he that in 1493–94 he encouraged and shadowed Charles VIII's invasion of Italy, planned (unsuccessfully) a new French invasion in 1496, and accompanied Louis XII in his campaign of 1499 and victorious entry into Milan. The *Julius Exclusus*, that damning dialogue written in about 1518, which ridiculed the 'Julian trumpet' of a pope in armour calling the world to war, was quoted in the Preface to this book, and will be further discussed below. It was not, however, the first literary attack on Julius as a warrior; even in the Pope's lifetime and before his famous storming of the castle of Mirandola early in 1511, a fictitious letter of Jesus Christ to Julius, dated 'in Heaven, 26 December 1509', circulated in Venice.[3] It reprimanded him over 'his abominable appetite for human and Christian bloodshed: so many ruins, rapes, robberies, acts of sacrilege and souls gone to perdition' were the outcome of his cupidity for temporal power. But none of these contemporary or near-contemporary attacks on Julius places him within the broader and long-sustained traditions of papal war-making.

Julius frankly declared, soon after his election as pope, that he intended to reclaim the territories in Romagna wrongly alienated from the Church.[4] Although he was at the time aiming to sound conciliatory towards the Venetians, who had seized as 'liberators' Cesare Borgia's territories in the Romagna, time showed that, as in the past, the Pope's aim could hardly be achieved without the use, or at least the overwhelming threat, of military force. Julius mounted a succession of campaigns of reconquest in the papal state. The first, in 1506, was directed against the families who effectively controlled two major papal cities, the Baglioni of Perugia and the Bentivoglio of Bologna; but it proved to be more a military demonstration than a conflict. The point is, however, that the Pope himself, and most of the cardinals – none of them is reported to have objected[5] – were to accompany the armed expedition. Julius had threatened to hire for it several thousand Swiss infantry to supplement troops of the Duke of Urbino and the King of France; when leaving Rome on 26 August, the expedition included 150 *stradiotti* (armed horsemen from Albania), as well as archers and gunners.[6] Niccolò Machiavelli joined the expedition as Florentine ambassador and found Julius at Nepi, where the Pope was inspecting with admiration the fortress designed for his predecessor by Antonio da Sangallo; he accompanied the papal party to Perugia, having witnessed Giampaolo Baglione's terms of submission, and was present at the ceremonial entry there.[7] Reinforced by troops commanded by the penitent Giampaolo Baglioni, Julius's army and retinue – still including the impressionable Machiavelli – then moved on through the Appenines. Julius evidently did not hesitate to play the commander; when they reached Forlì, for example, on 11 October, he inspected the munitions and other arms in the citadel.[8] Not surprisingly the Bentivoglio, like the Baglioni, also submitted without firing a shot, intimidated by much stronger forces, including the nearby French army, than Perugia had faced.[9]

Erasmus of Rotterdam had been staying in Bologna, but fled to Florence, expecting that there would be fighting and shocked that the Pope was playing the military leader, but he soon returned. Many years

Raphael (attrib.), Julius II: this drawing is thought to be a contemporary copy of the portrait in the National Gallery, London, rather than a preliminary sketch. Reproduced by permission of the Duke of Devonshire and the Trustees of the Chatsworth Settlement. Photograph: Photographic Survey, Courtauld Institute of Art, Devonshire Collection, Chatsworth.

later, when describing a thunderstorm in 1526, he recalled the time 'when our earthly Jupiter was hurling his thunderbolts at Bologna', but it is less likely that he heard guns fired in anger than in celebration of Julius's triumphal entry on 11 November.[10] The eviction of the Bentivoglio and establishment of direct government in Bologna by papal legates, in conjunction with a nominated civic senate, was to last for the next three and a half years. Two statues were commissioned to represent the personal victory of Julius. One enthroned figure was of painted wood or stucco, and erected on the crenellation of the palace in which the papal legate resided. The other, more famous, a huge figure cast in bronze by Michelangelo, was eventually erected in February 1508 over the main portico of the civic church of San Petronio. It expressed – so the anecdote goes, told by Michaelangelo's contemporary biographer, Ascanio Condivi, as well as by Giorgio Vasari – the Pope's ill-tempered demand that the sculptor should show him bearing a sword rather than a book, as he did not read (quite untrue). A Bolognese chronicle states, however, that both statues showed the Pope holding the keys of St Peter in one hand and blessing with the other. In any case, with or without sword, two formidable images of the conquering Pope dominated the centre of Bologna.[11]

Julius's next campaign was only a sideshow within the much larger war of the League of Cambrai, the European and Italian alliance against Venice that broke out into war early in 1509. Julius had his own quarrel with Venice in the Romagna over the republic's refusal to give up Rimini, Faenza, Ravenna and other places, but he had been cautious over supporting the League in its wider plan of hostilities in northern Italy. However, he had been attending to naval defences, in particular to an ambitious reconstruction of the fortifications of Civitavecchia. A medal was struck in December 1508 to commemorate the foundation of this 'rocca nuova', a vast rectangular structure with round corner towers rather than the angled bastions by then more usual; building work probably began the following April.[12] That same month, coinciding with Louis XII's invasion of Lombardy, a papal land force duly went into action against Venice in the Romagna. It was commanded by Julius's nineteen-year-old nephew Francesco Maria della Rovere, son of the former's brother Giovanni, whose military career and death in 1501 has been mentioned earlier. Francesco Maria was the adopted heir to Guidobaldo, Duke of Urbino, who had died in 1508, and also received the title of Captain General of the Church, but he was to prove a continuous disappointment to his uncle, and a thorn in the flesh to later popes.[13]

A certain share in the running of this campaign was held by Cardinal Francesco Alidosi, Julius's protégé and former secretary, now in his mid-fifties (b. 1455, made a cardinal in 1505), who had been legate of Bologna and the Romagna since July 1508. The partnership was stressful, and their army was a curious mixture of Spanish infantry, 867 of them, described at the time as 'beastly, badly equipped and robbers', and over twice as many Swiss.[14] Alidosi, however, lost no time in strengthening the fortress of Galliera, at the south-eastern entrance to Bologna, against possible Venetian attack. The Pope's instructions to him were explicit: to recover places in Romagna, especially Faenza, still occupied by the Venetians, 'those sons of iniquity'; to devastate the territory of Faenza if there was no submission; and to bring war machines to the walls of the city and destroy it 'by fire and iron'. Francesco Maria della Rovere took Solarolo, and Brisighella, north of Faenza in the Val Lamone, was besieged, and after its surrender on 29 April was subjected to a horrendous massacre by the Spanish troops.[15] Faenza presented greater problems, not least because the cardinal legate had allegedly failed to supply the Captain General with sufficient munitions; but Alidosi apparently gained the surrender of Faenza by the stratagem of subverting or corrupting some of its defenders. The Venetian governors of Faenza

Medal of Cardinal Francesco Alidosi, probably commemorating Romagna campaign, 1509, obv. and rev. (Warburg Institute).

were allowed to depart peacefully, but then, as was probably pre-arranged by either Alidosi or Francesco Maria della Rovere, were attacked and robbed on their journey.[16] 'We hope soon to have Ravenna, Rimini and Cervia,' Cardinal Alidosi wrote confidently to the Forty or Senate of Bologna on 9 May 1509;[17] a week later, Russi, with its strongly fortified castle, surrendered.[18] Soon after this, the cardinal and the Captain General entered the city of Ravenna, uneasily together. But Alidosi seems to have regarded himself as the single-handed conqueror of the Romagna. He made a ceremonial entry into Bologna by the Porta

## DE IVLIO.II.PONT.MAX.ORBEM CHRISTIA NVM IN ARMA CONCITANTE.

Pope Julius II in armour exhorting Emperor Maximilian, King Louis XII of France and King Ferdinand of Aragon to war on Venice (anon. print in Ulrich von Hutten, *Ad Divum Maximilianum bello in Venetos euntem Exhortatio*, 1517) (British Museum, Department of Prints and Drawings).

Maggiore in early June, and rode down a street decorated with triumphal arches and temporary statues of subjected towns. He even had a medal struck with his portrait as legate and on the reverse an image of Jupiter in his chariot putting birds to flight.[19] The outcome of the campaign was thus to bring as much joy to Julius as, or even more than, the French victory over Venetian forces at Agnadello on the river Adda, near Treviglio, on 14 May. 'Thus easily did the God of Victory give all to the Pope,' wrote Sigismondo de' Conti complacently.[20]

Another of Julius's cardinals who was detailed to play an active role in this war was Sigismondo Gonzaga (appointed in December 1505), son and brother of the professional military captains Federico and Gianfrancesco Gonzaga II, successive Marquises of Mantua. Sigismondo arrived in Ancona as cardinal legate of the March in March 1509. Immediately Francesco Maria della Rovere was ordered to recruit for the cardinal's service a company of 'four hundred infantry with a good corporal' to be stationed at the port of Fano and be totally under the cardinal's command.[21] In early May Sigismondo was instructed by the Pope to give all possible assistance to the officer in charge of coastal defences, since it was expected that the Venetians would probably try to mount an attack by sea; a few weeks later the cardinal declared that attempts at Fano and Senigallia had been resisted, and he was confident that he could boldly defend Ancona from any attack.[22] Naturally he hailed with joy the news of Venice's defeats at Agnadello and in the Romagna. 'The victories of the Pope,' he wrote on 31 May, 'demonstrate how great and effective is the might of the two swords which the vicar of Christ holds in his hand – the temporal and spiritual – to castigate and punish the enemies and rebels of Holy Church.'[23] One could hardly want a more explicit citation, in direct and physical terms, of the idea of the two swords, and the justification of using military force against a secular power that had usurped supposed rights and possessions of the Church. But the striking spectacle of the Pope in aggressive alliance with the Emperor and the Kings of France and Spain and other rulers, against a Christian power, did not fade quickly from collective memory, and soon became a target for anti-papal satire.

Even more actively committed than Sigismondo Gonzaga was another princely cardinal, Ippolito d'Este, on whom the red hat had been bestowed in 1493 at the age of fourteen. He was the brother of Duke Alfonso d'Este of Ferrara, and of Isabella d'Este, Marchesa of

Mantua, Cardinal Sigismondo's sister-in-law. Ippolito had some previous experience under arms; his role in the defence of Sforza Milan in 1499 has already been mentioned, and he also played a part in resistance to the Bentivoglio attempt to re-enter Bologna in 1507.[24] Together with his brother the duke, he now directed the attack on the Venetian river fleet on the river Po at Polesella, above Ferrara, in December 1509. This inland naval campaign by Venice against Ferrrara, a papal dependency and supporter of the League, had been intended to avenge the catastrophic defeat by the French army at Agnadello the previous May. Instead it was another disaster for the Venetians; thanks to the Ferrarese heavy gunners, aided by heavy rain and the rising level of the river, all but two of seventeen war galleys were destroyed and many oarsmen (*galeotti*) lost their lives. It was a turning point of the war.[25]

The Este family acclaimed the young cardinal as the hero of the battle. On 22 December Duke Alfonso wrote to their sister Isabella at Mantua that he and Ippolito had destroyed the Venetian armada and gained fifteen galleys as well as many other boats;[26] Ippolito himself wrote a febrile short message: 'By evening the whole Armada will be wrecked, with the help of God.'[27] A Mantuan eye-witness, Gianfrancesco di Bagno, who had been in the field with Cardinal Ippolito since 11 December, reported more fully: 'You cannot see the Po for all the fragments of ships, captured or sunk, and survivors swimming. [Together with the Duke] the Most Reverend Monsignor has been out on campaign throughout the night, playing the perfect captain. Such a glorious outcome was owing to the will of God.'[28] Next day the cardinal was again leading the attack, this time accompanying an advance party of foot soldiers and light cavalry right beneath the Venetian-built bastion, before the gunners were instructed to move into position. One hour before sundown he gave the order to open fire; he remained in the saddle all night directing operations in this dramatic offensive; Venetian galleys were again smashed and their rowers' heads were observed 'like birds in the water.'[29] The poet Ludovico Ariosto, who wrote to congratulate his patron, Cardinal Ippolito, on Christmas Day,[30] alluded to this victory in his epic *Orlando Furioso*, stressing that Ippolito's glory was not only in vanquishing the enemy, but in suffering no loss to his own forces.[31] After a victory procession and a sung *Te Deum* on 27 December, Ippolito had a great number of captured Venetian war banners hung in the cathedral of Ferrara.[32] His reputation as a soldier was to remain with him, though he had to keep in the background when the Pope declared war next year upon his brother. This did not deter him in November 1510 from ordering a new, made-to-measure suit of armour, including breastplate, from a Milanese manufacturer.[33]

## 'OUT WITH THE BARBARIANS' (1):
## FAILURE AGAINST FERRARA, 1510–11

It was after Julius switched his policy to oppose France, and its loyal ally Ferrara, forming the so-called Holy League in the summer of 1510, that his pursuit of war became implacable. Julius's avowed policy was now the total eviction of foreign or 'barbarian' forces from Italy even though he himself had been one of those most responsible for inviting these forces into the peninsula since the 1480s; by January 1511 Paris de Grassis, the papal master of ceremonies, declared that Julius's aim was not only to liberate Italy, but 'to exterminate the French King and all Frenchmen'.[34] The result of the Pope's almost fanatical determination was a long war, or series of wars. Hostilities had already begun in July 1510; anathemas were pronounced on Duke Alfonso d'Este, and once again those uneasy partners in arms, Cardinal Alidosi and Duke Francesco Maria della Rovere, went into action together. Both the papal (again, mainly Spanish) and Ferrarese troops inflicted destruction and robbery over a large area round Bologna, but on 3 September Alidosi received the surrender of Modena and shortly afterwards Francesco Maria took Carpi, San Felice and Finale.[35] Charged with preparing a scheme to invade Ferrara, Alidosi sent several urgent letters to the Marquis of Mantua, who was soon to be appointed Gonfaloniere of the Church. The main task envisaged was to establish a bridge of boats over the Po, and, when the Marquis asked what sort of boats Alidosi intended, the legate replied disingenuously, 'Your excellency, who is very expert in these matters, knows better than we do, because this is an exercise in military art more than one of priestcraft, so we remit it to your own wise judgement.'[36] It seems that this operation with river boats, about which the Marquis was dubious and probably resented Alidosi's rather sardonic tone, was not put into practice after all. In September, impatient for victory, Julius again left Rome with most of the papal court and returned to Bologna as the base for military operations. Shortly after their arrival, Alidosi's secular colleague, Francesco Maria, lost patience with him altogether and had him arrested for misgovernment and suspected treasonable dealings with the French. Julius, though desperately ill with fever, reinstated Alidosi, but he was to be less trusted in future with military operations.[37]

Other cardinals were brought into this furious campaign in the region of Emilia; indeed, the Sacred College now came to be used by Julius almost as though it were a cadre of staff officers. In mid-October, when he seemed near to death with acute fever, but according to an anonymous Portuguese agent[38] still absolutely determined to fight, Cardinals Luigi d'Aragona and Pedro Isvalies were charged to restore order in Bologna and confront the French. Both of these cardinals, appointees of Alexander VI, must have been regarded as safe pairs of hands, politically above suspicion. Luigi d'Aragona, appointed at the age of twenty in 1494 – by 1510 he was therefore in his mid-thirties – was a prince-cardinal, grandson of the late King Ferrante, living in hope of the restoration to Naples of his family, who had been dispossessed by the French first in 1495 and again finally in 1501, thanks to the collusion of France, Spain and the Pope. Isvalies, appointed in 1500, who also originated from the southern kingdom, where he was Bishop of Reggio, had served as legate in Poland and Hungary, and as recently as May 1510 was cardinal legate of Perugia, with the specific job of raising infantry there.[39] These two assuredly anti-French cardinals, protected by body armour under their vestments, apparently succeeded in rallying the population of Bologna to support and defend the papal government.[40]

In November another cardinal brought onto the scene of action was Marco Corner. Also appointed in 1500, he was the son of the hyper-rich Venetian noble Zorzi Corner, brother of Caterina, Queen of Cyprus. Corner was favoured by Julius presumably on account of his relative youth (he was only twenty-eight in 1510) but, above all, for his political reliability as a subject of the main allied power in the campaign. He not only acted as the Pope's go-between with his nephew, Duke Francesco Maria della Rovere, encamped at Castelfranco, but even accompanied the duke on a reconnoitre of the defences of Modena, now again in French hands, and was present at the siege and capture of Sassuolo.[41] It is small wonder that Alidosi resented him, and on one occasion actually pulled his beard in public,[42] a particularly shocking form of insult. Yet another appointment of a cardinal to a military post was made on 15 December

1510, when Cardinal Marco Vigerio, Bishop of Senigallia, became legate specifically to the papal army.[43] A Franciscan protégé of Sixtus IV, as he emphasised in an autobiographical letter some years earlier,[44] Vigerio was somewhat old for the battlefield – like Julius himself he was in his sixties, though he had been a cardinal only since 1505. He was a loyal creature of the della Rovere family network, and since he had served as castellan of Sant'Angelo in Rome was not without some useful experience. Shortly after his appointment two small fortresses, Spilimberto and Concordia, were captured,[45] but Julius scorned Vigerio's warning at the end of December that the severe weather conditions made it impossible to take Mirandola or indeed to carry out any military operations at all. According to the Mantuan Stazio Gadio, the Pope lost his temper and declared that he would go in person, at least as far as San Felice. Various persons tried to dissuade him, saying it would be 'of little honour to the Church', but he was adamant, and declared he would take at least three cardinals with him.[46]

As is well known, Julius's direct participation reached its climax in January at the siege of Mirandola, but in this episode, even if he was the star performer, he selected the same recently tried and trusted cardinals to accompany him:[47] Marco Corner, Luigi d'Aragona and Pedro Isvalies. Vigerio, as legate to the army, was also involved in spite of his previous misgivings, and even Alidosi was to join the party, in his capacity still as legate of Bologna. Yet another cardinal to play a part in the campaign was Sigismondo Gonzaga; while still continuing as papal legate in the March of Ancona, his legation had recently been extended to Mantua and to the military campaigns against Ferrara in which the Pope himself was taking part, 'not without danger to our person'. A papal letter to Sigismondo, dated at Bologna 23 October 1510, recited all this, and noted that the cardinal's brother, Marquis Gianfrancesco Gonzaga, as Gonfaloniere, was also employed in 'the war affairs of the Church' ('res bellicae ipsius ecclesie').[48] One of Sigismondo's main duties was to galvanise his brother into action, and to ensure that supplies or reinforcements came from Mantua.[49] Evidently Sigismondo felt the need to increase his martial appearance, for in December he obtained the Pope's permission to follow his example and grow a beard.[50]

Mirandola was a strong castle between Bologna and Ferrara, defended by the young widow of its lord or count, Lodovico Pico. The Pope was specially enraged against her because, as daughter of the governor of

French-occupied Milan, Giangiacomo Trivulzio, she had put herself under French protection, but the fact that his fury was directed against a woman, and that he was ready to go to such lengths in the worst winter weather in living memory ('so cold that bread and wine froze'), added to the eternal notoriety of this campaign, and – according to a local chronicler – at the time fuelled much gossip in Bologna.[51] As well as the record in local chronicles, the events are described graphically in dispatches preserved at Mantua, also in Venetian dispatches and private letters transcribed in Marin Sanudo's diaries. On 2 January Julius set off from Bologna with his selected trio of cardinals to the castle of San Felice, south of Mirandola, furious – in spite of the blizzard conditions – that his army and its Venetian allies, encamped to the west at Concordia, were inactive.[52] He was said on 3 January to have come with the 'greatest rage in the world'; with his beard, 'he resembled a bear'. Julius castigated with crude abuse his nephew and idle commander, Francesco Maria, declaring that he should simply go back to the brothel.[53] He was also censorious, if less crudely, of the Marquis of Mantua; when told he was in bed with a bad leg, the Pope allegedly replied, 'Tell him to get up or I'll come and fetch him.'[54] On the morning of 6 January 1511, when the snow ceased for a while, Julius ordered the buglers to summon the troops, and it was reported that everyone trembled when he berated them as rogues and robbers, and yelled compulsively: 'Mirandola! Mirandola!'[55] After days more of snow, on 12 January Julius had himself brought close to the walls.

A suit of armour once believed to have been worn by Julius at Mirandola still exists in the Vatican Museum. At a fancy dress ball given by Prince Borghese in February 1866, 'young Bolognetti Cenci borrowed the armour of Julius II from the Pope for the occasion'.[56] The historian Ludwig Pastor noted that it was in the Vatican Palace in the 1880s, and the intention was to display it in the Borgia Apartments,[57] but in later editions of his *History of the Popes* he expressed doubt about its authenticity; when its association with Julius began is not clear. Recently, it has been identified as Brescian of the late sixteenth century.[58] But even if the connection with Julius is spurious, perhaps dating only from the nineteenth century, at least it demonstrates his long-standing reputation as the active warrior Pope. Not that the possession of armour by a pope or cardinal – or any lesser prelate or cleric – is in itself wholly shocking, since armour is defensive rather than offensive equipment.

Julius made several statements that make clear that he understood how indecorous or scandalous his activity might seem, but nevertheless he insisted that it was justified. On 1 January he was reported to have said, 'If the Marquis of Mantua had come here, I would have been spared this trouble of going to the camp myself, because we should have sent him to put things in order if he had been willing to go.'[59] On 12 January, addressing those cardinals and others who had joined him, he declared, 'You will be my witnesses that we did not come here to Mirandola to cause the spillage of Christian blood, but if some enormous cruelty be committed, we excuse ourselves, having been forced to this against our will.'[60]

At Mirandola on 12 January Julius ordered the artillery into position. There were rumours that the papal gunpowder was of such poor quality that it hardly enabled the cannon balls to reach the walls, but in any case the bombardment went on for a week and the Pope even threatened to sack the town if it did not surrender.[61] Cardinal Isvalies's recommendation to offer a negotiated surrender for payment was turned down with contempt. Julius retorted that it would mean the poor soldiers got nothing and the Duke of Urbino would get everything.[62] He was undeterred by a direct hit by the defenders of the town upon the convent where he had his sleeping quarters (the Bolognese chronicler, however, says it was in a 'wretched peasant's hut'); two of his grooms were injured, and a huge cannon ball that closely missed him he later presented to the Madonna of Loreto in thanks for her protection,[63] rather as Pope John Paul II offered the bullet that almost killed him in 1981 to the Virgin of Fatima. Julius moved to Cardinal Isvalies's lodging place, but soon found that equally vulnerable.[64] Meanwhile he ordered a non-stop battering and fire-bombing of Mirandola until it surrendered on 20 January; finally he climbed up a ladder through a breach in the wall, which was also criticised in Bologna as quite unheard of and shocking.[65] His lack of decorum also perturbed the Venetian observer of these events, Hironimo Lippomano, who had commented to Cardinal Alidosi that a Pope, just recovered from severe illness, on the battlefield and in deep snow was a sight unknown to history.[66] It is worth noting, however, that Julius's conduct also inspired some praise. The Marquis of Mantua judged that the presence of the Pope had been essential 'to the glorious victory of Mirandola',[67] and Giovanni Francesco Pico della Mirandola wrote that he thankfully was able to return home 'by the Grace of Almighty God and the work of His Holiness'.[68]

Elated by his very personal victory, Julius next urged a rapid advance upon Ferrara. A few mornings after taking Mirandola, he went out in the freezing dawn and banged on the doors of the billets where the infantry were quartered, ordering them out in the snow on penalty of hanging.[69] A Mantuan agent reported on 26 January that Cardinal Sigismondo Gonzaga had told him that he must ensure by the following evening the delivery of sixty pairs of oxen to draw guns to Sermide, the point on the Po from which it was hoped to mount a more direct attack on Ferrara. Cardinal Sigismondo was also harangued by Julius to supply in addition fifty sappers and bombards; the Pope, he reported, was in bed, 'and in my judgement he did not feel very canonical'.[70] Even less 'canonical' was the tirade reported on 4 February, the day after Julius had conducted a review of the troops at Finale: 'I want Ferrara; I'd sooner die like a dog than ever give it up.' Five days later he allegedly declared, 'If by any chance I am beaten, then I will raise another army and so wear out [the French] that I'll chase them out of Italy.'[71]

Julius probably planned to lead the final assault on Ferrara himself,[72] but in the meantime returned to Cento and Bologna in early February and designated two cardinals to stay with the army. One of these was Vigerio, in spite of his previous caution, and the other Marco Corner, who was young (twenty-nine) and, it was believed, 'equally expert in war'.[73] The campaign did not go well; the weather continued to be atrocious, with torrential rain following the snow and flooding the flat countryside. Julius and his entourage left Bologna again on 11 February. Cardinal d'Aragona and Cardinal Vigerio, whose age was beginning to tell, were based at Finale, where Alidosi also came and went, and the rest of the papal entourage were stationed at different places. Julius planned to advance with Cardinals Isvalies and d'Aragona by way of Lugo and a key fortress, the Bastia of the Fossato Zanniolo, after which he hoped to capture Argenta and proceed to Ferrara itself.[74] This strategy failed: instead of a papal advance, Duke Alfonso d'Este descended on the Bastia in a daring assault just before sunset on 27 February; his force inflicted heavy losses on the papal army – several hundred Spanish troops were killed – and seized banners and guns.[75] Julius had meanwhile made his new base at Ravenna, having entered the city on 18 February and summoned the cardinals to join him there; unperturbed by failure, he was said to be in excellent spirits and health, stimulated by the sea air.[76]

The image of the fighting Pope in the Ferrara campaign is indelible, but we must repeat that it was not only Julius's participation that personified the military power of the Church so forcibly, but also that of his cardinals. As well as those mentioned already, in March a new red-hatted warrior appeared on the scene in the person of Christopher Bainbridge, Archbishop of York and ambassador of Henry VIII, who as a signatory to the League was expected to launch a second front against France. Bainbridge was made a cardinal on 14 March 1511, and a few days later was appointed special papal legate 'to instigate the military campaign' to capture by land the Bastia of the Fossato Zanniolo and close in upon Ferrara from the south in conjunction with Venetian forces.[77] A letter of 22 March 1511 informs us that the Cardinal of England, legate to this campaign (*impresa*), had been dispatched with 4200 foot soldiers, and others still being rounded up, 350 men at arms, 600 light cavalry, two large cannons and five other pieces of artillery, although Bainbridge protested that he could not operate without further reinforcements, and by early April torrential rain and floods made any action beyond occasional skirmishes impossible.[78] Recalled to Bologna, where he arrived on 4 May with about 4000 infantry, about 200 lances and 300 light cavalry, twelve carts of ammunition, eight pieces of heavy artillery, two cannons, and other guns, Bainbridge was immediately reappointed, this time as principal legate to the papal–Venetian army to oppose the French and prevent them from crossing the river Panaro towards Bologna, which proved a hard assignment.[79] From 16 to 18 May he was appealing desperately for supplies to Cardinal Alidosi and the civic authorities in Bologna, pointing out, with down-to-earth practicality, that the papal army could not operate at all without teams of sappers and, above all, adequate food supplies.[80]

When Julius II rode into Ravenna on 8 April, with sixteen cardinals, a great retinue and accompanying bursts of gunfire, an observer described him as looking cheerful and well, appearing 'not like a pontiff and an old man, but a fine, strong knight'. The master of ceremonies similarly described him as still looking warlike.[81] Nevertheless, in spite of all the efforts to launch an offensive against the French, the papal campaign collapsed. On 20 May Bologna surrendered to French forces, and on the following day the Bentivoglio returned; as a symbolic and defiant insult, the wooden effigy of the Pope on the palace overlooking the main piazza was decapitated, thrown down and burnt by two demonstrators.[82] Later, in December, Michelangelo's massive bronze statue of Julius on the façade of San Petronio was also toppled and destroyed; according to the fullest chronicle account it was broken up or partly melted down – except for the head – by fires lit on the ground beneath the church of San Petronio. Afterwards some of the metal, perhaps including the head, was sent to Ferrara at the duke's special request, and it may have been recast there as guns, though the story might be a fabrication that it was turned into a huge cannon called 'Giulio', or even (according to a much later source) 'La Giulia'.[83] Somehow it seems unlikely that Alfonso d'Este, in spite of everything, would have wished to insult the Pope quite so undiplomatically, just as the restored Bentivoglio government in Bologna dissociated itself in May from the destruction of the wooden statue, punishing by banishment those responsible and even commissioning a replacement.[84] Such humiliating setbacks in 1511 might well have suggested to Julius – supposing he ever entertained such a doubt – that God was not supporting his efforts, and they also call into question Machiavelli's dictum about his invariable success in war through impetuosity.[85] But Julius's martial resolution did not desert him, and he would prove to be as good as his word about bringing another army to evict the French from Italy and to regain Bologna.

The reverse image of a belligerent cardinal was in the end provided by Francesco Alidosi, in spite of his pretensions as hero of the Romagna campaign of 1509 and apparent commitment to the campaign against Ferrara and Mirandola. He had finally lost his nerve in April 1511, when things were going badly, and his intrigues with the French cost him his life at the hands of his resentful colleague in arms, Francesco Maria della Rovere. After fleeing from Bologna on 21 May, Alidosi turned up to meet the Pope in Ravenna three days later, only to be slain, not on the battlefield but in the street, and by the hand of the Duke of Urbino, the Pope's own nephew.[86]

## 'OUT WITH THE BARBARIANS' (2)
### THE ROAD TO VICTORY, 1511–13

The disasters of May 1511 did not abase Julius for long. On the way back to Rome in June, he consoled himself by remembering his successful pacification of Spoleto thirty-seven years earlier.[87] Although he was struck down by illness again late in the summer, he was soon planning a new campaign in northern Italy. His fury against the French was aggravated by the schismatic General Council that Louis XII had summoned to Milan, and which had transferred itself to Pisa, where it threatened to depose Julius and elect an anti-pope. Julius responded by planning a large-scale war, to be launched by the allied powers in an invigorated Holy League, com-bining principally the papacy, Spain and England. Cardinal Giovanni de' Medici, no soldier but a figure of political significance as the son of Lorenzo il Magnifico, living in hope of his family's restoration to Florence, was appointed the new legate in Bologna and Emilia on 1 October 1511.[88]

Meanwhile Julius brought in as shock troops of the League the fierce and devout Swiss mountain infantry, a number of whom already served as his security guards. He had papal war banners presented to Swiss contingents, and he also sent them the papal sword and cap;[89] a banner was also sent to the allied commander Ramon de Cardona, Spanish viceroy of Naples. Inspired by the German-speaking, French-hating Bishop of Sion, Matthäeus Schiner, who had been made a cardinal at the same time as Bainbridge in March 1511 and appointed legate to the Swiss on 9 January 1512,[90] these Alpine troops largely brought about the rout of the French by their effectiveness after the Battle of Ravenna (11 April 1512), which had been acclaimed at first a French victory.[91] Only a week after Ravenna, Julius urged Schiner to rally the Swiss for a new onslaught against the French, insisting that the papal army, in spite of getting the worst of it in the battle, was now more robust and vigorous than ever.[92] Schiner wrote at the end of April to the Marquis of Mantua to inform him that 25,000 Swiss had descended the valley of the Adige to join his forces against the French, and appealed for supplies, making the same point that Bainbridge had done, about the need for troops to eat if they were to fight.[93] He managed in early June to handle the united armies of Swiss and Venetians, stopped them from plundering Cremona, and led them to decisive victory at Pavia in June over the French, who were then pursued towards the frontier.[94]

It is remarkable that at the Battle of Ravenna there had been no fewer than three cardinals in the field. On the papal or Holy League side, as well as Cardinal Schiner, was Giovanni de' Medici, 'cardinal legate of Bologna and to the army of the Holy League'; although he was taken prisoner by the French, Julius insisted it was after a heroic resistance:

'While urging the forces [of the League] to fight on manfully, he was intercepted by the enemy.'[95] On the French side was the renegade Cardinal Federico Sanseverino, who, it will be remembered, was the son of the professional *condottiere* Roberto Sanseverino. His great stature and physical strength were confirmed by the writer Paolo Giovio, who maintained that it was Cardinal Sanseverino, towering over Giovanni de' Medici on the field of battle, who assured the latter's physical safety (the future Pope Leo X, who had been taken to Milan, subsequently on the way to France escaped from his captors disguised as a soldier).[96] Sanseverino, assuming total victory for the French at Ravenna, was reported as saying that it would be enough to have 200 lances and 3000 infantry and some light horse subsequently to enter Rome – no one would resist.[97]

But Cardinal Sanseverino was wrong. Thanks to the Swiss infantry the French had retreated in spite of winning the Battle of Ravenna, and were defeated and driven out of Italy a few months later. Ravenna became a papal city again, and for the second time Bologna submitted to Julius, who permitted Cardinal Sigismondo Gonzaga, as vice-legate, to take possession without recriminations, in fact to ride into the city with the rehabilitated Francesco Maria della Rovere, on 10 June.[98] The papal master of ceremonies described the jubilation in Rome, where a torch-light procession crossed the city on 27 June.[99] The political map of Italy was redrawn at the Diet of Mantua in August, a sort of peace conference of the victors attended by the Emperor Maximilian's ostentatious representative Cardinal Matthäeus Lang, who came with a huge military escort. The republic of Florence was to be punished for its alliance with France and restored to the Medici, and the papacy was not only confirmed as controlling power of the whole of Romagna and the March of Ancona – the object of over two centuries of conflict achieved at last – but made some almost undreamt-of acquisitions. From the former French-occupied duchy of Milan – now to become briefly a debilitated Sforza princedom – the Church appropriated Parma and Piacenza and their territories. It is not clear whether any legal claim was put forward in justification; recent writers have alleged that the Pope invoked Matilda of Canossa's legacy from way back in the eleventh century, and this may be what the Mantuan agent Folenghino meant, in quoting the Pope that the Church's legal claims were 'so old that it was shameful even to discuss them' ('le ragion de la Chiesa sono tante vecchie che è vergogna ad parlarne') – a crushing and significant line of argument on which protagonists of the papal state may often have relied. From Alfonso d'Este the Church meanwhile took the dukedom of Modena and the lordship of Reggio, both former Matildine territories that Alfonso held from the Emperor.[100] The future of Ferrara itself remained uncertain; Julius still longed for Alfonso's eviction from there as well, in spite of having allowed him a safe conduct to visit Rome in July 1512. Letters from the Mantuan agent Folenghino record Julius's inflexible determination to have Ferrara and his urgent orders to Francesco Maria della Rovere to apply himself boldly to this aim, but Francesco Maria showed his habitual lassitude.[101] The papal state, nevertheless, now extended far into northern Italy. On the eve of Julius's death, in February 1513, the Church under his leadership seemed triumphant, a triumph based on armed force.

* * * * *

Julius's obsessive fascination with war was not – in addition to its practical use as a political instrument – literary and historical like Pius II's, but he seems to have had a certain taste for its expression in visual artefacts and works of art. Thus conquest by and submission to ecclesiastical authority was probably one of the intended themes of his projected tomb by Michelangelo, even though the original commission pre-dated the Pope's first military expedition to Perugia and Bologna in 1506. Michelangelo's biographer Condivi[102] corrected Vasari, who in the first version of his *Life of Michelangelo* (1550) had declared that statues of Victory with conquered provinces at their feet were meant to be among the figures adorning the pediment; the ferocious Moses, later erected in the church of San Pietro in Vincoli, and a figure of St Paul were to be placed above. According to Condivi, who was presumably told this by Michelangelo himself, the intended theme of the monument was the expected death of the liberal arts after the Pope's decease, though this does not explain what Moses, in his role as lawgiver and leader, was doing there. Examples of the intervention of divine force on behalf of the Church's priesthood and possessions seem, however, to be a main theme in the Stanza of Heliodorus, the second of Julius's palace apartments to be decorated by Raphael: including the miraculous release of St Peter from prison and the Punishment of Heliodorus (Macabees, II) for attempting to rob the temple of its treasure. A third scene, the Repulse of Attila, portraying military confrontation averted thanks to the aerial intervention of St Peter and St Paul, may have been conceived in Julius's time but was completed under his successor.[103]

This taste was also reflected in several episodes illustrating Julius's infatuation with the Marquis of Mantua's young son Federico, who had been sent to Rome as a pledge or hostage for his father's loyalty, after the Venetian government released the marquis from captivity in 1510. In May 1512, when Isabella d'Este had requested that Raphael should paint a portrait of her son in armour, the Pope gave him a tunic (*saglia*) of cloth of gold that had belonged to Cesare Borgia;[104] a few months later Julius insisted that Federico, although only twelve years old, should dress up in his armour and accompany him to inspect the papal artillery. In a letter from Rome on 15 August 1512, Stazio Gadio, the Mantuan agent who kept an eye on Federico, wrote, 'When they reached the place where all the guns were kept, Julius showed them off one by one, telling Federico their names, "the bull", "the lion", "the wolf", "the dog"' – at least the Pope, for all his gloating over big guns, had not, like Pius II, named them after his parents. Finally Julius showed Federico a fine piece that he wanted to have cast in the foundry, and said: 'Federico, we want to have this one cast very soon, so that you can write and tell your father you have seen something he has never set eyes on.'[105] There is another account of Julius's super-gun in a letter of about a month later; it was apparently the brainchild of a Ferrarese gunsmith, maestro Andrea, who was on a charge because 'this very beautiful piece of artillery, very long and thick, did not come out well from the foundry because not enough metal was put into it'.[106]

During the Roman carnival early in 1513, only two weeks before Julius died, his victories were celebrated again in an extraordinary series of tableaux and processions, which Stazio Gadio described in another letter to Isabella d'Este.[107] This was a civic event, and as such was unusually deferential in its expression of support for papal authority and military success. There were chariots – devised 'in imitation of ancient Roman triumphs and all constructed in praise of Pope Julius'. On the first was 'a woman captive tied to a tree', probably the della Rovere emblem of an oak tree, surrounded by 'spoils of war and weapons of the conquered enemy', thus following the ancient custom of Roman triumphs always to place at the head of the processions enemy prisoners and spoils. The second chariot was Italy, painted on canvas with her boundaries shown, and above was written 'Italy liberated'. On the third was a mountain, on the summit of which was the head of a bearded old man, with snow on the top of his head: according to the inscription, this represented the Appenines. The fourth portrayed a city, and there was a captive woman tied to an oak tree, indicated as 'Bologna, cause of so many evils'. The fifth was the city of Reggio, with a priest sacrificing a bull. The sixth was the city of Parma, according to the inscription, which said 'Golden Parma'. On the seventh was a woman who presented the city of Piacenza to the Pope, and the inscription said 'Piacenza, faithful Roman colony'. On the eighth was the river god Po, with a chariot in the water on which were the seven sisters of Phaeton turned into poplars; above it was the ruined Phaeton, the wrecked chariot of the sun with horses scattered. Above the ninth was a woman crowning another, supposed to be Genoa crowning Savona (this was presumably meant to represent the triumph of the Pope's native city). The tenth showed Moses, who in the desert had exalted the image of a serpent, which had in its mouth the mulberry tree to make the Sforza arms. On the eleventh was St Ambrose on horseback with an orb in his hand and men under his feet. Above the twelfth was an obelisk or needle erected in honour of Pope Julius, as could be seen from the inscription, in Greek, Hebrew, Egyptian and Latin, almost all with the same meaning. The Latin said 'Julius II, Pontifex Maximus, Liberator of Italy and Extinguisher of Schism'. The temple of the Delphic Apollo followed on the thirteenth chariot. The fourteenth showed Aaron sacrificing to God and disobedient Jews struck down by the sacrificial fire. The fifteenth bore the hydra, above which was a man with a sword to cut off heads. On the sixteenth was the (Fifth) Lateran Council, the General Council of the Church called into session in December 1512 to end schism and debate reform, with the Pope, Emperor, kings, cardinals, bishops and lords. On the seventeenth was a huge oak tree, on the top of which was the Pope, in the middle the Emperor, lower down were the Kings of Spain and England, and at the foot the arms of the Holy League.

* * * * *

In justice it must be noted that Julius himself declared at various points that his warmongering in Italy in defence of the rights of the

Church was only the prelude to a great campaign against the infidel. It was reported, for instance, he had said that Agnadello was nothing to the victory he would win against the Turks.[108] Cardinal Sigismondo Gonzaga reported in June 1509 that the Pope was commissioning many galleys at Civitavecchia, and that he himself had ordered six at Ancona which should be ready within a few weeks. He understood that Julius was determined to set forth in person; his plan was to give thanks to the Madonna of Loreto, then to tour the conquered lands in Romagna and make Bologna his base for organising the crusade; he hoped to celebrate Mass in Constantinople within a year.[109] This objective was never entirely lost to sight. Even in his lowest hours in the Romagna in the spring of 1511, Julius allegedly asked the King of Scotland's ambassador to persuade Louis XII to make peace and to launch a campaign against the infidel, in which the Pope would take part in person.[110] It was in line with this papal resolve to settle the problems of Christendom expeditiously in order to face the long-standing external enemy that Cardinal Ximenes de Cisneros (1436–1517; a cardinal since May 1507, founder of the University of Alcalá and commissioner of the first polyglot Bible) vigorously led the troops – much to the annoyance of regular officers – at the siege of Oran in 1509, and declared that the smell of gunpowder was sweeter to him than all the perfumes of Arabia.[111]

It should be clear that, even if Julius's excesses of ferocious zeal and frequent lapses of self-control exposed him to serious criticism and mockery, he stood essentially within a long tradition, even a canonical tradition, that obliged the leaders of the Church to resort to arms – though preferably not to cause bloodshed by their own hands – when the Church was in danger. Even humanist writers endorsed this. In Julius II's own time Paolo Cortesi, in his book *De Cardinalatu* (*On the Cardinalate*), had drawn upon the canon law tradition to itemise the occasions that should rightly drive a cardinal to war. In the course of discussing the moral qualities desirable in a cardinal, Cortesi listed under the heading 'Fortitude' nine such occasions when it might need to be applied, among them schism, heresy, sacrilege, attack on or non-restitution of Church lands and cities, sedition, failure to pay taxes, etc. He gave as his example Julius II's recent declaration of war against Venice, and the Romagna campaign in the spring of 1509 led by Cardinal Alidosi,[112] even if fortitude was not a virtue very appropriate to Alidosi.

The portrayal of Julius in the famous anonymous dialogue *Julius Exclusus* is, of course, a gross if not wholly undeserved caricature. First printed in 1518, but previously circulating in manuscript, it was then and later usually attributed to Erasmus, in spite of his emphatic denials. Recently the English humanist Richard Pace has been nominated as the author,[113] and Pace in his dialogue on education, *De Fructu* (1517), indeed claimed to have written an anti-Julius text some time between the death of Julius and election of his successor (February–March 1513); other parallels between the two dialogues, including a certain theatricality characteristic of Pace, have also been detected.[114] Since Pace was Cardinal Christopher Bainbridge's principal secretary and even had the skill – unusual then for an Englishman – of being able to write Italian as well as Latin, which he did on the cardinal's behalf, and in an italic hand,[115] the attribution is particularly interesting. For Bainbridge, like Julius, was also a bellicose character, and, although Pace may not have been with him in the military campaign against Ferrara in the spring of 1511, he must have appreciated that on this account Bainbridge was highly favoured by the Pope. Bainbridge was still alive in February 1513; Pace dedicated to him his translation of Plutarch's *Lives* the following year, and mentioned him gratefully in *De Fructu*.[116] So the purpose and motivation of Pace (if it was he) in risking his career by writing such a malicious diatribe against his patron's patron remains obscure.

Various facets of Julius's behaviour under the stress of war, as we have seen from Venetian and Bolognese sources, provoked surprise and shocked comment among contemporaries. But in general he was proceeding on traditional lines, though with rather stronger personal commitment and less restraint than his predecessors. Even the idea of taking nearly the whole papal court with him to the war zone or expected battlefield, as in 1506 and 1510–11, was not an innovation: had not Pius II tried to do just the same when he set off for Ancona in 1464? In December 1512 the preacher at the opening of the fourth session of the Lateran Council praised Julius to the skies for his conduct of 'just war' and his territorial gains for the Church.[117] The neo-Latin poet Marco Girolamo Vida composed between 1511 and 1513 an epic 'Juliad' celebrating the Pope's martial deeds, though unfortunately no trace of it survives (he went on to write his epic about the life of Christ).[118] Fulsome praise for Julius's bellicose character and achievements, unlike the formulations quoted at the beginning of this chapter of Machiavelli and Giuicciardini, both of whom wrote from a semi-ironical or at any rate secular point of view, was the summation of the distinguished Jesuit theologian and historian Cardinal Bellarmine (1542–1621) at the end of the sixteenth century. Bellarmine praised Julius for 'recovering a great part of the ecclesiastical kingdom, which was done by diligence and virtue, imitating with great labour the virtue and diligence of famous and holy men, partly with his own armed forces, partly with the help of allies'.[119]

# 6 Post-Julius: the late Renaissance papacy and war, 1513–65

## LEO X: MORE WAR, 1513–21

If Julius II's pontificate was the high season of papal warfare, what followed was by no means an anticlimax. It is true that Leo X (Cardinal Giovanni de' Medici) was hailed in 1513 as a Pope of peace, the healer of Italy and of Christendom. This was expressed in the pageantry of his taking possession of the Lateran on 11 April; for instance, at the house of the Sienese banker Agostino Chigi there was a temporary triumphal arch with an inscription on both sides hailing Leo as 'the happy restorer of peace'.[1] There was also 'medical' punning on his family name, for instance in the verses written for the Roman students' poetry festival of 'Pasquino'; its theme in April 1513 was Apollo, whereas the previous year it had been Mars.[2] The acclamation of Leo as bringer of peace, particularly by Florentines, contained a degree of allusion, too, to his father, Lorenzo il Magnifico, who was already being mythologised as the statesman of a golden age, whose diplomacy might have been able to prevent the cataclysm of foreign invasion and wars of the period since his death in 1492.[3] The projection of Leo as the prince of peace was also helped by the dissimilarities in age, appearance and character between himself and Julius II. Even Erasmus fell for the promise shown by Leo's character and respect for learning, and in speculative quarters there were hints that he might turn out to be the angelic Pope destined to inaugurate a new age.[4]

But much was misleading in this image, and it did not prevail for long. The portly, short-sighted Leo was not essentially averse to the use of force. His passion for hunting is a clue to this, and there is a graphic description by a cardinal's observant secretary of Leo entering the netted enclosure into which a stag had been driven and, with his eyeglass in one hand and his sword in the other, giving the wretched creature a mortal thrust.[5] The idea that Leo initiated a golden age of peace depended on the last victories of Julius II, whose launching of war against the French was supported enthusiastically by the Medici and – in spite of the unfortunate capture of Cardinal Giovanni at the Battle of Ravenna – had brought about their own restoration to Florence in September 1512.

The spring of 1513 was only briefly an auspicious time for the new Pope to pose as the neutral champion of peace and moderation. Observers in the court of Rome were quick to note that Leo's underlying attitude conformed quite closely with that of his predecessor, whom he had served, loyally if not gloriously, in successive military legations. A Mantuan agent told his master the marquis on 13 March 1513 that the Pope was said to have sent a robustly worded letter to Massimiliano Sforza, the 'restored' Duke of Milan, about the attempted restitution of Parma and Piacenza, seized on his behalf by Ramon Cardona, viceroy of Spanish Naples, as a means of strengthening Milan against threats of a new French invasion. 'I do not believe,' he wrote, 'that Pope Leo will be any less tenacious concerning the Church's affairs than was Pope Julius of happy memory.'[6] Similarly, Cardinal Sigismondo Gonzaga wrote to his sister-in-law, Isabella d'Este, on 11 April, 'His Holiness has triumphed as the Captain [sic] and vicar of Christ.'[7]

Leo still tried to cultivate his image as a peacemaker, but it was difficult to sustain after an agreement between France and Venice to reconquer Milan – rather as in 1499 – had been revealed. Under pressure he renewed the anti-French 'Holy League', and even paid a covert subsidy to the Swiss. These intrepid troops defeated the French invaders at Novara in June 1513, and the news of their victory was hailed with rejoicing in Rome; Leo had a salvo fired from Castel Sant' Angelo and Cardinal Bainbridge reported talk in high places of the renewed desire for total 'extermination' of the French King. It was both a re-evocation of Julius II's triumphs of the previous year and a personal victory for Cardinal Schiner, so much so that the bells of Schiner's title church in Rome, Santa Pudenziana, were rung and there were shouts of 'Julio!' in the streets.[8]

Leo, nevertheless, still kept the door open for a reconciliation with France. In October the rebel pro-French cardinals, including Federico

Sanseverino, came in a state of repentance to Rome, and Leo forgave and readmitted them, in spite of the protests of Bainbridge and Schiner.[9] Meanwhile he had gained Modena by purchase from the Emperor, its overlord, which may have helped to reduce the case for another war against Alfonso d'Este, France's faithful ally. But he did not commit himself to a French alliance, strongly discouraging Louis XII from a new invasion of Italy and even making a secret anti-French agreement with Ferdinand of Spain. The path of papal diplomacy in 1513–14 was complex and inconstant and no attempt need be made to trace its course here. Among its more consistent threads, as the Florentine ambassador in Rome, Francesco Vettori, wrote to his friend Machiavelli in July 1513, were to preserve the papal state in the strong condition in which Julius had left it, and to provide for Giuliano de' Medici, the Pope's younger brother, and Lorenzo, the Pope's nephew (son of his elder brother Piero, who had fled Florence in 1494).[10] For Giuliano, it was already suggested, a principality might be found, perhaps formed out of Parma and Piacenza. Machiavelli, whose advice for Leo was at all costs to avoid neutrality – for which, he argued, even an ecclesiastical prince risked being despised – later commented that such a heterogeneous new princedom, including also Modena and Reggio, would be valuable but exceedingly difficult to hold together.[11] Leo's father, Lorenzo il Magnifico, might have been astonished that his warning in 1488 about the prospect for Italy of an overpowerful Church state had now come to mean a Florentinised version of the same, directed by his own son as pope. Not only this, but there even seemed to be an opportunity for a lay prince of the Medici family, allied with and sponsored by papal temporal authority, to found a central principality strong enough to stabilise the whole of Italy – as formulated by Machiavelli in the conclusion to *Il Principe*.

For there can be little doubt that Leo's true inclination – when not hedging or double-dealing – was to resume the belligerence of his predecessor as champion of papal authority. There is even a hint of this in the continuation of Julius's decorating programme in the papal apartments. In 'The Repulse of Attila' the design appears, by comparison with an earlier drawing, to have been slightly changed, with the intro-duction of Leo X himself in the part of Leo I, mounted on a white horse. It has been suggested that this was meant to be the horse he was riding when a cardinal at the Battle of Ravenna, but such a personal touch seems unlikely, particularly as that occasion was a humiliation; it was not as though he had escaped capture by a dashing ride on horseback. The next room, 'The Stanza del Incendio' (1514–17), contains more historical demonstrations of divine power exercised miraculously in favour of papal authority and on behalf of earlier popes with the name Leo. One of these is 'The Fire in the Borgo' (the district adjacent to St Peter's), where Leo III, with features resembling Leo X, appears at a window, blessing the Roman crowd as their benign bishop and apparently quelling the conflagration; another scene is 'The Victory over the Saracens at Ostia', in the presence of Leo IV.[12]

\* \* \* \* \*

At first there was little change in papal caution and the backing of both sides after Louis XII's sudden death on 1 January 1515, and the accession of Francis I. Giuliano de' Medici married in June the young King's aunt Filiberta of Savoy with a promised dowry of lands – supposedly that difficult combination of Parma, Piacenza, Modena and Reggio – which would have created a completely new power base for the Medici. But, when Francis I invaded Lombardy in July, bringing his army through the Alps by an unusual route, and threatened Milan, Leo had to appear to act decisively and oppose him, though he still carried on secret overtures and negotiations. Cardinal Giulio de' Medici, the Pope's cousin, was appointed legate to the papal army, over which Giuliano, now Duke of Nemours, was made Captain General; on 2 July 1515 Leo blessed and presented Giuliano with a baton and two standards – one bearing the papal cross keys, the other the Medici emblem of balls (*palle*) – but because of serious illness (Giuliano died in March 1516) the job passed to their young cousin, Lorenzo. Cardinal Schiner was again called to act as legate to the Swiss troops assembled to defend the papal state. But Cardinal Giulio and Giuliano were extraordinarily slow and evasive; the cardinal wrote unashamedly to Lorenzo on 30 August that, while they were expecting Cardinal Schiner's light cavalry, a much bigger Swiss commitment across the Po was needed if 20,000 papal troops were to be sent into battle. Evidently there were strong suspicions that the Swiss might be making a separate peace with the French; Cardinal Giulio wrote again when Schiner arrived at Pavia with 2000 troops, telling Lorenzo to send an emissary to meet him but not to offer any additional help.[13] Cardinal Schiner launched his independent attack on the French at

Marignano, near Milan, on 13 September, at first gaining some success, but on the second day the supposedly invincible Swiss were routed and Massimiliano Sforza fled.

After Marignano Leo had little choice but to turn pro-French, in order to save Bologna and the rest of the lands of the Church. At the concordat held at Bologna in December, he had the satisfaction of absolving French officers and soldiers who confessed their sinfulness in having fought against Julius II, and Francis I himself is said to have declared to Leo: 'Holy Father, do not marvel that all these men remain the enemies of Pope Julius, because he was indeed our very greatest enemy, and we have not known a more terrible enemy in war than Pope Julius, who was truly a very prudent captain, and better as the commander of an army than as pope.'[14] In spite of this acknowledgment of papal military genius, Leo had to hand back to the French, now reinstated as rulers of Milan, both Parma and Piacenza, those final and most spectacular gains of Julius. He became deeply resentful of this humiliation, and was supposed also to hand over Modena and Reggio, though he avoided doing so by making a financial arrangement with the Emperor.[15] Francesco Guicciardini, the Florentine lawyer and historian, was appointed papal governor first of Modena (June 1516) then also of Reggio (July 1517): these combined zones became the bastion of the extended papal state. It is remarkable that Guicciardini, who proved a tough and shrewd administrator, should have taken on this difficult job, for he professed in his writings strong views about the invalidity of papal temporal power.

Among the cardinals who were veterans of Julius's wars, either those of Leo's own vintage or created by Julius, Schiner was the longest-lasting and the most recurrently involved in military operations, almost the only one who continued to serve with armies in Leo's time. Bainbridge died in July 1514; Marco Vigerio and Federico Sanseverino died in 1516. Corner took no more part in wars, retired in 1517 to the estate at Asolo of his aunt Caterina, ex-Queen of Cyprus, and died in 1524; Luigi d'Aragona left Rome for long periods of travel and died in January 1519; Sigismondo Gonzaga lived in retirement at Mantua. Ippolito d'Este, who was described by the Venetian ambassador in 1517 as 'more suited to arms than anything else',[16] had not since 1509 given much in the way of armed service to either Julius or Leo, presumably because of the political hostility of both popes towards his brother, Duke Alfonso d'Este. He was, however, sent in 1518–19 as cardinal legate to Hungary, where he distinguished himself in ferocious bear hunts, if not in sorties against the Turks, of whose dangerous nearness to Buda and his bishopric of Eger he was well aware. To his brother-in-law, Gianfrancesco Gonzaga, Marquis of Mantua, Cardinal Ippolito sent as presents a handgun (*schiopetto*) and a Bohemian dagger.[17]

Out of the new intake of cardinals under Leo, two of the earliest, Giulio de' Medici and Bernardo Dovizi (both appointed in 1513), were appointed cardinal legates to the papal army in different wars but, as will be noted, were not wholly suited to this role. The exceptionally large creation of new cardinals in July 1517 was an act of Leo's partly or mostly motivated by the desperate need for loyalty in his entourage, after the discovery of a murderous conspiracy against himself that had implicated at least six cardinals. Of the new members, Pompeo Colonna was the most soldierly figure, as his turbulent later career was to prove. Scion of the turbulent Roman baronial clan that Alexander VI had attempted to overcome in 1501 by the confiscation of their property, Pompeo had had, for a young cardinal, a peculiarly violent past. According to Paolo Giovio, his contemporary biographer, Pompeo's education had consisted entirely of the arts of war; he had fought on the winning side at the Battle of the Garigliano in 1504 (when the French lost control of the kingdom of Naples to Spain) and in 1511 had led a civic rebellion against papal government of Rome.[18] Few of the other cardinals created by Leo stand out as conspicuously endowed with gifts of military skill and leadership, but these qualities, after all, tended sometimes to emerge in unexpected places.

Soon after his capitulation to Francis I in the second half of 1515, Leo narrowed his sights to direct an aggressive campaign in Italy, in some ways more brazenly aggressive than any of the campaigns of Julius II, although, unlike Julius, he did not participate in person. Probably acting on the insistence of Alfonsina Orsini, the mother of Lorenzo de' Medici, he sent an army in May 1516 to expel Francesco Maria della Rovere, Duke of Urbino, on grounds of disobedience, and to install Lorenzo in his place. This proved to be one of the most ruinously expensive and unsuccessful military ventures in the history of the papal state. For in February 1517 Francesco Maria, supported by Spanish troops, returned from his exile at Mantua to reconquer Urbino and much of its territory.[19] Huge sums were spent on papal reinforcements to no great advantage,[20] though at least Roberto Boschetti (a former protégé of Giuliano de' Medici), appointed special papal commissary at Fano and Ancona, was able to supply the defending forces with sufficient ammunition to fight off sea attacks by Francesco Maria.[21] Lorenzo, however, was wounded outside Mondolfo on 26 March, leaving the numerous papal forces without overall leadership. According to Machiavelli's friend Francesco Vettori, occasional skirmishes with the enemy only made matters worse; the *condottieri* were at logger-heads with each other; the infantry obeyed nobody.[22]

Leo sent in June as legate to the camp his former secretary Cardinal Bernardo Dovizi da Bibbiena, 'a man,' as Francesco Vettori put it, 'very clever in worldly dealings, but wholly inexpert concerning war', who was, moreover, closely bound by social ties to the evicted court of Urbino. Dovizi's main contribution, having arrived at Mondolfo, was to calm down a violent outbreak between the Gascons and Spanish troops in Lorenzo's army[23] and another row between Germans and Italians, which had begun over a half-barrel of wine. He also applied himself to the problems of securing supplies, defending the ports of Ancona and Pesaro, and equipping the papal fleet; he urged his friend Latino Juvenale to accept the post of captain of the galleys.[24] Although in July 1517 Francesco Maria's forces did much damage in a big operation near Urbino itself, they failed in their attempt to gain control of Pesaro, from where they had hoped to harass Lorenzo's supply ships.[25]

Ultimately it was Cardinal Dovizi who was entrusted with peace negotiations, but – according to an anecdotal source – when the cardinal invited Francesco Maria to a meal, the latter observed, menacingly, 'Priests kill with cups of wine; soldiers kill with the sword.'[26] Francesco Maria was of course on record for having killed another papal protégé, Cardinal Alidosi, not with a sword but a dagger. Dovizi was spared this, and did not, so far as the story goes, attempt in his turn to proffer a poisoned cup, but the peace terms negotiated were immensely expensive for the papacy, having to meet not only the costs and debts of the papal army and its overcharging *condottieri*, but also the expenses and damage claimed by Francesco Maria. True, Lorenzo was reinstated in Urbino, but he was said to be prepared to hand it back to the Church and was more interested in controlling Florence, where he lived, dominated by his mother, until his death in May 1519; he had been hoping perhaps to add to it Siena or even the Romagna.[27] Boschetti, meanwhile, already vicar of the duchy of Urbino from September 1517, took over as papal governor under Leo's direct rule.

At the same year as the war of Urbino reached its crisis and the murder plot implicating prominent cardinals was uncovered, Leo was also preoccupied with the Turkish danger. A crusade had always been among his serious plans. He declared in August 1514,[28] and repeated in November 1517, according to Cardinal Giulio de' Medici, that he would not fail in his duty, so far as he was able, and would go in person and lay down his life for his sheep.[29] Francesco Guicciardini wrote from his post at Reggio that, while he was pleased to hear that at Rome a crusade was being discussed, he himself would prefer first to hunt down 'the Turks on our own doorstep' and then go after those who were further afield[30] – echoing Pius II's statement of priorities over half a century earlier. Instead, it looked as though the bolder policy would prevail. An advisory council of war, set up in November 1517 and including Cardinals Giulio de' Medici, Corner and Farnese, resolved that it was necessary to take the offensive; Giulio de' Medici wrote urgently to the papal nuncio with the Swiss troops, stressing the danger that Christendom faced and hoping to count on their help. Leo had decided to cast himself as another Innocent III, as supreme organiser and judge; his proposals in the winter of 1517–18 included a five-year truce between the European powers, intercessionary prayers, legates and preachers dispatched far and wide, comprehensive taxation; altogether a greater degree of preparatory organisation than had been seen for many years.[31]

After the deaths of both Giuliano and Lorenzo, the relatives to whom Leo had felt he had obligations and whose careers had become entangled with papal policy, his aims became more openly reminiscent of his predecessor. Guicciardini observed in a comparison between the two popes that Leo's enmities were perhaps even greater than those of Julius, but he nursed them more secretly.[32] Urbino reverted to the direct rule of the papacy in 1519, and in January 1520 Leo sponsored a surprise attack on Ferrara. This failed, but new plans were laid with Cardinal Giulio de' Medici and Francesco Guicciardini to use political exiles and a corruptible captain of the ducal guard.[33] Ferrara had become an obsession with Leo, just as it had been with Julius II. Two months after this scheme collapsed, a lightning campaign was launched with greater success to rid the March of Ancona of its remaining semi-autonomous lords or 'tyrants' (as they were conveniently – and in most cases justly – designated). This little-noted campaign owed much to the example of Julius II, or even to the methods of Alexander VI and Cesare Borgia; its execution was largely in the hands of Niccolò Bonafede (1464–1534), Bishop of Chiusi and vice-legate of the March, who had started his career there under the Borgias.[34] Ludovico Uffreducci, Lord of Fermo, was defeated in combat at Monte San Giorgio; the rulers of Fabriano and Recanati were assassinated. Giampaolo Baglioni of Perugia, who had formerly escaped overthrowal by collaborating with Julius II, was persuaded to come to Rome for a judicial hearing (which would not have put him in serious danger), and once there was arrested, summarily tried and executed.[35]

By the summer of 1521, in the last six months of his pontificate, Leo was as single-mindedly committed to war against the French presence in Italy as Julius II had been, enthusiastic about his alliance with the Emperor Charles V and his appointment of the young Marquis of Mantua, Federico II Gonzaga, Julius's former hostage and favourite, as Captain of the Church. Letters of the Mantuan ambassador from Rome, Baldesar Castiglione – later famous for his book on the role of the courtier (*Il Libro del Cortegiano*) – record this papal euphoria. 'I have never seen the Pope happier about anything he has done than this *condotta* of your excellency,' Castiglione wrote to the Marquis of Mantua on 10 July, and a month later he reported Leo's delight on the news that Federico had promised to make available his own artillery, without even being asked.[36] It was expected that Cardinal Pompeo Colonna would be appointed legate to the army, but in the event Giulio de' Medici was again chosen for this role.[37] On 23 August Castiglione reported that Leo was in a very good mood and was certain of victory, having compared the forces on his side with those of the enemy,[38] and on the following day that he had blessed the flags and the baton of command of the Captain General of the Church;[39] he reckoned that the Swiss in French service would be recalled to their cantons, and that Cardinal Schiner would be leading a large force of them to join the papal side, in which case victory was certain.[40]

'I think the French know that the Pope has little wish to come to an agreement with them,' Castiglione wrote on 2 October;[41] the arrival of the papal army at Casalmaggiore on the river Po, and the meeting at Guastalla of Cardinal Giulio de' Medici as legate and Federico Gonzaga as Captain General, had given the Pope great pleasure, he wrote a few days later.[42] On 30 October Leo was delighted to hear of the arrival of the Swiss[43] to carry out a joint attack. Milan fell on 19 November, and Cardinal Giulio de' Medici gave thanks to God for Cardinal Schiner's triumphal entry there.[44] Milan was followed by other Lombard cities, including, ultimately, Parma and Piacenza, which had been among Leo's chief war aims.[45] Francesco Guicciardini later commented on the unseemly presence within the army of two cardinals, Giulio de' Medici and Matthäeus Schiner: '[T]wo legates travelling in the midst of that [army] with their silver crosses surrounded (so much today is reverence for religion abused) by so many weapons and guns, so many blasphemers, murderers and robbers.'[46] But Castiglione, a former soldier himself, who had known Julius II, shared the Pope's excitement: 'I think like Our Lord [the Pope] that God wills this victory to be the means of entirely ridding Italy of the French,' he wrote.[47] Leo's state of exaltation and exhaustion probably played a large part in weakening his resistance to the fever that led to his death on 1 December, robbing him and Rome of victory celebrations.

## THE INTERLUDE OF ADRIAN VI, 1522–23

That frugal Dutch scholar Adrian Florenzel of Utrecht, the outsider elected pope on 9 January 1522, was certainly no champion and exponent of papal militarism, and little needs to be said here about his brief reign, which extended for barely a year after his arrival in Italy in August. His first act, when he made a landfall at Portofino and was greeted by a small party of Tuscan cardinals including Giulio de' Medici, was to reproach them for bearing arms as well as wearing secular clothes.[48] Although, as Charles V's former tutor, he was obviously more inclined to an imperial rather than a French hegemony in Italy, he took no part in subsidising the continued fighting in northern Italy, where the French had suffered another major defeat near Milan at La Bicocca in April and soon afterwards lost control of Genoa.[49]

Adrian made clear that he had neither the wish nor the funds to engage in war, and it is only surprising that there was not a total breakdown of papal temporal government in Italy. As it was, Duke Alfonso of Ferrara took advantage of the situation to seize back Modena and Reggio, Francesco Maria della Rovere recovered Urbino, the Baglioni returned to Perugia, while Pandolfo di Roberto Malatesta and his son took back Rimini. As well as dismissing, no doubt with justification, many of Leo X's administrators, Adrian seems to have been content to confirm these acts of repossession, allowing a reversal of the whole trend of papal policy under Leo X, Julius II and their predecessors. There were two major exceptions: Bologna was prevented from reverting to the Bentivoglio, thanks to prompt action from Cardinal Giulio de' Medici (as will be noted below), and over Rimini the Pope reacted quickly, by dispatching in December 1522 the Spanish soldiers who had accompanied him on his journey to Italy. He nevertheless reinvested Alfonso d'Este with the dukedom of Ferrara, though the cardinals refused to allow the restitution to Alfonso of Modena and Reggio. He also re-invested Francesco Maria della Rovere with Urbino in March 1523, and according to a Venetian source was even prepared to hand back Ravenna and Cervia to Venice.[50]

Though he also had to face the prospect of Lutheran dissent spreading through northern Europe, it was only with regard to the Turks that Adrian expressed himself as aggressively as any of his predecessors. The threat to the Knights of St John in 1522 moved him to appeal directly to Charles V, declaring that he would willingly shed his own blood to save the Christian bulwark of Rhodes. The news that Rhodes had fallen on 22 December took a long time to arrive, and to be believed in Rome. It affected Adrian strongly. He did his utmost to try and raise money to support a task force to avenge this outrage to Christendom, as well as an army to go to Hungary. Regarding the troubles of Italy, meanwhile, on 3 August 1523 he finally signed a defensive alliance with the Emperor Charles V and other powers including Henry VIII of England, an agree-ment in which Cardinal Giulio de' Medici had played a strong part, aimed at opposing any renewal of French aggression in Lombardy.[51] The strain of all this, culminating in a ride through Rome to publish the signing up of the new defensive League in the great basilica of Santa Maria Maggiore, wearing full pontifical vestments and escorted by Swiss guards – the very image of the papacy he had not wished to foster – brought on a feverish illness from which he never properly recovered. He had a relapse and died on 14 September 1523,[52] a victim of warfare if not its perpetrator.

## CLEMENT VII: YEARS OF DANGER, 1523–34

Giulio de' Medici, who finally emerged as Pope Clement VII in November 1523, was not only a tried administrator but a prelate hardened by much experience of armed conflict. As a youth in 1497 he had taken part in an attempt to restore the family to power in Florence; indeed, Guicciardini, commenting on this, remarked that he was more suited to arms than to the priesthood.[53] He entered the crusading Order of Knights Hospitaller of St John, and joined the household of his cousin, Cardinal Giovanni de' Medici, accompanying him – and unlike him, avoiding capture – at the Battle of Ravenna in 1512. After Giovanni's accession as Leo X Giulio was promoted to the cardinalate and office of Vice-Chancellor, and – as already mentioned – served as papal legate to the army in the campaign against Francis I in Lombardy in 1515 and in the war of Urbino. He took part in crusade planning in 1517 and in the Marche campaign in 1520, and was again legate to the army in the war in Lombardy in 1521. He continued to be active under Adrian VI, and in April 1522 was credited with defeating an attempted Bentivoglio coup at Bologna. The English ambassador at Rome reported (quoted here in his own words with archaic spelling),

> Cardinal de Medicis, as legat of the said citie, made soche provision...that, the armye being within, with the aid of the peple issued out and slewe diverse of ther enemys...and put the whole [French and Bentivoglio] armye to flight so that the said Citie by the wisdom and diligence of the said Cardinall is savid for the Churche.[54]

Yet after he became pope in November 1523 Giulio was for ever stamped – thanks to contemporary writers such as Guicciardini and Giovio, who observed him closely – with the reputation of timidity and vacillation. This was the pope who in May 1527 would have to face the sack of Rome, the gravest, most terrifying and humiliating challenge of armed force faced by any pope throughout the whole history of the papal monarchy, worse than in 1084, 1112, 1303, 1413, 1494 or indeed 1798 or 1870.

It could be argued that Clement lacked several of the indispensable qualities to be an effective Renaissance pope, and could do little about it. Of these essentials, he lacked first large resources of money. Second he lacked an aspiring and dependable son, nephew or other close male relative anxious to make a career in the Church or the papal state. His second cousin Giovanni Salviati, on whom Leo had conferred the red hat in 1517, was to prove quite able as a diplomatist, but he was probably too Florentine and parentally dominated to be potentially a Machiavellian new prince. It is worth noting, however, that Machiavelli had sent him a copy of his *Art of War*, about which the young cardinal wrote appreciatively in September 1521, assuring the author that the defects in organisation of modern armies, including the army of the Church, could be overcome by adopting his precepts.[55] Another second cousin, Ippolito, who would become a cardinal in 1529, was altogether too young and too headstrong to fill the role of a prince within the papal state, and even he yearned in preference for power in Florence. Third, and most important of all Clement's deficiencies, the second Medici pope lacked *fortuna*.

This third deficiency was most evident from the course of war in Italy in 1524–25 between the forces of Charles V and Francis I. Having at first continued cautiously to support the imperial cause, Clement, much influenced by Gianmatteo Giberti, his former secretary now promoted to a major post ('datarius') in the papal chancery, wavered and switched to France. How can this fatal step be explained? The Pope had of course pro-French tendencies going far back in his career, and may have been dazzled by Francis I's successes in Lombardy in the autumn of 1524. He may even have had hopes, in spite of its dangers, about the foolhardy expedition to the south of James Stuart, Duke of Albany, or at least wanted to avoid exposing Rome to any threat from Albany's large army.[56] If only that adamant Swiss, Cardinal Schiner, had still been around, maybe Clement would have been dissuaded from switching to France, but Schiner had died at Rome in December 1522, a year before his former partner in anti-French campaigns became pope. An official agreement was signed with Francis in January 1525, but the timing could not have been worse, on account of the sensational defeat and capture of Francis in the Battle of Pavia at the end of February. This left Clement, by a stroke of extraordinarily bad luck, in a position of weakness from which it would take long to recover. Giberti, falling back on the argument that it was all a miraculous demonstration of God's will, encouraged the cardinal legate, Giovanni Salviati, to send a note of congratulation to Charles V and express the Pope's hope that peace would follow, that this was what he had always desired.[57] In fact, a treaty negotiated with the Emperor and signed on his behalf by Lannoy, viceroy of Naples, seemed to give Clement almost all he could want. It included the guaranteed integrity of the papal state, with Reggio and Rubiera, which had been seized again by Alfonso d'Este during the long papal vacancy in autumn 1523, handed back, and Francesco II Sforza accepted as Duke of Milan. Unfortunately for Clement, nothing was done to implement this treaty.

After the Peace of Madrid, in January 1526, when Francis I was released from captivity, and in turn proceeded to break the terms that had been agreed, Clement again needed to act decisively. In a long letter or harangue addressed to him in March Guicciardini reproached him for not being as firm and astute as he had been as a cardinal, and insisted that decisive action could still save the situation and 'liberate the Apostolic See and Italy from this atrocious and disgraceful servitude'. The Pope should act boldly, Guicciardini complained; for instance, he should retake Reggio 'or play some trick on Cardinal Pompeo Colonna', who was certainly the most aggressive, pro-imperial and ambitious member of the Sacred College. He (Clement) could yet emerge as 'the most glorious pope in two hundred years'.[58]

For brief periods Clement appeared to muster some strength. The signing in May 1526 of the Holy League of Cognac with Francis I, an avowedly aggressive alliance, seemed to signify a new beginning. In a letter of self-justification sent to the Emperor in June 1526 the Pope was emphatic that Charles should withdraw from Italy, reproaching him for the non-fulfilment of treaty obligations and his violations of papal territory including Parma, and his forcing Clement to seek other allies and to take arms in self-defence. In July Guicciardini, now commissary general of the papal army, saw that immediate action was imperative: a rapid move to capture Milan had every chance of victory over the unpaid, unprepared, numerically inferior imperial forces in Lombardy.[59] That this did not happen seems to have been mainly the fault of the Duke of Urbino, who first hesitated because the Swiss troops had not arrived, and then, having made in July several unsuccessful attempts to attack Milan, retreated; in August and September he lost more time, in spite of receiving French reinforcements, by carrying on the fairly pointless siege of Cremona, then held by imperial forces.[60]

Perhaps it would have made a difference if Clement VII had appointed a resolute cardinal legate to the army and applied himself with furious vigour, as Julius II would have done, to rallying the coalition and insisting on action. The blame, it has to be repeated, falls on the Duke of Urbino, that same Francesco Maria della Rovere who had failed his uncle Julius II in 1511 and been ousted from Urbino by Leo X, only to be reinstated in his dukedom under Adrian VI and – in spite of his known resentment against the Medici for the way they had treated him – reappointed Captain of the Church by Clement.[61] Meanwhile, as well as losing the military initiative, Clement received a crushing reply to his 'justification', aimed at depriving him also of the moral high ground. This reply, handed to Castiglione on 18 September 1526, took the argument back to fundamentals, even playing the Lutheran card. The Pope, the Emperor insisted, had drawn the sword that Christ ordered Peter to put up. It was beyond belief for the vicar of Christ to acquire worldly possessions at the cost of even one drop of human blood. No one was coming to attack the Holy See, so there was no need of weapons or troops.[62]

As for Guicciardini's suggestion to play a clever trick on Cardinal Pompeo Colonna, Clement was instead the victim of an outrageous demonstration by that overpowerful dissident, who in spite of the above assurance did come to attack the Holy See, and moreover did so in the Emperor's name. Pompeo had nearly been elected pope himself in 1523 but was finally persuaded to switch his votes (rather reminiscent of Ascanio Sforza in 1492) in exchange for the vice-chancellorship and other compensations; his fury at Clement's desertion of the Emperor in 1525 and signing later of the League of Cognac led him to call an armed march on Rome by the Colonna and their supporters in September 1526. Here was a cardinal – not only that, but the Vice-Chancellor of the Church, head of the whole machinery of papal government – declaring war on the Pope: it was one of the most bizarre and anarchic episodes in a long trend of violent behaviour on the part of a secularised minority in the Sacred College. According to Paolo Giovio, whose biography of Pompeo was highly partisan and stressed his love of family and military honour, 8000 knights and 3000 infantry commanded by Pompeo's brother were involved in this expedition, with artillery drawn by buffaloes and men, helped at difficult points by Pompeo himself.[63] When they reached Rome the cardinal shut himself up in his palace, leaving his followers do as much damage as they could, looting and terrifying the inhabitants of Rome, though they did not succeed in laying hands on Clement.

The Pope took his revenge on the Colonna in November 1526 with a punitive campaign worthy of Alexander VI, demolishing their fortresses and devastating their lands. According to the papal bull[64] condemning Pompeo, which was published in February 1527, the latter's purpose had been to seize Clement, alive or dead, and to rule as pope in his place, apparently without election by his peers, or any other of the normal formalities. It is hard to imagine how on earth Pompeo can have justified to his conscience and his confessor this treasonable presumption, or justified using force in a manner more calculated to endanger than defend the Church. Though formally deprived of his cardinalate and other offices, he was not punished for long. In fact, he was soon needed to intercede on Clement's behalf with much more fanatical enemies than himself, and give refuge to fellow cardinals and others in danger.

Meanwhile in September 1526 the Job-like Clement had also had to bear the shock of the Turkish victory at Mohács in Hungary, and news of the loss to Christendom of that country. Like Adrian and Leo before him when such tidings of disaster arrived, Clement declared that he himself would take part in a military expedition and as vicar of Christ was prepared to lay down his life.[65] It was no clearer than the avowals of previous popes, whether he meant by this simply to be ready for martyrdom, or was prepared even to fall in combat. A war-planning council of five cardinals was set up, but it is fairly clear that the Pope's distractions in Italy, quite apart from his shortage of money, meant that nothing would be done.

Worse than the Colonna raid was to come in the spring of 1527, with the League of Cognac coalition not only continuing to do nothing, but even failing to protect Rome from the mainly Spanish army advancing under the Duke of Bourbon's command and the horde of Lutheran 'landsknechts' under George von Frundsberg. The latter were mercenary foot soldiers, first raised by the Emperor Maximilian in the early years of the century from the south German lowlands. Less disciplined than the Alpine Swiss on whom they were supposedly modelled, landsknechts were a brutal new phenomenon in European warfare.[66] Armed with huge pikes and swords, swaggering in feathered hats and slashed breeches, inspired by Lutheran slogans but furious for want of food and wages, Frundsberg's undisciplined troops were a terrifying prospect for Rome, even if the Spaniards, demoralised after Bourbon's death, proved to be equally brutal and avaricious.

For all his military experience, Clement did not strike a heroic pose as he cowered in the Castel Sant'Angelo amid the horrors of the sack and the passive experience of hearing and watching Spanish sappers under-mining it; one correspondent in Rome wrote in horrified anticipation of seeing 'a pope and a whole flock of cardinals blown into the air by fire'.[67] Most of the cardinals, those not with the Pope in the safety of the castle, fared much worse in the terrible months of May and June 1527, suffering torture and mockery to extort from them money and valuables, not only from the landsknechts but also from the Spanish captains whom some had paid handsomely for protection. Few offered physical resistance, in spite of their well-stocked armouries, guards and military retainers. An exception may have been Cardinal Giovanni Piccolomini, who probably considered himself untouchable, having a solidly pro-imperial and pro-German family background from his great uncle Pius II onwards. Nevertheless, according to one of the most reliable accounts – a letter of Cardinal Scaramuccia Trivulzio of Como to his secretary, sent later from Civitavecchia – Piccolomini suffered twice over. After he had bought off the Spaniards, the cardinal's palace was then assaulted by landsknechts. Since the latter were said to have kept up the attack for four hours before the cardinal surrendered, it sounds as though there was counter-fire from within, and the dead piled up on both sides. Cardinal Piccolomini was paraded through the streets, bare-headed and in a shabby garment, kicked and punched and forced to make another ransom payment, before gaining refuge with Cardinal Pompeo Colonna.[68]

In December 1527 Clement eventually bought his escape to Orvieto, and by then could again pin some hope on relief by the forces of the League of Cognac. For a French army, led by Odette de Foix, Vicomte de Lautrec, had gained much success in Lombardy and Emilia; early in 1528 it advanced down the Adriatic coast; it won many more victories before laying siege to Naples in April. There Lautrec was deadlocked. The city, defended by imperial forces, was still holding out in August when Lautrec himself died of disease; the remnants of his army had to withdraw northwards.[69] Once again *fortuna* had been cruel to the Pope. Or had the papacy met its deserts as the victim of military force, hoist by its own petard after itself sponsoring so much war and slaughter?

The debate about the sack of Rome – whether it represented scandalous sacrilege and disaster or a providential judgement of God on a corrupted body – was only just beginning. One writer in the court of Charles V, Erasmus's friend Juan de Valdés, made a pretty clear case for the latter point of view, in a polemical dialogue that attacked the whole concept of papal war and deplored all the horrors it had perpetrated. The protagonist, called Lactancio, is answered by an apologetic archdeacon, who uses the old argument of necessary defence of the Church; at one point he concedes, 'I agree that all those things are very cruel, but the people of Italy would look down on a pope who didn't wage war. They would think it a great insult if a single inch of Church land were lost.'[70]

Whether or not there was any truth in the fictitious archdeacon's assertion, it is paradoxical that, relatively soon after Clement VII's return to Rome in October 1528 and reconciliation with Charles V in the Treaty of Barcelona (29 June 1529), the Pope seems to have recovered more purpose than he had shown for years. Charles, not without a tinge of remorse for what had happened, now stood as guarantor of both the papal lands in Italy and of a Medici principate in Florence, to replace the popular republic that had been set up there in 1527. After the successful imperial siege of Florence (1529–30) and final overthrowal of the republic, Clement endeavoured to take a strong line with cities in the papal state that had again tried to throw off papal rule during the period of crisis. Ancona was one example. On the strength of allegations that Ancona was threatened by Turkish naval attack – allegations strongly denied by the city's own ambassadors – he sent a force to take it in 1532, suppressed the ancient civic constitution and appointed as cardinal legate and governor Benedetto Accolti. Archbishop of Ravenna and a papal secretary since 1523, Accolti had been made a cardinal in 1527, and commanded a troop of 4000 Spanish infantry in the siege of Florence. At Ancona he supervised the building of a new fortress complete with its own gun foundry, and his government was reputedly so oppressive that he was eventually removed and put on trial under Clement's successor.[71] His interests appear to be neatly expressed by the inventory of his possessions, drawn up after his arrest in 1535, where scarcely any devotional objects, books or works of art are listed (one of the few exceptions was a portrait of Julius II), but several swords and daggers and six or seven handguns.[72]

Perugia also had to be dealt with. Clement appointed as legate in Umbria his second cousin Ippolito de' Medici, the bastard son of Giuliano, Duke of Nemours, who had been raised to the purple at the age of eighteen in January 1529. The purpose of his legation was to dispossess Malatesta Baglioni of Perugia, who was then serving the republic of Florence as military commander against the besieging imperial and papal army. Ippolito never went there, and delegated the administration to a series of vice-legates, the first of whom in 1529–30 was

Ennio Filonardi, Bishop of Veroli,[73] but the condition of Perugia deteriorated and reached a point of crisis under Clement's successor.

Ippolito de' Medici's opportunity for greater glory came in 1532 when he was sent as papal ambassador to Charles V's brother Ferdinand, Archduke of Austria and King of Hungary. Ippolito arrived in Ratisbon (modern Regensburg) with a retinue of five prelates, ten secretaries and an armed guard of thirty to forty gentlemen, most of whom were former military captains, and with 5000 ducats in hand with which to enrol troops.[74] His office was extended to that of papal legate to Ferdinand's army against the Turks in Hungary, and the Venetian ambassador reported on 1 September that he had set off by boat down the Danube accompanied by ten gunners (*arquebusieri*).[75] Ippolito was described as 'dressed like Jupiter' – modified in a subsequent letter to 'wearing military habit'. Unfortunately, a portrait by Titian showing him in full armour does not survive; Vasari mentions it in his life of the artist[76] as painted at Bologna at the same time as the well-known portrait of the Cardinal in the costume of a Turkish warrior (which it seems unlikely that he was wearing on the above occasion). Ippolito intended to select horses at Vienna and proceed at once to the battlefront, but when he reached the imperial army, which was on full alert, the Turks on the other side of the river made no move. Eventually the campaign was called off and Ippolito was said to have expressed his disappointment with such rage that Ferdinand imprisoned him for a day.[77] The Mantuan agent in Rome, Fabrizio Peregrino, whose graphic and opinionated dispatches will frequently be quoted in the following pages, heard of this episode and commented that Ippolito had wanted madly to play the part of a war captain ('voleva pazzamente fare il capitano di guerra').[78] After the papal election in 1534 he quickly left the Apostolic Palace and planned to leave Rome altogether, according to Peregrino, to reduce the expense of maintaining so many military captains and *bravi*.[79]

## PAUL III: WAR, PEACE, RECONSTRUCTION, 1534–49

The pontificate of Alessandro Farnese, Paul III, in many ways represented a return to the traditional programme of the Renaissance papacy. Above all it represented continuity. The brother of Giulia Farnese, Alexander VI's mistress, Paul was a grandfather aged sixty-seven when elected pope on

13 October 1534 (Julius II had been nine years younger at his election), and over eighty when he died: it is hard to think of any previous pope except perhaps John XXII with such a venerable lifespan. He came, moreover, from a professional military family of the Roman Campagna; no pope since Martin V could have claimed so many military forebears. Although never on a battlefield himself, he had plenty of experience of the martial side of the papacy; he had ridden into Rome beside Cesare Borgia in February 1500 when the latter returned in triumph from his first Romagna campaign, and had carried out the tough assignment of legate to the March of Ancona from 1504 to 1508 under Julius II. He had joined Julius in his military expeditions to Perugia and Bologna in 1506–7, and was again with him at Bologna during the Ferrara campaign in the winter of 1510, and at Ravenna and Cervia throughout the military setbacks and terrible weather conditions of March 1511.[80] In the famous portraits of him painted by Titian he looks a choleric and sharp-witted old man, who might as easily have been a superannuated general as a religious leader.

Almost immediately Paul began promoting members of his own family to responsible positions, a long-standing convention that Adrian VI and Clement VII had broken not so much on ethical grounds as for the lack of any aspiring and suitable brothers, sons or nephews. Thus Paul's son Pierluigi Farnese was made Gonfaloniere of the Church in January 1535; his fourteen-year-old grandson Alessandro became a cardinal the same year and Ranuccio, Alessandro's brother, also became a cardinal in 1545; two nephews of the Pope were similarly promoted.[81] The Gonfaloniere Pierluigi was appointed on 2 February 1537 to the office of Captain General, an unusual and possibly unprecedented fusion of the papacy's highest military titles.[82] The Mantuan ambassador commented soon afterwards, perhaps expecting a crusade to be announced, 'It is the opinion here that Our Lord the Pope ought to be planning some great project if the war with France and Lutheran matters do not hinder it.'[83] But Paul's great project (or not the least of his projects) was to raise members of his family to princely status – the same design as all his predecessors had cherished, to a greater or lesser extent, since Pius II, only excepting Paul II, Adrian VI and Clement VII.

Thus in 1537 Pierluigi was made Duke of Castro and Count of Ronciglione, and in 1540 the Pope's nephew Ottavio Farnese was made Duke of Camerino. The biggest event was the creation of the dukedom of Parma and Piacenza for Pierluigi Farnese in 1545, the title passing to Ottavio in 1547 after Pierluigi's assassination. The Farnese thus appropriated that northernmost province of the papal state, acquired after the defeat of French Milan by Julius II and lost or regained with such agonising frequency by the Medici popes. It was perhaps the greatest success story of papal military force and nepotism operating as a stabilising factor in Italian politics; apart from one brief interruption, the Farnese retained Parma and Piacenza until the eighteenth century; no other papal dynasty set up as regional rulers, not even the della Rovere at Urbino, lasted so long, and most of them barely outlasted their founders.

Papal authority was forcefully reasserted and extended in central Italy under Paul III, as one would have expected from one who, as a young cardinal, had followed the standard of Julius II. Perugia was the first trouble spot, since 1529 governed arbitrarily by the vice-legates of the absentee cardinal legate Ippolito de' Medici, and still unstable. Even before his coronation in October 1534 Paul had sent troops there under the control of a special commissary. When the vice-legate and his staff were murdered and the legatine palace burnt down[84] there had to be a more severe military response. In August 1535 Cardinal Ghinucci flatly refused to take up the resident post of legate, knowing only too well, Fabrizio Peregrino wrote, the unstable and bizarre character of the Perugians ('ello che cognosse i cervelli perusini, quanto siano fantastichi et bizarri'). Meanwhile the Pope resolved himself to spend a week in Perugia, setting off, Julius-like, with some of the cardinals, and intending – so it was believed in Rome – to subject it in such a way that it would no longer rise against the papal state ('per volere asettare quella città, di modo che più non habbia da piezzare in sollevarsi contra del stato ecclesiastico').[85] In spite of this, in the spring of 1540 there was a further rebellion in Perugia, provoked by the tax on salt. Throughout April and May Fabrizio Peregrino wrote about Paul's determination this time to chastise and crush the city. On 18 April, he wrote, 'There is no other course he can take for the sake of his honour and that of the Apostolic See.' On 1 May he reported that a force of landsknechts and Spanish troops from the kingdom of Naples, together with 10,000 Italian infantry, had been recruited, and artillery was being moved into Castel Sant' Angelo. Pierluigi Farnese was appointed as supreme commander to be accompanied as papal legate by Uberto Gambara (made a cardinal in 1539), whose experience of military operations included the siege of Florence in 1530. A few weeks later Peregrino revised the numbers involved as 3000 Spanish and 8,000–10,000 other infantry, reflecting, 'The Perugians will have the punishment they deserve.'[86] The city duly submitted and was saddled – initially by the use of forced labour – with a colossal and impregnable fortress, to be known as the 'Paolina', designed by Antonio da Sangallo the Younger.[87] Similarly oppressive was the fortress which Sangallo built for Paul III at Ancona: its function in each case was not just military defence, but also civil and penal administration.

Meantime, in rather different circumstances, Camerino was also brought under direct papal authority.[88] Here the issue in 1535 was a proposed marriage between Guidobaldo della Rovere, son of Francesco Maria, Duke of Urbino, and Giulia Varano, daughter of the late Duke of Camerino, Gian Maria Varano; a marriage unacceptable to the Pope as it would lead to an inconveniently large union of the two duchies. The forbidden marriage went ahead, however, and Camerino was duly joined to Urbino, but Paul was adamant. Upon the death of Francesco Maria in 1538, and against the advice of some of the cardinals, a punitive expedition was dispatched under Cardinal Ennio Filonardi and the parties quickly surrendered. Filonardi, who had only recently become a cardinal at the age of seventy-two in December 1536, was an old hand at military operations. He had acted back in 1512–13 as papal liaison officer and collaborator with Cardinal Schiner, and in 1535 he had been made Prefect of Castel Sant'Angelo. Camerino passed under direct papal rule, until the dukedom was reinvented and conferred on Ottavio Farnese two years later.

Parma and Piacenza, the new duchy bestowed on Pierluigi Farnese, stood in even greater need of the papacy's military protection, since both France and the empire still had claims to those cities and their territories. Interestingly, Pierluigi Farnese wrote to Paul III that the defence of Parma and Piacenza should be entrusted to a strong vassal, i.e. himself, rather than to an ecclesiastic 'not too expert in military matters'.[89] This advice, so unlike what Angelo Geraldini recommended to Innocent VIII only half a century earlier, may be read as a sign of the times, and a wider reaction that seems to have developed against the use of military prelates, a theme that will be further discussed below.

But, in spite of Paul III's use of force to subdue or threaten Italian dissidence, he was on the whole wary about wider involvements, apart from the perennial urge to destroy the Ottoman Turks. In January 1535, when he sent Charles V the papal sword, to embolden him to fight Muslims, Peregrino reported that the Pope was offering to go in person on crusade.[90] The vainglorious if chastened Cardinal Ippolito de' Medici might have hoped that his hour had come at last for some heroic fighting, but in August 1535 it came instead for his death, not in battle but by squalid murder at the hands of a former servant. His armour, and perhaps other martial equipment, was acquired by Pierluigi Farnese ('l'armatura che vano al Signor Pierlugi').[91] Paul III, if he remained pacific for the time being, evidently continued to cherish thoughts of war against the infidel. When Charles V, fresh from his victory against the Sultan of Tunis, asked the Pope for a loan of 50,000 ducats for military purposes (i.e. war against France), the Pope was said to have replied that he would not give him a single soldo to wage war against Christians, but against the infidel it was another matter; the Pope was only too ready to promote an offensive war.[92]

In 1537, however, there arose the biggest threat to Italy for many years of a Muslim invasion, with reports of Turkish military and naval forces assembling in great numbers in the southern Adriatic and Albania. Throughout that year the letters to Mantua of Fabrizio Peregrino vividly reflected the state of near-panic affecting some quarters in Rome, as well as the grumbling resentment of courtiers like himself who saw themselves being taxed more and more steeply for the costs of defence. In January 1537 Peregrino reported that Paul dared not leave Rome for fear of starting a panic, and there were rumours nevertheless that he was planning to escape because he had not provided for its safety. At the beginning of May he spent some days at Civitavecchia watching the galleys prepare to leave for Naples, where they were to join with those of the Emperor. Papal orders were issued, meanwhile, for the strengthening of Civitavecchia, Ostia, Terracina and other ports; the cardinals were told they must provide money to pay for 8000 infantry.[93] A massive Turkish attack on Ancona was expected; forces were assembled in Rome and repairs to the walls undertaken.[94] In early August reports arrived of a Turkish landing in Apulia and of a siege followed by a massacre at Castro, but, instead of attempting to advance, the Turks then withdrew across the Adriatic.[95]

Echoing several of his predecessors since Pius II, Paul told a Venetian ambassador in 1538 that he wished to go on crusade in person.[96] The preparations had reached the point in February of the appointment of a 'legate, over the armada of His Holiness and the Holy See against the infidels',[97] in the person of Marco Grimani, patriarch of Aquileia. This appointment seems to echo the appointment of Trevisan, also patriarch of Aquileia, nearly a century earlier; even if Marco Grimani was not himself a cardinal – and not even in holy orders – he was brother to Cardinal Marino Grimani. The baton of command, banners and a cross were blessed by the Pope and presented to him on 7 February.[98] Paul was to provide thirty-three galleys in a combined papal–Venetian armada; oarsmen were to be recruited in the March of Ancona by the papal commissary, Marco Vigerio II, Bishop of Senigallia. The papal galleys, somewhat fewer than planned and short of manpower, attacked the castle of Prevesa beyond Corfu, but were beaten off. Marco Grimani wrote over-optimistic reports on the campaign to Cardinal Alessandro Farnese, who eventually ordered him to withdraw to Ancona; little had been achieved apart from a modest defiance.

There appeared to be a new dimension to papal warfare developing by the 1540s, or, if not exactly new, the resurrection of one that had been rather dormant since the crusades against the Hussites: war against organised heretics in Europe. Talks aimed at peaceful reconciliation with the Lutheran and other Protestant movements broke down. In 1546–47 the War of the League of Schmalkalden – a linkage of Lutheran principalities and cities formed over ten years earlier in this small town in Hesse (north Germany) – looked like the start of military conflict with Catholic forces supported by the Pope and Emperor. In June 1546 Cardinal Alessandro Farnese was appointed papal legate to the Catholic army, and set out with his brother Ottavio as commander. The cardinal was taken ill on the way at Trento; he reached Ratisbon in August but was recalled to Rome in October, so he failed to share the triumph of Charles V at Mühlberg the following April.[99] But such direct clerical participation or leadership – reviving the precedents of Cardinals Beaufort or Cesarini against the Hussites – did not after all become the pattern in the religious wars of the sixteenth century. Even military campaigns against the Turks, though blessed to Heaven by the Church, would in future generally be run by the secular Catholic authorities.

\* \* \* \* \*

The diffusion of satirical writings, including the dialogue *Julius Exclusus* to which reference has been made, no doubt played their part in forming opinion about the papacy's warlike inclinations. Even more powerful, perhaps, were means of visual mockery; in fact, one early German edition of the *Julius Exclusus* – exceedingly rare – was furnished with a woodcut illustrating the famous encounter with St Peter of Julius and his army (see the Prologue to this book).[100] For already in the early 1520s in Germany woodcuts by Cranach and other German artists were heaping Lutheran ridicule and ill-repute upon the papacy, suggesting its approaching overthrowal in an apocalyptic context, which a few years later the sack of Rome had seemed to vindicate.[101] The portrayal of the Pope as the legendary Antichrist, the harbinger of the end of the world, and both Pope and cardinals as diabolical figures engaged in warfare against Christ, was a favoured theme in some of this defamatory material. Cranach's *Passional Christi und Antichristi*, a small picture book containing twenty-six woodcuts, published in 1521, went into many editions. It presented on facing pages themes contrasting the life of Christ with that of Antichrist (identified with the papacy), each picture including an explanatory note by Philip Melancthon.[102] In the first pair of woodcuts, the Antichrist page alludes directly to the papacy's ancient claim to supreme political authority, depicting a pope with two cannons, accompanied by cardinals and soldiers, challenging beyond a chained doorway the emperor, who is also leading an army. Were St Peter shown in place of the latter figure, this picture might have served as an alternative and rather more striking frontispiece to the *Julius Exclusus*. The eighth pair of woodcuts contrasts the humble nativity of Jesus with an armed pope apparently preparing to capture a town, because the legend below refers to the Church's presumed right to shed blood in order to regain possession of its temporal property. The ninth pair juxtaposes Christ's entry into Jerusalem on an ass with the pope and cardinals riding to hell with foot soldiers. Papal propensity for war is therefore one of the themes to which Cranach deliberately draws attention. Other prints appeared in subsequent years satirising the pope as a warrior or displaying popes and cardinals wearing armour and equipped with guns for the slaughter of innocent Christians. One published in 1528 depicted the forces of papists and evangelists lined up for battle; they appear rather evenly matched until one notices that the papal guns are being fired by demons.[103]

The employment of prelates on the battlefield risked becoming victim to the general Protestant assault not just on Catholic doctrine and discipline but on the whole traditional comportment of the hierarchy. The practice had therefore to be modified or abolished altogether in the interests of decorum and gravity, so as not to provide the enemy with more of the very ammunition (so to speak) that justified its propaganda. After all, Luther himself declared in his tract *On War against the Turk* (1529): 'If I were a soldier and should see a priest's banner in the field or a banner of the cross, even if it were a crucifix, I should run as if the devil himself were chasing me.' He argued that military campaigns against the Turks were justified but had to be led by Christian laymen, above all by the Emperor, never by the Pope and clergy. In the same context Luther added some memorable asides about the leadership in war of two popes of his own time, emphasising – not without certain distortions of history – the limitations of their success, showing that God had disapproved.

> Even Pope Julius the evil hot-headed bully ['dem bösen Eisenfresser': literally 'iron eater'], who was half devil, did not succeed but finally had to call in Emperor Maximilian and let him take charge of the game, despite the fact that Julius had more money, arms and people. I think too that this present pope, Clement, who people think is almost a god of war ['einen Kriegs Got'], succeeded well in his fighting until he lost Rome and all its wealth to a few armed soldiers.[104]

In the same tract Luther had suggested that not only were popes and cardinals inefficient in war but, because their participation was unrighteous, they brought down disaster upon their allies. He harked back to Giuliano Cesarini's failure against the Turks at Varna in 1444: 'The Hungarians themselves blamed Cardinal Julian and killed him for it.' He also cited the disaster which befell Francis I at Pavia in 1525: 'I have heard from fine soldiers who thought that the King of France, when he was defeated and captured by the Emperor before Pavia, had all of his bad fortune because he had the Pope's, or as they boastfully call them, the Church's army with him.'

Paul III, nevertheless, still seems to have been relatively undeterred by, or perhaps unaware of, these trends in Lutheran propaganda. He revived or continued, generally with lasting success, a number of the policies of Leo X and his predecessors. His firm policy of control in the papal state, and placement there of his relatives, has illustrated this; he even renewed war against the Colonna in 1541, as a punishment to Ascanio Colonna for refusing to give help for the defence of Rome; after several months of resistance the castle of Paliano was taken and other Colonna possessions confiscated.[105] Even the summoning of a general council,

Print showing a pope with cardinals, cannon and armed men confronting the Emperor (Cranach, *Passio Christi et Anti-Christi*, 1521) (Warburg Institute).

so long as it was done by the Pope and the agenda was approved by him or on his behalf, followed the rule laid down by Pius II in his bull *Execrabilis* of 1460 and previously put into practice by Julius II with the Fifth Lateran Council called in 1512. In any case, Paul did not hurry this matter, and the first assembly at Trento took place only three years before his death.

Another aspect of the continuity under the Farnese papacy was the revival on a grand scale of commissions for building and decorating palaces in and around Rome. This cannot be discussed in detail here, except for one aspect rather peculiar to the Farnese, for which the pope was less responsible than his relatives, although he was the thematic centre of it all. This theme was the celebration of the Farnese dynasty, and its services to the papacy in war and peace. Much was made of the pope as peacemaker, as for instance in Vasari's *Hall of a Hundred Days* painted for Cardinal Alessandro Farnese in 1546 in the Palazzo della Cancelleria, where the fury of war is chained up, in spite of the campaign planned that year against the Schmalkalden League.[106] At about the same time, the governor of Castel Sant'Angelo commissioned a series of frescoes from Perino del Vaga and his assistants that related the Pope to his namesake Alexander the Great, a name synonymous not with pacification but with military conquest on the global scale, though of these the only ones that are specifically scenes of war are the building of a ship and a battle with King Porus and his army of elephants.[107] The tomb of Paul III in St Peter's, however, persists in portraying the Pope as peacemaker ('in atto di pacificatore'),[108] in spite of all the aggressive military operations that he authorised, and another example of the Pope portrayed in this guise is the scene in Palazzo Farnese showing him at the signing of the treaty between Charles V and Francis I at Nice in 1538. This was painted later for Cardinal Alessandro or his brother Cardinal Ranuccio, and the programme by Francesco Salviati to which it belongs laid greater stress on the glorious service in war rendered to the papacy by the Farnese family in general. In one scene Mars appears with a fierce dog, wearing a sword and buckler decorated with a thunderbolt; there is also a scene (curiously adjacent to one that alludes to the Council of Trent) that represents Cardinal Alessandro riding to war with Charles V against the League of Schmalkalden.[109] These mural paintings were executed in the early 1550s, some time therefore after Paul's death, but their point of reference was still his long reign as pope. A rather similar, but less allegorical, programme was painted at Caprarola, the palatial pentagonal fortress near Viterbo, designed for Cardinal Alessandro by Sangallo the Younger, and started only in 1553. Here, from about 1562, Taddeo Zuccari painted historical events, some distant such as the liberation of Bologna by Cardinal Albornoz in 1363 and Eugenius IV's appointment of Ranuccio Farnese as Captain General of the Church in 1435; but some very recent, such as Pierluigi Farnese's similar appointment in 1535, Paul III praying as the imperial fleet set forth for Tunis, the suppression of the Perugia salt tax rebellion of 1540 and the campaign against the League of Schmalkalden in 1546–47, where Cardinal Alessandro appears much more explicitly in battle formation, on horseback and carrying a papal banner.[110]

## THE LAST PHASE OF THE RENAISSANCE PAPACY, 1549–65

Many features and priorities of the ecclesiastical *ancien regime* continued to thrive in the period after Paul III's death. His immediate successor, Julius III (pope 1550–55), formerly Cardinal dal Monte, nephew of one of Julius II's cardinals and a lavish building patron, showed himself, although no warrior in character, to be a strong champion of direct rule by the papacy over its Italian lands. Perhaps reflecting northern fears of an impending papally led war against Protestantism, rather than an allusion to the Italian context, a German woodcut even portrayed Julius in armour, wielding an enormous sword, alluding apparently to a medal he had struck with the provocative inscription 'The nation and kingdom that will not serve me shall perish' (*Isaiah*, LX, 12).[111] In reality, Julius waged war only in Italy, and on a much more modest scale than his namesake. Having first reinstated Ottavio Farnese at Parma, with the support of the Emperor in May 1551 he re-deprived him of it, on grounds of disobedience, for his acceptance of military backing from Henry II of France. A French-sponsored invasion of the papal state ensued, with devastation of the region north of Bologna. Although at least two cardinals (Morone and Cresenzi) were opposed to a papal counter-offensive, a joint papal and imperial army was formed in June 1551. In keeping with tradition, a cardinal was appointed legate to the army (Cardinal Giovanni Angelo Medici, later Pius IV) and an abbot accompanied him as commissary general. But it proved impossible to retake Parma, and the main event was another siege of Mirandola, which had served as a French military base since 1548. Unlike his predecessor, Julius did not take part in the hostilities, but his nephew Giambattista del Monte did so as Captain General. It was a much bigger and longer-lasting siege than Julius II's, claiming the lives of at least 300 soldiers and costing the Pope about 300,000 scudi.[112] But, by July 1552, the military expenses, the exploitation of the situation by Turkish fleets threatening the coast of Italy, and successful French intervention at Siena led Julius III to abandon this fruitless war and make peace.

The fanatical Gianpietro Carafa, created a cardinal in 1536, inquisitor and deviser of the first index of prohibited books, set a new tone of disciplinary severity after his election as Paul IV (pope 1555–59). But his external policy was dominated by a hatred of Spain – as one might expect of a Neapolitan nostalgic for the former monarchy – which led him to support the cause of Henry II of France against Charles V. A Venetian report in February 1556 quoted the Pope saying, 'We greatly fear we shall have to proceed to the ultimately terrible thing,' and before long he was threatening war against Naples even if he himself had to lead the army in person, bearing the cross.[113] The campaign that ensued was much less heroic than this in style. Writing in the late eighteenth century, the historian Edward Gibbon ridiculed it as a 'hasty quarrel when the vicar of Christ and the Turkish sultan were armed at the same time against the kingdom of Naples'.[114] Hostilities were begun by the Duke of Alva on behalf of Charles V in September 1556 and he soon conquered most of the Campagna, including key places such as Anagni, Frosinone and Terracina; on 18 November even the fortress of Ostia surrendered.[115] The war ended with a stalemate treaty, but the French defeat by imperial forces at St Quentin in August 1557 was a greater blow for Carafa policy. This decisive military event not only brought to an end three centuries of French ambition in Italy, but also ended at last the pose of Renaissance popes as champions of 'Italian liberty' and players of politics and war with the secular powers of Europe.

Paul IV's nephew Carlo Carafa had encouraged and assisted the Pope in his war policy. Probably the most unscrupulous papal relative since Girolamo Riario and Cesare Borgia, his career had started long before as a page in the service of Cardinal Pompeo Colonna; later a hit man and professional soldier (he enrolled in French service in the war of Siena

Chriſtenlicher Leſer / vernem die vrſach / warumb wir den Bapſt Iulium III. auff diſe weiß abgemalet haben. Dann er hat jüngſt ein Silberinne Müntz laſſen ſchlagen / In wölcher auff der einen ſeitten ſein bildnuß / auff der andern aber diſe wort auß dem Propheten Eſaia am lx. Capittel / geſchlagen warden / Gens & regnũ quod mihi non ſeruierit peribit, das iſt / Das volck vnd Reich ſo mir nicht dienet / würdt vmbkommen. Diewil er dann alſo raſende vnd wietiget / allen den jenigen den todt trewet / die ſich vnd einer Tyrannei nicht vnderwerffen / künden wir jhne in ſeinem wieten vnnd trewen auff ein beſſere weiß abmalen. So aber jemands bei im ſelber gedencken wolte / warumb er eben jetzt der zeit ſo hefftig den Glaubigen vnd Außerwölten trewete / der ſoll vnder andern auch die vrſach wiſſen. Nach dem jhme etlicher maſſen in Engelland gelungen / das ſie ſich mit verleügnung des h. Euangeliums widerum vnder ſeinen gehorſam ergeben / hat er auch ſeine gedancken auff Teütſchland gewendet / vnnd verhoffet / es ſolle bald dem Künigreich Engelland nachvolgen / vnd ſich jme auch wider vnderwürflich machen. Derhalben trewet er auff diſe Müntz / er wölle der malſten eins mit Hörskrafft ſampt ſeinen Sapanniern vnnd Italienern / villeicht auch mit etlichen Legionen der Türcken / in Teütſch Land fallen / vnd ſie mit Schwert vnd Feür verderben / wo wir jhne nicht für vnſern aller heiligſten vatter vnnd Statthalter Chriſti erkennen würden / an ſtatt Chriſti der vns vnſere ſünd verzeihe. Demnach wir auch bedencken ſollen / was vns gebüren will. Gott iſt vnſer vatter / wölcher vns allein die ſünd verzeihet durch vnſern herren Jeſum Chriſtum / der da ſitzt zů der gerechten des Vatters / vnd regiert mit ſeinem wort vnd h. Geiſt alles in Himel vnd auff erden / ſo jhme vom vatter übergeben / vnd bedarff keines Statthalters. Diſem einigen Gott / Chriſto / dem Vatter vnnd heiligen Geiſt / ſollen wir anhangen / vnd vns weit weit abſündern von dem vnreinen vnd ſchantlichen menſchen / wölcher an Gottes ſtatt will angebettet werden / Ja wir ſollen ehe tauſent mal ſterben / dann von Chriſto zů dem Antichriſto abfallen / ſein trewen aber vnd gewalt ſollen wir nicht fürchten / diewil Gott mit vns iſt ein Künig aller Künigen / vnd Herr aller Herren.

Pope Julius III as a demonic warrior (anon. print from a contemporary broadsheet, Staatsbibliothek, Handschriftenabteilung, Berlin).

in 1552), Carlo was made a cardinal in 1555. His particular contribution to the anti-imperial hostilities, in spite of his former obligation to Pompeo Colonna, was to conduct a final campaign of destruction and confiscation against the Colonna family, while his intrigues with Henry II of France were tied to his ambition to gain Siena as a principality for himself. In November 1556 he had even tried to barter the Colonna castle of Paliano in exchange for Siena.[116] Carlo's failed career, like the failed papal war, also marks the end of a long era; papal nephews in future would need to be more discreet in pursuing their ambitions. Under the next pope, Carlo was to be deprived of all his goods and titles, condemned on numerous charges including homicide, and hanged, or rather strangled, by a bungling executioner.

Paul's successor in 1559 was the Milanese Cardinal Medici (no relation of the famous Florentine family), one of the last cardinals created by Paul III. He took the name Pius IV, perhaps in conscious tribute to the memory of the two Piccolomini popes, and reverted in most respects to a more relaxed style, but was far from renouncing the papacy's military aspects, of which he had some experience in his earlier career. Before becoming a cardinal in 1549 he had served as general commissary to papal troops in Germany in 1543 and again, accompanying Cardinal Alessandro Farnese, in 1546; his service as a cardinal legate in Julius III's Parma war has already been mentioned. Though papal policy was no longer directed aggressively against Spain and Spanish Naples, Pius was evidently convinced of a need for military preparedness and was allegedly planning to restructure the papal army in August 1564, so that there would be a reduced dependence on mercenaries. He envisaged instead a standby militia like that of Duke Cosimo I of Florence ('fare una nuova militia nel stato ecclesiastico, conforme a quello del duca di Firenze, che sarà sempre in pronto ad ogni sua voglia'). It would be composed of anyone in the papal state who could bear arms and owned a horse, obliging them, in return for a modest retaining fee, always to be ready to respond to papal commands.[117] This initiative came to nothing.

In the meantime papal policy was being aimed in practical ways against religious enemies, Protestants and Muslims. Money was sent to encourage the Catholic Swiss cantons to attack Calvin's Geneva, and to aid Charles IX of France against the Huguenots; troops as well as money were sent to strengthen the Knights Hospitallers' defence of Malta, helping them to overcome the long siege by the Turks in 1565.[118]

Corresponding to this realistic military side of Pius IV's papacy, spectacular war games continued to be played out in the Vatican. The last military tournament[119] was held in 1565, to celebrate the marriage of Annibale Altemps, son of the Pope's sister Chiara Medici and commander of the papal militia, to Ortensia Borromeo, sister of the Pope's nephew Carlo, the future saint. The event did not begin until sunset, but crowds were filling the space in the Cortile Belvedere from dawn onwards. It was preceded by a military review and started with a deafening salvo of artillery and blowing of trumpets, which terrified many of the audience; the proceedings were so genuinely ferocious that three men were killed and another unhorsed in the very first event. The Pope and cardinals, at least twenty-two of them, watched from windows of the Vatican Palace; it was a show worthy to delight any Renaissance pope, not least perhaps Pius IV's Sienese predecessor of a century earlier.

# 7  A farewell to arms?

The mid-1560s were only an approximate watershed. If much was changing, with new regulations and institutions, the impact of the Council of Trent and the pervasive influence of the Jesuit Order, some things were still barely changing at all. Certainly the papacy was nowhere near renouncing war; in fact it has been reckoned that the papal military establishment and outlay, in proportion to total income, were at a peak in the late 1560s, though the whole subject of papal recruitment and payment of armies and defence expenditure, from the sixteenth to the nineteenth centuries, calls for further study, based on the huge amount of archival material not yet exploited.[1] After the death of Pius IV, the accession as Pius V (pope 1566–72) of Cardinal Michele Ghislieri, a protégé of Paul IV, resumed the control of the papacy by extreme 'counter-reformers', which was to last, this time without a break, for a quarter of a century. Conformity of belief, pastoral discipline and the rooting out of heresy were now among the highest priorities, while Protestants and Turks received increasing attention as military targets. Although defence expenditure remained high, papal warfare in Italy became less recurrent; in part because the papal state was now a more stable, cost-effective[2] and complete entity within Spanish and imperial-dominated Italy, and was no longer threatened by invading foreign armies.

No pope henceforth would profess himself ready to face the battlefield in person; even the appointment of cardinal legates to papal armies in the field became less common, though lay nephews of a reigning pope continued to be preferred for high command until the end of the seventeenth century.[3] As has been suggested in the previous chapter, there may also have been an element of prudent decorum behind this withdrawal of the top clergy from military encounters. The Church had to be guarded against the abuse of a critical world, with its new medium of derision and destruction, the printing press. An extraordinary battlefield scene printed in the 1560s showed, for example, the Pope once again as Antichrist aided by the cardinals, in particular by two tall figures in soutanes and tasselled hats labelled the Cardinal of Lorraine (Charles De Guise, cardinal 1547–74) and Cardinal Granvelle (Antoine Perrenot, cardinal 1561–86). These leading agents in the repression of Protestants on behalf respectively of Charles IX of France and Philip II of Spain were depicted firing heavy artillery against the True Church.

Pius V – later to be canonised – was notable for his encouragement of force in defence of the Church. He urged Philip II to repress with utmost severity the militant Protestants and iconoclasts in the Netherlands, and highly approved of the Duke of Alva's ruthless methods. When Alva wrote reporting his victory over Louis of Nassau in August 1568, Pius ordered bonfires and processions of celebration and thanksgiving in

The True Church under attack from battling popes and cardinals (anon. print, late 1560s) (Warburg Institute).

Rome, following up his letters of congratulation to Alva with the gift of the sword and cap the following December, together with the golden rose for his wife.[4] Meanwhile he increased active papal support to Charles IX of France against the Huguenots. Papal permission was granted to sell Church property to raise funds, under the supervision of Fabio Frangipani, the new nuncio sent in August 1568. Subsequently a special papal division was raised in Italy, consisting of 4500 foot soldiers and 500 cavalry under the command of Ascanio Sforza, Count of Santafiore. Ready by January 1569, it was accompanied to France by Lorenzo Lenzi, · Bishop of Fermo, as pontifical commissary, with five assistants, to keep strict control of discipline and morals; among the Pope's particular orders was an instruction to take no prisoners but to slay them all. The papal troops contributed to the Catholic victory in the Battle of Moncontour on 3 October, and Pius continued his hard line, telling the Cardinals of Lorraine and Bourbon on no account to negotiate with the Huguenot leader Coligny; he strongly condemned the Treaty of St Germain.[5] A prominent feature of Pius V's tomb in Santa Maria Maggiore, commissioned later by his admirer and protégé Sixtus V, the former Cardinal Felice Peretti, would be relief sculptures relating to the victorious military and naval campaigns against Protestants and Turks, including the Battles of Moncontour and Lepanto.[6]

Ever since his election in the summer of 1566, Pius had been urging war against the Turks. His nephew Michele Bonelli, a cardinal from 1566 to 1598 and known, as his uncle had been, as 'Alessandrino' or the Cardinal of Alessandria, was engaged in correspondence about this with the court of Philip II of Spain. Pius and Bonelli had even proposed that don García de Toledo should set off from Brindisi with his entire fleet, but don García refused to do more than defend the coasts of the papal state.[7] From July 1570 onwards endless discussions took place, often in the apartment of Cardinal Alessandrino, about the proposed Holy League intended to sweep the Turks from the Mediterranean. Gondola, Philip II's emissary in Rome, reported difficult discussions over sharing costs, though finally it was agreed that the papal contribution should be one-sixth, to three parts from Philip II, and two parts from Venice.[8] The question of appointing a supreme commander also provoked much debate. The Venetians proposed their own Cardinal Alvise Corner, but Pius vetoed this, interestingly on the grounds that the post was not suitable for a cardinal. As commander of the papal fleet he had already appointed Marcantonio Colonna in May 1570, conferring the papal war banner and baton of command in an elaborate ceremony.[9] Remarkably, it never seems to have been proposed in Rome that either Michele Bonelli or any other cardinal, much less the Pope himself, should accompany the joint war fleet. Philip II's war council would in any case have strongly objected had it been proposed; early in 1571 Cardinal Alessandrino had been firmly told that in their opinion the Pope could not play the principal role like a secular prince, nor even appoint generals. He should just appoint a prelate to give blessings and spiritual comfort.[10] Pius V does not appear to have contested this. The great naval victory at Lepanto in October 1571 was of course regarded as a papal triumph, and the celebrations in Rome lasted for weeks;[11] this was the culmination of Pius V's pontificate, for he died on 1 May 1572.

It was therefore his successor, Gregory XIII (pope 1572–85), formerly Cardinal Ugo Buoncompagni of Bologna, who acclaimed that other violent victory for the Church, the Massacre of St Bartholomew's Night (24 August 1572). On that notorious occasion in Paris several thousand persons, mainly Huguenots, were slaughtered, shortly after the marriage of Catherine de' Medici's daughter to Henry of Navarre. It has never been proved that the papacy, or even the Cardinal of Lorraine and other extremists, had engineered this bloodthirsty disposal of so many Huguenot leaders and others, or that it was the outcome of a 'grand design' initiated by Pius V and his predecessor.[12] Nevertheless, the cardinal, who was in Rome when it happened, allegedly broke the news by asking the Pope what he would best like to hear, and got the expected reply; Gregory and the cardinals celebrated a *Te Deum* in St Peter's.[13] Giorgio Vasari, who had been commissioned to paint in the Sala Regia, the Pope's principal audience chamber in the Vatican Palace, his rendition of the Battle of Lepanto, which shows Turks slaughtered and drowning, was invited in November 1572 to paint scenes relating to St Bartholomew's Night. Of the three he rapidly executed, one is particularly shocking: it includes the throwing of Coligny's naked body from a window and unarmed people being slain.[14] There was also a medal commissioned, with the Pope's head on one side, and on the reverse an avenging angel bending over corpses; it bears the inscription *Strages Ugunottorum* ('Massacre of the Huguenots').[15]

The invasion of England was a more open military design of Gregory XIII's papacy, a sequel to Queen Elizabeth's condemnation by his predecessor, though in the end it never happened. The exiled theologian and would-be missionary William Allen – who was finally appointed a cardinal under Gregory's successor in 1587 – had already drawn up plans for it in 1576. 5000 musketeers, all expertly trained, well-disciplined and zealous Catholic soldiers, would suffice for the job, so he reckoned. They should land at Liverpool, having been paid by the Pope for several months, and be led by a prudent and pious papal legate (Allen himself?) preceded by a banner of the cross. This was the original plan that Allen placed before Gregory XIII and the Spanish ambassador in Rome.[16] Promised the bishopric of Durham, in 1583 Allen was advising the victor of Lepanto, Don John of Austria, on strategy, but the papacy lost confidence in the project and withdrew all promises of financial backing upon the crushing defeat of the Spanish armada in 1588.

The reputation of Sixtus V (pope 1585–90) depends largely on his lavish building programme in Rome, but he was also a pope who believed passionately in the employment of force to secure and defend the Church. This was shown in his government of the papal state. A native of the March of Ancona, statues and inscriptions still commemorate him there like some populist dictator, and even his tomb, which accompanied the tomb he erected to Pius V in his Capella Sistina in Santa Maria Maggiore,[17] expresses the success of his iron-fisted government: the sculpted relief representing Justice depicts the campaign against bandits, with soldiers displaying the severed head of a bandit chief, a surprisingly brutal detail for a papal tomb. But Sixtus's ambitions were wider than this, and too wide to have any chance of fulfilment during his reign of only five years: he had hopes of overcoming by force both the Protestant north, including a swift campaign from Savoy against Geneva, and the Muslim east.[18] His two immediate successors had even less time to spare for the realisation of war projects; Urban VII, the former Cardinal Castagna, died after only a couple of weeks in September 1590; Gregory XIV, in his one year on the papal throne (December 1590 to November 1591), made an effort to strengthen the papacy's support of the League against the Huguenots and collected thousands of Swiss troops for this purpose.[19]

It was, however, the former cardinal Ippolito Aldobrandini, Clement VIII (pope 1592–1605), another native of the March of Ancona, who displayed in practice the greatest belligerency in this period after the Council of Trent. His persistent attempts to build up a huge coalition against the Turks, involving Poland, Christians in the Balkans, and even Persia, came to nothing,[20] but in Italy his aggressive annexation of Ferrara in 1597 at last fulfilled the desire of Julius II and Leo X. After Duke Alfonso II d'Este died (27 October 1597) without a son to succeed him, the Pope refused to allow Ferrara to pass to Alfonso's cousin Cesare d'Este, the designated heir;[21] with the support of most of the cardinals, he decided to implement this ruling by force. While the Pope's brother, Pietro Aldobrandini, was Captain General of the papal army, several cardinals were directly involved in the war machine in ways reminiscent of the past. Cardinal Cesi was put in overall charge of supplies, including arms; Cardinal Bandini, the papal legate in Romagna with headquarters at Forlì, had regional responsibility. Late in November another prelate, Girolamo Matteucci, was appointed 'general commissary of the papal army for the recovery of Ferrara'.

The first forecasts turned out to be overconfident, assuming that within one month Clement VIII could have invaded the duchy of Ferrara with 3000 horse and 20,000 foot soldiers. Cardinal Bandini found that the stores of artillery, gunpowder, cannon balls and other munitions held in castles throughout the Romagna were insufficient for a major campaign. Matteucci then planned to harness oxen to drag artillery all the way from Civitavecchia, Perugia and Castel Sant'Angelo in Rome, while Cardinal Aldobrandini, the Pope's nephew, suggested melting down the bells of St Peter's to cast into cannon balls and purchasing small arms from Genoa, Brescia and Milan. These rather desperate proposals, and the startling inadequacies of the arsenal, all suggest there was an element of sham in the papacy's outward appearances of strength in Italy. However, the true situation may not have been widely perceived and was not confirmed in any military encounter; moreover, the Pope obtained assurances of military support from Henry IV of France. But ultimately the spiritual sword proved, as in the medieval past, to be the stronger weapon in the papal armoury. Cesare d'Este suddenly gave up his defiance after sentence of excommunication was proclaimed in late December 1597, and on 28 January left in tears for Modena, the other seat of the Este regime.[22] Fire and bloodshed on behalf of St Peter had been avoided. 'Since that time,' wrote Gibbon nearly two centuries later, 'the papal arms are happily rusted.'[23] This was nicely expressed, if not entirely true, as we shall see; the papal farewell to arms would remain a long time coming.

The two long-lived, lavish popes of the earlier seventeenth century – Camillo Borghese, Paul V (pope 1605–21) and Maffeo Barberini, Urban VIII (pope 1625–44) – were far from pacific. Paul V continued Sixtus V's erection of bellicose papal tombs in Santa Maria Maggiore in his own Capella Paolina. Clement VIII was commemorated there with reliefs depicting the siege of Esztergom (Hungary) and the conquest or

Pope Paul V approving the plan for a fortress at Ferrara (tomb of Pope Paul V, Santa Maria Maggiore, Rome) (Courtauld Institute of Art, Conway Library).

submission of Ferrara, and Paul's own tomb there showed another success against the Turks in Hungary and his personal approval of the plans for a papal fortress to secure Ferrara.[24] The idea of the Church as an army or a fortress, subject to a supreme commander and staffed by field officers, who might indeed be involved in bloodshed, was still current, and not only in a metaphorical sense. Among its proponents was Tommaso Campanella, whose Latin tract *The Monarchy of the Messiah* (*Monarchia Messiae*) – written in 1606 to confound the semi-independent standpoint of Venice – quoted Micah, V and other scriptural sources to justify an ecclesiastical principality with no earthly superior, armed with the material sword and lance, for use against both infidels and gentiles ('Now gather thyself in troops, O daughter of troops... I [the Lord] will execute anger and fury upon the heathen, such as they have not heard').[25] Paul V managed to vanquish Venice and Paolo Sarpi without the material sword but by means of spiritual sanctions, notably the interdict lasting from May 1606 to April 1607, but it was not without some threats, or possibly bluff on both sides, about resorting to force. In August the Mantuan ambassador in Rome reported the Pope as saying that his predecessors had dealt on different terms with Venice, particularly Julius II, who had treated them as they deserved.[26] Papal military preparations were begun and the Venetians put the fleet on alert and increased the size of their army, hiring Albanians and negotiating the hire of Swiss and other mercenary troops.[27]

Intellectual opinion was divided over this crisis and its implications, but there was no lack of positive thinking about the physical strength of the papacy. The Piedmontese Giovanni Botero (1544–1617) wrote[28] that the 'Church State' had never been stronger, since the acquisition or direct control over Ferrara as well as Romagna and the March of Ancona, 'heavily populated regions containing the most warlike people in Italy, while Umbria could be described as a fortress in itself, with its narrow passes and steep sites... Ferrara is so strong that from that direction the Church State is almost impenetrable. The Bolognese is weaker; Castelfranco should be fortified.' Campanella, in some later reflections about ecclesiastical government,[29] published in 1633, advised Urban VIII to be warlike, indeed to raise two separate armies, a marine force in the name of St Peter and a land force, somewhat like the Ottoman Sultan's janissaries, in the name of St Paul. 'For an armed religion has never been vanquished.'

In fact, Urban VIII was much more bellicose than Paul V. He first made his brother Carlo Barberini Captain General of the Church 'and all that appertains to the army, to fortresses or the galleys', then his nephew Antonio became the principal adviser in such matters. Antonio Barberini (1607–71), created a cardinal in 1624, developed an almost obsessional interest in military affairs. He enlarged Paul V's arms factory at Tivoli, and planned to exploit the· iron ore of Monteleone near Spoleto, having visited the mine in June 1629 and been assured that it was highly suitable for the manufacture of small arms and armour, such as corslets, arquebuses, etc.[30] He strengthened key fortresses to protect the papal state (from what enemy it is not clear) – Sant'Angelo in Rome, Bologna, Tivoli among others – and, following Botero's proposal, planned to make Castelfranco an impregnable stronghold renamed Forte Urbano.[31]

With or without Forte Urbano, huge military citadels, thick low walls and state-of-the-art bastions continued to express the authority of St Peter throughout central Italy. The long gallery of topographical painted maps in the Vatican seems to have been devised deliberately to illustrate the formidable strength of the lands of the Church, and the safety of the surrounding sea provided by papal war galleys and strongly fortified ports.[32] The inscriptions suggest that most of the credit for this was owing to Urban VIII, even though, for instance, the citadel overlooking the harbour of Ancona had been designed for Paul III by Antonio da Sangallo a century earlier, and Civitavecchia likewise contained the work of a long series of architects and military engineers.

As for war in reality, admittedly Urban VIII's wish to revive the Enterprise of England came to nothing,[33] and when the prospect arose of another direct major annexation to the papal state, owing to the lack of an heir to Francesco Maria II della Rovere, Duke of Urbino, no war occurred.[34] Had there been resistance, no doubt Cardinal Antonio Barberini would have been ready for it; instead, all went peacefully according to the agreement made – not without some threats of military intimidation – soon after Urban's accession in 1624. By the following year the papacy had already appointed a clerical governor and taken possession of the main fortresses of the duchy, while the Camera Apostolica bought up the ducal artillery and stores of weapons. After the death of the duke in April 1631 Urbino lost its last vestiges of independence; Taddeo Barberini became governor, and first Cardinal Antonio and then their brother Cardinal Francesco Barberini were appointed as legates.

There was, however, a proper outbreak of war in the papal state in 1642–44, the so-called War of Castro, against Odoardo Farnese, Duke of Parma and Castro. Even during the previous year preparations for an offensive were going ahead, in response to Odoardo's aggressive fortification of Castro and harassment of surrounding territory within the papal state. Soldiers were recruited for papal service and great quantities of artillery amassed; Cardinal Antonio Barberini undertook in person an inspection of fortresses.[35] Odoardo claimed that his quarrel was with the Barberini, not the papacy, but Urban nevertheless opened hostilities in the name of the Church. Cardinal Antonio and his brother Taddeo, Captain General of the Church, took charge of military operations; Castro was captured and partly demolished. Odoardo, however, received help for the defence of Parma from Venice and France, and on the papal side the campaign went ingloriously. In the Battle of Fortezza Lagoscuro in March 1644 Cardinal Antonio only escaped capture thanks to the speedy horse on which he fled.[36]

As might have been foreseen, this reversion to the style and policy of the early sixteenth-century papacy was not only unsuccessful on the battlefield but also in its effect upon opinion. A pasquinade circulated in 1642[37] ridiculing Urban and carrying some echoes of the *Julius Exclusus*. Its title, *Baccinata* or *Battarella for the Barberini Bees on the occasion of our Lord the Pope taking up arms against Parma*, alluded to the practice of beating kettles or pans to disperse a swarm of bees, and so to the Barberini family emblem and the desirability of putting a stop to the war. It was in the form of a defamatory letter addressed to the papal nuncio in Venice. 'The pope does not imitate Christ, who wanted to bring peace to the world,' declared the author, one Ferrante Pallavicino;

> Christ shed his own blood, and Our Lord [the Pope] sheds the blood of others and promises eternal life to those who shed the most Christian blood…and if the shepherd is only permitted a thin rod with which to control the sheepfold, or better still, nothing at all, as Christ said to the Apostles, 'Do not carry any rod with you on the way,' what can be said of Our Lord and Pastor [the Pope], who scatters the herd of the Church with swords, guns, archebuses and cannons?

Needless to say Ferrante was made to suffer for this; arrested on papal territory in November 1642, he was eventually executed in March 1644.

In spite of Barberini policy, the belligerent tradition of Roman Church leadership seems to have been losing much of its impulse and justification as the seventeenth century progressed. Although a fair-sized army was still maintained, with particularly large garrisons in Rome, Civitavecchia and Castelfranco Emilia,[38] it must have become evident that the papal state in Italy was threatened by no other power to justify the high level of expenditure on defence. Meanwhile a certain *modus vivendi* between Catholic and Protestant regimes was achieved by the Peace of Westphalia in 1648, so that even the papacy's potential scope for mediation became irrelevant.[39] In the west, the dominance of Europe by France under Louis XIV, in spite of Jansenism, Gallicanism and other problems, was on the whole reassuring for the Church over the next half-century. In the east, despite Venice's defeat and loss of Crete in the long War of Candia (1645–69), in which the papacy had provided only marginal support, the decline or stagnation of Ottoman power was confirmed by the failure of the last Turkish siege of Vienna in 1683 and the Venetian successes in southern Greece of Francesco Morosini between 1684 and 1693. Overall, therefore, the papacy had less need to worry about war or self-defence than it had done for centuries. In the new age of enlightenment the Monsignori Eminentissimi flaunted powdered wigs and shoe buckles, rather than body armour and spurred boots.

Even so, the papal farewell to arms was a very slow process, and should a threat to the power of the Church erupt in any area the response was not necessarily pacific. In the Spanish succession crisis Clement XI, who supported Philip V and France, refused in 1708 the imperial demand for unrestricted overland access to Naples. The papal legate in Ferrara was ordered to put that city in a heightened state of defence, and troops were enrolled in Rome. War broke out in October between pope and emperor; imperial troops occupied Ferrara and other papal towns before a treaty was signed in January 1709, which amounted to a papal climbdown.[40] The short 'war' in 1739 of Clement XII (pope 1730–40) against the semi-independent republic of San Marino furnished another late blast of the papal war trumpet. The cause of the attack was violation of a legal immunity, the prosecution of a San Marino citizen who claimed papal protection, therefore a supposed defiance of St Peter's rightful authority.[41] Cardinal Giulio Alberoni (1664–1752) – better known from his earlier career in Spanish diplomacy – was ordered, as papal legate in the Romagna, to advance on San Marino with 200 Romagnol troops and others locally recruited; the republic's governing council called out the militia but failed to prevent the papal force from advancing destructively into their territory. Alberoni was implacable, ordering the destruction of the houses of 'the mad dogs' (recalcitrant councillors who refused the oath of total obedience to the papacy), though subsequently Clement XII greatly modified the terms of submission, and San Marino remained virtually autonomous within the papal state.

## TOWARDS MODERN TIMES: THE ARMED CHALLENGES OF NAPOLEON AND THE *RISORGIMENTO*

By the end of the eighteenth century, however, new and boundless dangers appeared to threaten both the spiritual and temporal properties of the Church, and it is perhaps surprising that the papacy was caught so ill-prepared. The ill wind blew from France, not only bringing godless republican secularism but also military invasion. Pius VI (pope 1775–99) had duly urged Louis XVI not to submit to revolutionary demands, but was strangely silent upon the fall of the monarchy in the autumn of 1792 and execution of the King in January 1793, and unresponsive even to the seizure of the papal enclaves in Provence (Avignon and the Comtat Venaissin). He seems to have assumed that the outbreak of war between revolutionary France and Austria in 1792 and the invasion of Piedmont might only affect northern Italy; in general he depended on protection from the Bourbon kingdom of Naples, and paradoxically looked to two non-Catholic powers, Britain and Russia, to provide him with naval defence if required. He wrote with some exaggeration to Catherine the Great, 'We have neither troops nor naval fleets.'[42] In November 1792, when asked what he would do if the French attacked Rome, he replied serenely that his post would be at the doorway of St Peter's. The Venetian ambassador who reported this stressed the inadequacy of belated defence measures being attempted, 'military matters not being what priests know about'.[43] By 1796, however, Pius was aroused to a more warlike stance, in the face of Napoleon Bonaparte's first Italian campaign on behalf of the Directory. Cardinal Ercole Consalvi (1757–1824) was appointed to head the congregation in charge of military affairs, and in September 1796 it was announced, 'The peace-loving soul of the Holy Father is wholly opposed to hostilities…however, he will not desist from seeking tranquillity for his beloved subjects, and if the French think otherwise, he does not intend to leave them [his subjects] defenceless…if any of their troops should cross the frontier, His Holiness is determined on resistance.' Instructions were issued to ring the church bells in any place entered by the French, to call the people to arms and man the defences.[44] Military help was promised from the kingdom of Naples, and the papal nuncio in Vienna actively negotiated there for help; Cardinal Gianfrancesco Albani, one of the most instransigent of the cardinals, instructed him to say that the Pope was the only Italian power that could continue to resist Napoleon. Meanwhile, artillery was sent to defend Perugia and volunteers assembled in the Romagna.[45] From Rome itself at the beginning of January 1797 it was reported that papal uniforms and cockades were to be seen everywhere and even children were playing war games.

Armed confrontation occurred at the river Senio between Imola and Faenza on 2 February 1797. The papal troops were encouraged by a number of priests bearing crosses who mingled in the ranks, exhorting them to fight hard, but within a few hours they faced defeat. Napoleon acted magnanimously, declaring that, although many priests and a Capuchin friar had been involved and some were wounded, he would not punish the people of Faenza; he even sent a message to the Pope through the Abbot of Camaldoli to reassure him 'Bonaparte is not an Attila'.[46] Fourteen (out of the total of seventy) cardinals still opposed any compromise, and Cardinal Albani wrote a letter to the Pope on 5 February exhorting him not to give in. 'The throne of Truth, upon which Your Holiness is seated, has many times been bathed in the glorious blood of your predecessors in defence of the same Truth,' he declared rhetorically, without citing any historical evidence, 'while as for ourselves, the very colour of our vestments reminds us to what point our constancy should reach.' After this he turned briefly to history, citing Leo I and Gregory the Great, but then jumped to 'the more recent example of Pius II', who did not cringe in the face of the terrible danger Italy and Christendom faced from Mohammed the Conqueror. Cardinal Albani suggested that Pius VI might imitate the earlier Pius by writing a reproachful letter to Napoleon; at least this would gain time to prepare for the ultimate showdown.[47]

Pius VI was well aware of the essential weaknesses, not least in financial resources, of the papal state, and at this point of confrontation his will seems to have failed; in any event, he was not prepared to emulate Pius II nor to repeat the fulminations and physical commitment of a Gregory VII or a Julius II, nor even the evasive cunning of an

Alexander VI. By the Treaty of Tolentino in February 1797 he confirmed that about half of the papal state – the legations of Bologna, Ferrara and Romagna – not to mention Avignon and the Comtat Venaissin – should remain under French control. The Italian lands were to be incorporated within the new Cisalpine Republic, while French troops were also to be stationed in the legation of Ancona and in Rome itself. A huge indemnity in money, pack animals, works of art, manuscripts and other items had also to be paid. Worse was to come; in February 1798 there was a republican rising in Rome followed by a full-scale French military takeover. The Pope refused to cede his sovereignty, and was told to leave within three days. He was allowed first to take refuge in Tuscany, then in France. Meanwhile two cardinals resigned, much to the annoyance of the Pope, who suggested that this act made them eligible to fight and shed their blood for the Holy See; ten cardinals meanwhile escaped to the kingdom of Naples, including Cardinal Albani, whose villa was sacked and his goods confiscated by the French. Those remaining were arrested, among them Cardinal Consalvi, who was imprisoned for two nights in Castel Sant'Angelo. They were then taken under military escort to Civitavecchia and deported.[48]

In these dire circumstances, or at least in the south, where the royal government of Naples was also replaced early in 1799 by a short-lived republic, the Church finally struck back. Cardinal Fabrizio Ruffo (1764–1827) distinguished himself in the most robust tradition of ecclesiastical military leadership. Ruffo was formerly treasurer of the papal state, a forceful and practical administrator who had been responsible, among other things, for strengthening the military citadels of Ancona and Civitavecchia in 1791–92 and for introducing his own invention of a more effective device (*fornello*) for firing mortars from cannon. His distinction as an enlightened economic manager led to his employment by the King of Naples and appointment as special royal commissary in the crisis of early 1799. Supplied with arms from Naples, Ruffo raised in the wilds of his native Calabria a peasant army to fight for monarchy and religion, who became known as the 'Sanfedisti', warriors of the Holy Faith. 'Brave and courageous Calabrians,' he declared in his recruitment manifesto of February 1799,

> unite now under the standard of the Holy Cross and of our beloved sovereign. Do not wait for the enemy to come and contaminate our home neighbourhoods. Let us march to confront him, to repel him,

to hunt him out of our kingdom and out of Italy and to break the barbarous chains of our holy Pontiff. May the banner of the Holy Cross secure you total victory.[49]

His correspondence with Sir Henry Acton records his cool commitment as military commander. 'I beg the king [of Naples] to order at least a thousand handguns and many loads of lead shot to be sent to me,' he wrote on 12 February 1799; 'I think it would be expedient to send a frigate with a mortar against Cotrone and to destroy it absolutely' (26 February); 'Catanzaro has really surrendered; many of the worst types have been massacred, others taken prisoner' (8 March); 'Cosenza has been taken and sacked' (19 March).[50]

Ruffo's campaign aroused and still arouses controversy. Direct participation in bloodshed and cruelty was attributed to him by his enemies, much of it unjustified, though even his apologists can only manage to excuse the sack of Altamura on the grounds that the republican garrison there had previously massacred royalist prisoners; he did his best to restrain the looting and to restore discipline.[51] If not quite in the mode of the notorious military cardinals of the fifteenth century, such as Vitelleschi or Forteguerri, or indeed Giuliano della

Cardinal Ruffo, protected by St Anthony, leading the Sanfedisti, 1799 (popular print).

Rovere, Ruffo was a charismatic leader. Fearless in action, hazardously conspicuous on his white charger, he was said to have shouted to the crowd outside the walls of Altamura on 9 May, 'Keep clear of me, the bullets won't harm me' (indeed they didn't) 'and I'd be sorry if any of you were hurt.'[52] Within a few months in the spring of 1799 Cardinal Ruffo's irregulars were largely responsible for the overthrowal of the Neapolitan republic, aided by the intimidatory British naval force commanded by Horatio Nelson, who was less inclined than Ruffo to recommend mercy for the defeated.

Pius VI's death in exile at Valence in August 1799 was followed by the even greater eclipse of papal political and military power. Pius VII (pope 1800–23), a more timid character than his predecessor, was elected at Venice in March 1800. After the concordat was signed in August 1802, there was a brief period of easier relations, while Napoleon's uncle, Cardinal Joseph Fesch, acted as French ambassador in Rome and quasi-supervisor of the Pope;[53] Pius agreed to witness Napoleon's self-coronation as emperor in Paris in December 1804, and then was allowed to return to Rome. But, with the renewed outbreak of European war, what remained of papal temporal power was again compromised. Napoleon wanted total control of the Italian coast against possible Russian or British attack, and in November 1805 ordered the military occupation of Ancona. Even Cardinal Fesch supported the protestations against this violation of papal neutrality, and by the end of 1807 all pretence was abandoned. Papal plenipotentiaries were recalled from Paris, and in February 1808 Rome was again subjected to French military occupation. Cardinal Fesch returned to Paris, while Pius VII lurked in the Quirinal Palace.[54] In July 1809 he was arrested and transferred to Savona, where he remained until 1814.

For thirty years or so after Napoleon's fall, the papacy – restored to Rome and its lands in Italy – fell under the control of reactionaries, those who had always wanted to defy Napoleon and now wanted to abolish even his better reforms and reject the more pragmatic policy of Cardinal Consalvi, sheltering themselves behind the weapons of foreign soldiers and Neapolitan police agents. One of the most powerful and determined of these reactionaries was Tommaso Bernetti, a canon lawyer by training, who came from Fermo in the March of Ancona. Bernetti received the red hat only in 1826, but he had had experience in papal administration ever since 1801, including – in the immediate restoration period – the posts of 'assessore alle Armi' (1816–20), assistant legate in the March and at Ferrara, and governor or police chief of Rome (1820–23). He distinguished himself by exceptional harshness towards Carbonari and other dissidents; he even raised irregular bands (called 'Centurioni'), who were allowed a free hand in raids and executions. Under Leo XII (pope 1823–29) and his short-lived successor Pius VIII (pope 1829–31), Bernetti came into his own as the leading figure in papal diplomacy, cementing close relations with the Habsburg empire under Metternich's direction and the French monarchy of Charles X; he even travelled to Moscow, though he received rather less encouragement there. In May 1828 Bernetti's industry was rewarded with the office of cardinal secretary of state. The zenith of this repressive and backward-looking career[55] came under Gregory XVI (pope 1831–46), a monk from the Veneto whose outlook was rooted in the pre-revolutionary eighteenth century and may have chosen his name as a deliberate if wishful allusion to Gregory VII, the champion of clerical against secular authority.[56] In 1831 it was Cardinal Bernetti who supervised the crushing of the liberal-inspired risings in the March of Ancona and other legations. He first dispatched Cardinal Giovanni Antonio Benvenuti as legate to accompany a division of the papal army, but this force proved unable to suppress the rebellion, much less to impose the ferocious counter-revolution that it transpires had been planned. Cardinal Benvenuti was captured and held as a hostage, while he negotiated terms that were rejected in Rome; Cardinal Albani, meanwhile, was sent as special commissary, and in February 1832 Metternich, who was much less inflexible than Cardinal Bernetti, was again asked to send Austrian troops to do the job.[57]

The policy of Cardinal Bernetti and his colleagues, of opposition to all reform and ultimate reliance on Austrian military power, was in time discredited; he was deprived of his military responsibilities in 1835 and, although he lived until 1852, lost influence. The more liberal and pragmatic faction grew in power in the early 1840s, and triumphed with the election as pope in 1846 of Cardinal Giovanni Maria Mastai-Ferretti, yet another robust character originating from the March of Ancona. In his youth, according to unconfirmed tradition, he had wanted to be an officer in the papal guard, but as a priest and bishop he committed himself to pastoral work, not politics; at all events he was not part of the old establishment in Rome.[58] Taking the name Pius IX ('Pio Nono') the new pope was at first wildly popular for issuing a general amnesty, a relaxation of some of the more oppressive controls and a constitution that to a limited extent reduced clerical power.[59] After only two years, however, the experiment ended abruptly with the outbreak of revolutions all over Europe. Pius categorically refused to become the champion of liberal-minded Italian patriots. Resisting all pressures to declare war on the Habsburg empire, on 29 April 1848 he made an allocution to the cardinals declaring that it was not lawful for the pastor of the faithful to enter into war to shed Christian blood (disregarding all the precedents). He remained passive after the Austrians took the offensive, occupying Ferrara and advancing elsewhere into papal territory, then winning a decisive victory over the Piedmontese army at Custoza (25 July).[60] Nor could Pius face any longer the seditious atmosphere in Rome after the murder of his competent first minister, Pellegrino Rossi, in November 1848.[61] Instead he fled to Gaeta and the protection of Bourbon Naples. Even if the secular Roman republic (February–April 1849), inspired and led by Giuseppe Mazzini, was doomed to collapse, the Pope's flight and the arrival of French military forces bent on restoring him were not events likely to foster much reverence or loyalty. During the French bombardment in June 1849 ordinary Romans had allegedly shouted 'There goes a Pio Nono' as the shells whizzed over their heads or onto their homes.[62]

Pio Nono, having returned to Rome in 1850 as a disillusioned reformer, never a 'liberal' but at least a pragmatic conservative, henceforward became intransigent. In the face of the Italian *Risorgimento*, soon to be sponsored by the Savoyard monarchy, the papacy at last tried to regain some of its old belligerence and autonomy. Pius refused to consider renouncing any of the temporal claims, and even went on the offensive. When the challenge to the rights of St Peter became really serious from 1859 onwards, he did all he could to save them, aided by his Secretary of State, Cardinal Giacomo Antonelli (1806–76).[63] A cardinal since 1847, this astute curial prelate had soon come to dominate papal policy, sharing many of the views of the reactionary Cardinal Bernetti. Their first priority was to build up an independent papal army, and to require the withdrawal of French and Austrian troops of occupation. In March 1859 Antonelli was talking of an army of 18,000, and was particularly keen to recruit a whole battalion of Swiss riflemen.[64] In June of that year, when the Piedmontese were gaining widespread support in Umbria, Romagna and the March of Ancona, the unaccredited British agent in Rome, Odo Russell, reported that about 4000 Swiss troops had been sent by the Pope to intimidate Perugia, where they shot everyone in sight, including old men and women, on the strength of which the Pope promoted their colonel to the rank of brigadier general.[65] In another letter, Odo Russell wrote that Cardinal Antonelli assured him that

> the people were getting daily more disgusted with the terrorism exercised over them by the agents of Sardinia [i.e. the kingdom of Sardinia, with Savoy–Piedmont, under Vittorio Emanuele II and his Prime Minister Camillo Cavour] [...] The Papal Army was daily increasing and the Swiss soldiers enlisted on their way from Naples to the north now seemed animated with the most excellent military spirit. All now tended to make His Eminence hope that the Papal army would ere long be able to commence operations in the Legations...the success of the butcheries of Perugia has instilled a military ardour into his Holiness the Pope and his Eminence Cardinal Antonelli, which appears to me as ill-judged and misplaced as it is revengeful and bloodthirsty.[66]

The German historian Ferdinand Gregorovius, a long-standing resident in Rome, also had feelings of revulsion. He had written in his diary on 26 June: 'The capture of Perugia was sanguinary. These foreign mercenaries, the scum of the whole of Europe, rioted as in a Turkish city...and even outraged nuns... Had the Pope only waited three days, Perugia would have voluntarily submitted. The longing once more to act the temporal prince will cost him dear.'[67]

In this mood of military ardour, Cardinal Antonelli was reported to be recruiting hard and raising new regiments to increase the size of the papal army, with Swiss and other 'volunteers' recommended by their bishops, including many Irish (not a great success). The hope was that the French army of 'protection' would no longer be needed.[68] In April 1860 the Pope appointed General Lamoricière, a famous veteran of French campaigns in North Africa, who had trained in Algeria a force of Arab auxiliaries known as Zouaves, as supreme commander of the independent papal army. Odo Russell wrote that this had in fact been against the advice of Antonelli, 'who was overruled by an intriguing prelate and confidential friend of His Holiness, Monsignor de Mérode, a distant relation of General Lamoricière'. This Belgian chamberlain of the Pope, who had in his time served as a soldier under Lamoricière in Algeria, shortly afterwards replaced Antonelli himself as papal War

Minister or 'Pro-Minister of Arms'.[69] By July 1860 General Lamoricière was planning to concentrate the army (henceforward known as the papal Zouaves) into two enormous camps at Spoleto and Pesaro, in anticipation of a great campaign to win back the March of Ancona and Romagna, in the footsteps of the armies of earlier popes. Pio Nono tried for the time being to sound wary: 'The duty of the Pope,' he observed

Pius IX reluctantly surrenders the material sword to King Vittorio Emanuele II, but insists that he retains the keys (cartoon in *Punch* magazine, 1870).

to Odo Russell, 'is to wait, defend the rights of the Church and not give way to his enemies.'[70]

The defeat of the papal army at the Battle of Castelfidardo, near Ancona, in September 1860 brought this revival of papal belligerence to the verge of collapse. There was even talk of Pio Nono going into exile. Odo Russell now commented that the Pope's 'attempt to make a Military Power of the Holy See, his belief in the obnoxious Antonelli, his neglect and contempt of the Sacred College...have tended to render him more an object of contempt and pity than anything else'.[71] Yet there was no weakening of conviction on the Pope's part. 'The Temporal Dominion was given by God to his Vicar Upon Earth,' he assured Odo Russell two years later. 'I cannot by any act of my own give up the States of the Church which I hold in trust.'[72] Cardinal Antonelli repeated much the same diehard standpoint in November 1865, satisfied by the replacement of French by pontifical troops to guard the frontiers of Church territory and of Mérode by a level-headed professional soldier, General Kanzler, at the papal war ministry. Meanwhile the papal Zouaves continued to receive new recruits, perhaps of mixed quality, but apparently their morale was high.[73] There was even some sign of a possible turn of fortune in November 1867, when papal and French troops routed the Garibaldini at Mentana. In March 1868 the Pope, in one of his humorous and boastful moods, declared to Odo Russell that Garibaldi had compelled him to become a military prince and now he had a larger army than any other sovereign in the world in proportion to the number of subjects left to him, and all his soldiers were animated with the true spirit of crusaders. 'If the interests of the Church ever required it,' His Holiness added, laughing loudly, he would even 'buckle on a sword, mount a horse and take command of the army himself like Julius II'.[74] As late as October 1869 something of this mood of defiance still lasted, when the papal dragoons held a mock battle and assaulted a 'fortress' in the Villa Borghese.[75] So much for papal vainglory. The French, facing war with Prussia, withdrew their military support after the Vatican Council approved the Pope's decree of infallibility, and on 20 September 1870 there was virtually no resistance when the Piedmontese army arrived at Porta Pia. While Pius IX and his immediate successors remained indignantly confined to the Vatican, the remnants of the papal army were relegated to guard duties, their weaponry merely ceremonial, and the last ship of the papal navy was sold off in 1878.[76]

# Epilogue

In the present political climate, when apologies are in vogue,[1] not least on behalf of those long dead whose deeds, often piously and sincerely motivated, cannot be undone (the 'crusades', for example, are now a cause for collective guilt), we have yet to hear a word of recantation or apology for the centuries of warfare over the lands of the Roman Church. Instead the Vatican beatified Pio Nono on 3 September 2000; and there may even be some ultras who still deplore the compromise reached with the Italian Fascist regime in 1929, confirmed by the post-war republic, under which all but minimal papal territorial and temporal claims were renounced.

Fortunately, one can leave to the imagination what might have happened, how violently the Church or its leaders might have responded, had events turned out differently in the twentieth century. 'The Church in danger' – mainly from Communism – was of course a prevailing theme for most of the time, and another book would be needed to illustrate the many ways in which counter-attack by force was envisaged or indeed, in some countries, put into practice by clerical authority. The twenty-first century has already seen some extreme versions of other, older enemies on the offensive. How far can the Church allow itself to be pushed, even though it no longer has temporalities to defend, before its leaders, or some of them, reach again for the sword? What if the Vatican were to be bombed? Perhaps the root trouble has always been that Christian teaching is so ambiguous and flexible about war and peace. Erasmus wrote in his *Complaint of Peace*, 'What has a mitre to do with a helmet, a crozier with a sword, the Gospel with a shield?'[2] Alas, the answer, in a word, is: much. This book, if mainly limited to distant centuries, and concentrating unashamedly upon one aspect of ecclesiastical policy and government, in only one – albeit the largest and most highly organised and prevalent – body in Christendom, has aimed to show the Roman Church's leadership being drawn, almost inevitably, into processes of war rather than peace.

# Notes

## FOREWORD

1 E.g. the *Longman History of Italy*, various authors, 6 vols; UTET *Storia d'Italia*, various authors, 24 vols. For a lively discussion entitled 'The Problems of Italian History' see Denys Hay, *The Italian Renaissance in its Historical Background* (Cambridge, 1961).
2 See below, Chapter 5, nn. 100–101.
3 Here the reader might be directed to the long, dense, difficult but rewarding fourth chapter, 'Political Revolution', in Philip Jones, *The Italian City State: From Commune to Signoria* (Oxford, 1997).

## PROLOGUE

1 Transl. with commentary by M.J. Heath, 'Julius Excluded from Heaven: a Dialogue' ('Dialogus Julius Exclusus e coelis'), in *Collected Works of Erasmus*, vol. 27, ed. A.H.T. Levi (Toronto, Buffalo and London, 1986), pp. 155–97 (at p. 169). See also discussion in Chapter 5, 'The Julian trumpet' (below).

## CHAPTER 1

1 Ep. 20, 21 (*PL* 16, cols. 1043, 1050); C. Erdmann (1935), transl. Marshall W. Baldwin and W. Goffat, *The Origins of the Idea of Crusade* (Princeton, 1977), p. 15 n. 26; J.H. Russell, *The Just War in the Middle Ages* (Cambridge, 1975), pp. 14–15, 72, 78.
2 Erdmann, *Origins*, p. 25; Russell, *Just War*, pp. 28–29; letter of Gregory I, 27 September 591, in *Gregorii I Registri*, ed. P. Ewald, G. Hartman (Berlin, 1890), vol. I (no. II, 7), pp. 105–6.
3 Russell, *Just War*, p. 78; P. Partner, *The Lands of St Peter* (London, 1972), pp. 58–60.
4 F. Gregorovius, transl. A. Hamilton, *A History of the City of Rome in the Middle Ages*, vol. III (2nd edn revised, London, 1903; repr. New York, 2001), pp. 171, 181–83.
5 P. Fedele, 'La battaglia del Garigliano, 915', *ASRSP*, 22, 1899, pp. 181–211 (at p. 193); Erdmann, *Origins*, p. 25; the letter is in L. Jaffé, *Regesta Pontificum Romanorum … ad 1198* (2nd edn, Berlin, 1881–88) no. 3556.
6 The complicated history of donations and origins of papal temporal claims in Italy are outlined by D. Waley, *The Papal State in the Thirteenth Century* (London, 1961), pp. 2–22; P. Partner, *The Papal State under Martin V* (London, 1958), pp. 1–8.

7    J.M. Wallace Hadrill, *The Frankish Church* (Oxford, 1983), pp. 186–87.
8    W. Ullmann, *The Growth of Papal Government in the Middle Ages* (2nd edn, London, 1962), pp. 229–38.
9    *The Works of Liudprand of Cremona*, transl. F. A. Wright (London, 1930), pp. 223–26.
10   Waley, *Papal State*, p. 7.
11   Ullman, *Growth of Papal Government*, esp. pp. 193–203.
12   Ibid., pp. 420–37.
13   K. Cushing, 'Anselm and Coercion. A Legal Form of Persuasion', in *The Papacy and Law in the Gregorian Reformation: The Canon Law Work of Anselm of Lucca* (Oxford, 1998), p. 127.
14   Erdmann, *Origins*, pp. 74, 118–23.
15   H.E.J. Cowdrey, *Pope Gregory VII, 1073–85* (Oxford, 1998), passim.
16   Ibid., p. 27.
17   E. Caspar, *Das register Gregors VII* (Berlin, 1920), vol. I, p. 166; Cowdrey, *Gregory VII*, esp. pp. 485, 652.
18   W. Ullmann, *The Growth of Papal Government in the Middle Ages*, revised edn (London, 1965), p. 304; Cowdrey, *Gregory VII*, pp. 310–11, 485, 652.
19   Erdmann, *Origins*, pp. 202–23.
20   Ibid., p. 256; Cowdrey, *Gregory VII*, pp. 310–11.
21   Erdmann, *Origins*, pp. 144–45.
22   Cushing, *Papacy and Law*, pp. 132–40 and p. 217, n. 66; Cowdrey, *Gregory VII*, p. 653.
23   L. Duchesne, ed., *Le Liber Pontificalis* (new edn Paris, 1981), III, esp. pp. 147–55; F. Gregorovius, *A History of the City of Rome in the Middle Ages*, transl. A. Hamilton, vol. IV (2) (2nd edn, revised, London, 1905; repr. New York, 2002), pp. 317–75.
24   I.S. Robinson, *The Papacy 1073–1198: Continuity and Innovation* (Cambridge, 1990), pp. 367, 386, 390.
25   P. Munz, *Frederick Barbarossa: A Study in Medieval Politics* (London, 1969), pp. 85–86.
26   Ibid., pp. 166–67, 198; Waley, *Papal State*, p. 12.
27   Ibid., pp. 196–204.
28   Munz, *Frederick Barbarossa*, pp. 14–15, 18–19.
29   S. Runciman, *History of the Crusades*, vol. I (Cambridge, 1951), pp. 186, 220–25, 252–53; J.A. Brundage, 'Adhémar of Le Puy: The Bishop and his Critics', *Speculum*, XXXIV, 1959, pp. 201–12.
30   *De Consideratione Libri Quinque ad Eugenium Tertium*, vol. IV, 3, in *Opera Omnia*, vol. I, ed. S. Mabillon and J.-P. Migne (Paris, 1879), col. 776; *Five Books of Consideration: Advice to a Pope*, transl. J.D. Anderson, E.T. Kennan (Kalamazoo, 1976), p. 118; Ullmann, *Growth of Papal Government*, pp. 423–32.
31   M. Chibnall, ed., *John of Salisbury: Memoirs of the Papal Court* (London, 1956), p. 60.
32   J. Riley-Smith, *The Knights of St John in Jerusalem and Cyprus 1050–1310* (London, 1967), pp. 235–36, 382–87 and passim.
33   Russell, *Just War*, pp. 77–82.
34   Ibid., p. 107.
35   S. Kuttner, 'Cardinalis. The Growth of a Canonical Concept', *Traditio*, 3, 1945, pp. 129–214 (esp. pp. 172–78); J.F. Broderick, 'The Sacred College of Cardinals: Size and Geographical Composition', *AHP*, 25, 1987, pp. 7–71 (esp. pp. 8–10); Robinson, *The Papacy*, Chapters 2, 4 passim.
36   Robinson, *The Papacy*, p. 169.
37   Runciman, *History of the Crusades*, vol. III (Cambridge, 1955), p. 5.
38   E. McNeal in K.M. Setton et al., *A History of the Crusades*, vol. II (Philadelphia and London, 1962), pp. 154–55.

39    Ibid., p.176.
40    Innocent III, *Regestorum Libri* in *Opera Omnia, PL* 216, col. 139; A.P. Evans in Setton, *History of the Crusades*, vol.II, p.289n.; P. Belperron, *La Croisade contre les Albigeois et l'union du Languedoc à la France* (Paris, 1942; new edn 1959), p.166.
41    Setton, *History of the Crusades*, vol.II, p.437, quoting Palmer A. Throop, *Criticism of the Crusade* (Amsterdam, 1940), p.32; E. Siberry, *Criticism of Crusading 1095–1274* (Oxford, 1983) pp.34–35, quoting 'Le Besant de Dieu' by Guillaume le Clerc. On Pelagius's leadership, Runciman, *History of the Crusades*, vol. III (Cambridge, 1955), pp.155–70.
42    Russell, *Just War*, p.282.
43    N. Housley, *The Italian Crusades: The Papal–Angevin Alliance and the Crusades against Lay Powers 1254–1343* (Oxford, 1982), p.169n., and see below.
44    Throop, *Criticism*, pp.135–36.
45    Ibid., pp.190–93.
46    Housley, *Italian Crusades*, pp.1–9 and passim.
47    Waley, *Papal State*, pp.27–34.
48    Ibid., p.40.
49    E. Kantorowicz, ed. E.O. Lorimer, *Frederick the Second* (London, 1931), p.177.
50    Waley, *Papal State*, pp.287–96; idem, 'Papal Armies in the Thirteenth Century', *EHR*, LXXI, 1957, pp.1–30.
51    *Commentaria Innocenti Quarti Pont. Max ... Super Libros Quinque Decretalium*, lib.3, tit.34 c.8 (Frankfurt-am-Main edn, 1570, pp.430–31). I owe this reference to Magnus Ryan.
52    G. Moroni, *Dizionario di erudizione storico ecclesiastico*, vol. LXX (Venice, 1845), p.24.
53    Kantorowicz, ed. Lorimer, *Frederick the Second*, p.615.
54    Ibid.
55    Waley, *Papal State*, pp.146–47; E. von Westenholz, *Kardinal Rainer von Viterbo* (Heidelberg, 1912).
56    Waley, *Papal State*, pp.147–48; F. Reh, *Kardinal Peter Capocci: Ein Staatsmann und Feldherr des XIII Jahrhunderts* (Berlin, 1933), pp.84–121; A. Paravicini Bagliani in *DBI*, vol.18 (Rome, 1975), p.606.
57    Salimbene, ed. G. Scalia, *Cronica* (Bari, 1966), vol.I, pp.560–63; *The Chronicle of Salimbene de Adam*, ed. J.L. Baird (Binghamton, 1986), pp.194–95, 389–91.
58    J.L.A. Huillard-Bréholles, *Historia Diplomatica Friderici Secundi*, vol. VI (Paris, 1861). pp.771–75.
59    E. Jordan, *Les Origines de la domination angevine* (Paris, 1909), pp.xii–xiv.
60    Saba Malaspina in *RIS*, vol.VIII (Milan, 1726), cols. 794–96; Jordan, *Les Origines*, pp.xiv, 176.
61    Salimbene, ed. Scalia, *Cronica*, vol.I, pp.568–72; *Chronicle of Salimbene*, pp.396–99; Housley, *Italian Crusades*, pp.167–69; O. Canz, *Philipp Fontana, Erzbischof von Ravenna: ein Staatsmann des XIII Jahrhunderts* (Leipzig, 1910); G. Zanella in *DBI*, vol.47 (Rome, 1997), pp.757–62.
62    Salimbene, ed. Scalia, *Cronica*, vol.I, pp.571–72; *Chronicle of Salimbene*, pp.397–98.
63    Gregorovius, *History of the City of Rome*, transl. Hamilton vol. V (2) (repr. New York, 2003) gives the fullest account of Charles of Anjou's campaigns in the 1260s (pp. 335–453; pp. 452–53 for his conclusion). But see also Housley, *Italian Crusades*, pp. 16–19, 152–55.
64    S. Runciman, *The Sicilian Vespers* (Cambridge, 1958), pp.65–116; Partner, *Lands of St Peter*, pp.266–68.
65    Waley, *Papal State*, pp.184–85.
66    Salimbene, ed. Scalia, *Cronica*, vol.II, p.871; *Chronicle of Salimbene*, p.604.
67    Runciman, *Sicilian Vespers*, pp.223–25.

68 Salimbene, ed. Scalia, *Cronica*, vol. 1, pp. 632, 755–56; *Chronicle of Salimbene*, pp. 443–45, 526–27.
69 C.A. Willemsen, *Kardinal Napoleon Orsini 1263–1342* (Berlin, 1927), pp. 7–8; Waley, *Papal State*, p. 245.
70 L. Mohler, *Die Kardinäle Jakob und Peter Colonna* (Paderborn, 1914); T. Boase, *Boniface VIII* (London, 1933), pp. 163–85; Partner, *Lands of St Peter*, pp. 288–89.

## CHAPTER 2

1 G. Soranzo, *La Guerra fra Venezia e la Santa Sede per il dominio di Ferrara 1308–13* (Città di Castello, 1905), esp. pp. 138–60; Housley, *Italian Crusades*, pp. 24–25.
2 W. Bowsky, 'Clement V and the Emperor-elect', *Medievalia et humanistica*, XII, 1958, pp. 52–69; *Henry VII in Italy: The Conflict of Empire and City State, 1310–1313* (Lincoln, Nebr., 1960).
3 On the *De ecclesiastica potestate* of Augustinus Triumphus (d. 1328) see M.J. Wilks, *The Problem of Sovereignty in the Middle Ages* (Cambridge, 1963); Housley, *Italian Crusades*, pp. 36–37.
4 Marsilio of Padua, *Defensor Pacis*, transl. A. Gewirth, Chapter 26, 'Roman Bishop and Roman Empire' (New York, 1956; repr. 1967), pp. 358–59.
5 Petrarch, ed. U. Dotti, *Epistolae Sine Nomine*, vol. XVII, 6 (Bari, 1974), pp. 181–84; transl. N. Zacour, *Petrarch's Book Without a Name* (Toronto, 1973), pp. 102–3.
6 H. Finke, ed., *Acta Aragonensia*, Bd. 1 (Berlin and Leipzig, 1908), no. 262 (at p. 395).
7 On du Poujet, see L. Ciccio, *Il cardinale legato Bertrando del Poggetto in Bologna* (Bologna, 1902).
8 A. Luttrell, 'The Crusade in the Fourteenth Century', in *Europe in the Late Middle Ages*, ed. J.R. Hale, J.R.L. Highfield, B. Smalley (London, 1965), pp. 122–54 (at pp. 142–44); K.M. Setton, *The Papacy and the Levant (1204–1571)*, vol. I (Philadelphia, 1976), pp. 184–87, 190–94, 216–23.
9 Setton, *Papacy and the Levant*, vol. I, pp. 266–73; J. Smet, *The Life of St Peter Thomas by Philippe de Mézières* (Rome, 1954), pp. 128–34.
10 E. Cornides, *Rose und Schwert im päpstlichem Zeremoniell* (Vienna, 1967), p. 33; C. Burns, *Golden Rose and Blessed Sword: Papal Gifts to Scottish Monarchs* (Glasgow, 1970), pp. 11–12.
11 G. Moroni, *Dizionario di Erudizione storica-ecclesiastico*, vol. XXXI (Venice, 1845), pp. 271–72; vol. LXX (Venice, 1845), pp. 22–23.
12 F. Filippini, *Il cardinale Egidio Albornoz* (Bologna, 1937), pp. 2–3.
13 A. Theiner, *Codex Diplomaticus Dominii Temporalis Sanctae Sedis*, vol. II (Rome, 1862), no. CCXLII, p. 247.
14 J. Glénisson and G. Mollat, *Gil Albornoz et Androin de la Roche, 1353–67* (Paris, 1964), pp. 36, 39.
15 Theiner, *Codex*, vol. II, no. CCCXXX, p. 351; cf. on recapturing Forlì, August 1359 (ibid., no. CCCXXXVI, p. 357).
16 J. Larner, *The Lords of Romagna: Romagnol Society and the Origins of the Signoria* (London, 1965), pp. 92–93, 96.
17 Filippini, *Albornoz*, p. 228 and passim; Partner, *Lands of St Peter*, p. 351.
18 Filippini, *Albornoz*, p. 162; Partner, *Lands of St Peter*, p. 342.
19 Giovanni da Legnano, ed. T. Erskine Holland, *Tractatus de bello, de represaliis et de duello* (Oxford, 1917).
20 *Epistolario di Santa Caterina da Siena*, ed. E. Dupré Theseider (Rome, 1940), vol. I, Ep. LXVIIII, pp. 288–89; (? April 1376); LXXXVIII, pp. 354–58 (December/January 1376/77); *The Letters of St Catherine of Siena*, transl. S. Noffke (Binghamton, 1988), vol. I, pp. 218, 266; G. Mollat, *Popes at Avignon* (London, 1963) pp. 170–71.

21    Text in G. Gori, 'L'Eccidio di Cesena dell'anno 1377', *ASI*, n.s. VIII, part IIa (1858), pp. 3–37 (esp. p. 19); see also R. Sassi, 'Il vero nome del notaio Fabrianese autore del *de casu Caesenae*': *atti e memorie della R. deputazione di Storia Patria per le province delle Marche*, 6th ser., vol. II, 1942, pp. 149–55; Partner, *Lands of St Peter*, pp. 362–65.

22    Gregorovius, *History of the City of Rome*, trans. Hamilton, vol. VI (2), (repr. New York, 2004), pp. 494–520; E.G. Léonard, *Les Angevins de Naples* (Paris, 1954), pp. 453–59; Partner, *Lands of St Peter*, pp. 368–69.

23    R. Swanson, '"The Way of Action": Pierre d'Ailly and the Military Solution to the Great Schism', in W.J. Sheils, ed., *The Church and War*, Studies in Church History, 20 (Oxford, 1983), pp. 191–200.

24    E.-R. Labande, *Rinaldo Orsini, Comte de Tagliacozzo et les premières guerres suscitées en Italie par le grand schisme* (Monaco and Paris, 1939), pp. 201–26, 259–60; Partner, *Lands of St Peter*, pp. 369–70.

25    E. Perroy, *L'Angleterre et la France pendant le grand Schisme d'Occident* (Paris, 1933), pp. 166–209.

26    A. Cutolo, *Re Ladislao d'Angio-Durazzo*, 2 vols (Milan, 1936), vol. I, pp. 94–95; on the confusing sequence of events after Urban's election, see also Léonard, *Les Angevins de Naples*, pp. 453–76.

27    P. Stácul, *Il cardinale Pileo da Prata* (Rome, 1957), pp. x, 129, 195–211.

28    Labande, *Rinaldo Orsini*, pp. 259–60; Partner, *Lands of St Peter*, pp. 373–74.

29    P. Partner, *Papal State under Martin V*, p. 16.

30    Stácul, *Pileo da Prata*, pp. 218, 363n.

31    G. Romano, 'Niccolò Spinelli da Giovinazzo, diplomatico del secolo XIV', *Archivio storico per le province napoletane*, xxiv–xxvi, 1899–1902 passim (especially at xxvi, pp. 482–97).

32    Labande, *Rinaldo Orsini*, p. 258.

33    Partner, *Lands of St Peter*, p. 376; A. Esch, *Bonifaz IX und der Kirchenstaat* (Tübingen, 1969), pp. 594–95.

34    P.J. Jones, *The Malatesta of Rimini and the Papal State* (Cambridge, 1974), p. 120.

35    Ibid., pp. 121–22.

36    Theodoricus de Niem, *Historia de vita Johannis XXIII Pontificis Romani* (Frankfurt-am-Main, 1626), pp. 1–2. Partner, *Papal State under Martin V*, pp. 20–22, 30, defends Cossa. Under 'Giovanni XXIII' see also Uginet in *DBI*, vol. 55 (Rome, 2000), pp. 621–27.

37    Partner, *Papal State under Martin V*, pp. 22–26.

38    Ibid., pp. 29–31.

39    H. Finke, *Acta Concilii Constanciensis*, vol. II (Münster, 1923), pp. 672–73; vol. IV (Münster, 1928), pp. 561, 582 (*capitula agendorum*); Partner, *Lands of St Peter*, p. 394.

40    Partner, *Lands of St Peter*, pp. 25, 29, 39.

41    See e.g. R.R. Betts, *Essays in Czech History* (London, 1969), esp. pp. 176–94.

42    Especially P. Prodi, *Il sovrano pontefice* (Bologna, 1982; repr. 1999); transl. as *The Papal Prince: One Body and Two Souls: The Papal Monarchy in Early Modern Europe* (Cambridge, 1987).

43    Prodi, *The Papal Prince*, pp. 80–85.

44    A. Black, *Monarchy and Community. Political Ideas in the later conciliar Controversy 1430–50* (Cambridge, 1970), pp. 87–8, 102–4; A. de Vincentiis, *Battaglie di Memoria: gruppi, intellectuali testi e la discontinuità del potere papale* (Rome, 2002), esp. pp. 107–19; Prodi, *The Papal Prince*, pp. 15–16.

45    Prodi, *The Papal Prince*, pp. 38–51, supporting Delumeau's argument.

46    Ibid., pp. 9–10, 65.

47    N. Housley, *The Later Crusades 1274–1580: From Lyons to Alcazar* (Oxford, 1992) pp. 405–7, 434–35.

48    Partner, *Lands of St Peter*, pp. 26, 71.

49  Partner, *Papal State under Martin V*, pp. 67, 70, 73, 78, 89.
50  Ibid. pp. 78–79.
51  D. Girgensohn in *DBI*, vol. 22 (Rome, 1979), pp. 69–74.
52  G. Holmes, 'Cardinal Beaufort and the Crusade against the Hussites', *EHR*, 88, 1973, pp. 721–50.
53  Joannis de Segovia, ed. E. Birk, *Historia Gestorum Generalis Synodi Basiliensis, in Monumenta Conciliorum Generalium*, vol. II (Vienna, 1873), pp. 27–28; A.A. Strnad and K. Walsh, in *DBI*, vol. 24 (Rome, 1980), pp. 188–95 (at p. 192).
54  R. Aubert in *DHGE*, vol. 27 (Paris, 2000), pp. 621–22. On Segovia's conciliar theories, see Black, *Monarchy and Community*, passim.
55  Theiner, *Codex Diplomaticus*, vol. III (Rome, 1862), no. CCLXIV, p. 315; a similarly worded commission of 1431 is noted by Prodi, *The Papal Prince*, p. 51, n. 58.
56  M. Miglio, 'Un problema storiografico', in G. Mencarelli, ed., *I Vitelleschi: fonti. realtà e mito* (Tarquinia, 1998), pp. 11, 14, 16.
57  A. da Mosto, 'Ordinamenti militari delle soldatesche dello stato romano dal 1430 al 1470', *QF*, vol. V, 1903, pp. 11–34 (at p. 28).
58  Miglio, as above; see also J.E. Law, 'Profile of a Renaissance Cardinal', ibid., pp. 69–83 (esp. pp. 70–74); idem, 'Giovanni Vitelleschi, "prelato guerriero"', *Renaissance Studies*, 12 (1998), pp. 40–66 (esp. pp. 64–65).
59  Miglio, 'Un problema', p. 13, citing the *Mesticanza* of Paolo di Lello Petrone.
60  A. Esch, 'Il progetto di una statua equestre per il Campidoglio del 1436: il problema della tradizione', *I Vitelleschi*, pp. 21–22.
61  Seated portrait reproduced as the cover of the collected papers (*I Vitelleschi*, ed. Mencarelli, as above) of the colloquium held in 1996; equestrian portrait in white, ibid., Pl. XV, and see G. Tiziani, 'Un ritratto di Giovanni Vitelleschi committente e guerriero ed alcune emergenze vitelleschiane', ibid., pp. 149–74 (esp. p. 149).
62  Quoted by G. Lombardi in *I Vitelleschi*, p. 31.
63  Miglio, 'Un problema', p. 12; Law, 'Profile', pp. 73–74.
64  I am grateful to John Law for this detail.
65  P. Paschini, *Lodovico Cardinal Camerlengo* (Rome, 1939), pp. 41–42; Law, 'Profile', pp. 74–76.
66  Paschini, *Lodovico Cardinal Camerlengo*, pp. 48–51.
67  G. Hill, *A Corpus of Italian Medals before Cellini* (London, 1930), no. 756, pp. 197–98.
68  See below, n. 87.
69  Paschini, *Lodovico Cardinal Camerlengo*, pp. 56–58.
70  Ibid., pp. 65–67.
71  Niccolò della Tuccia in I. Ciampi, *Cronache e statuti della città di Viterbo* (Florence, 1872), p. 207; Vespasiano de' Bisticci, ed. A. Greco, *Le Vite*, vol. I (Florence, 1970), p. 56.
72  G. Manetti, *Vita Nicholai Quinti*, in L. Muratori, *RIS*, vol. III, (2) (Milan, 1724), cols 921–22; transl. and ed. A. Modigliani, *Vita di Nicolò V* (Rome, 1999), pp. 109–12.
73  B. Platina, ed. G. Carducci and V. Fiorini, *De vita Christi ac omnium Pontificum*, in *RIS*, vol. III (1), n.s. (Città di Castello, 1914), p. 339.
74  Manetti, *Vita Nicholai Quinti*, cols 914, 916; ed. Modigliani, *Vita di Nicolò V*, pp. 95, 99–100.
75  Discussed by D.S. Chambers, 'Tommaso Parentucelli vice-camerlengo: problemi attorno la Camera Apostolica e il governatorato di Roma', *Papato, stati regionali e Lunigiana nell'età di Nicolò V* (Atti delle Giornate di Studio, maggio 2000), ed. E.M. Vecchi (La Spezia, 2004), pp. 59–71.
76  Manetti, *Vita Nicholai Quinti*, cols 929–30; ed. Modigliani, pp. 128–32.
77  Manetti, *Vita Nicholai Quinti*, col. 944; ed. Modigliani, *Vita di Nicolò V*, pp. 164–68; Pastor, ed. Antrobus, vol. II, pp. 288–99 (at p. 293).

78　A.S. Piccolomini to Filippo Maria Visconti, 13 December 1444, quoted by K.M. Setton, *The Papacy and the Levant*, vol. II (Philadelphia, 1978), p. 91.

79　Pius II, ed. A. van Heck, *Commentarii*, 2 vols (Vatican City, 1984), lib. XII, p. 744; transl. F.A. Gragg and L.G. Gabel, *The Commentaries of Pius II*, Smith College Studies in History (Northampton, Mass., 1937–57), pp. 797–98.

80　Pastor, ed. Antrobus, vol. II (London, 1899), p. 387n.

81　Pastor, ed. Antrobus, vol. II, pp. 390–98; L. Gómez-Canedo, *Un Español al Servicio de la Santa Sede: Don Juan de Carvajal, Cardinal de Sant' Angelo, legato en Alemania y Hungria (1392–1469)* (Madrid, 1947), esp. pp. 153–85.

82　Paschini, *Lodovico Camerlengo*, p. 182.

83　Ibid., pp. 184–88; Setton, *Papacy and the Levant*, vol. II, pp. 185–89.

84　R. Lightbown, *Mantegna* (Oxford, 1986), cat. no. 11, p. 410; R. Signorini, 'Alloggi di sedici cardinali presenti alla Dieta', in *Il sogno di Pio II e il viaggio da Roma a Mantova*', ed. A. Calzona et al. (Florence, 2003), pp. 315–89 (at p. 340).

85　Pastor, ed. Antrobus, vol. II, p. 258; J. Gill, *Personalities at the Council of Florence and other Essays* (Oxford, 1964), pp. 65–78; Setton, *Papacy and the Levant*, vol. II, p. 147; the basic story is in Pius II, *Commentarii*, lib. XI, p. 690; transl. Gragg and Gabel, *Commentaries*, pp. 746–47.

86　Housley, *Later Crusades*, pp. 384–85; J. Hankins, 'Renaissance Crusaders: Humanist Crusade Literature in the Age of Mehmed II', Dumbarton Oaks Papers, 29 (1995), pp. 111–201.

87　F. Flamini, 'Leonardo di Pietro Dati: poeta Latina del secolo XV', GSLI, 16, 1890, pp. 1–107 (esp. pp. 49–56, and 101–4 for extract from the unpublished text, Florence, Biblioteca Riccardiana, MS 1207).

88　Paschini, *Lodovico Cardinal Camerlengo*, p. 51.

89　*Historiarum ab inclinatione Romani imperii decades III, libri XXXI*, ed. B. Nogara, *Scritti inediti e rari di Biondo Flavio* I (Rome, 1927), pp. lv–lvii.

90　P.E. Sigmund, *Nicholas of Cusa and Medieval Political Thought* (New Haven, Conn., 1963), pp. 196–97.

91　Poggio Bracciolini, *Facetiae*, no. XIX, *Opera Omnia*, vol. I (facsimile reprint of 1538 Basel edn, Turin, 1964), p. 427.

92　Idem, *De varietate fortunae*, lib. 3, in *Opera Omnia* (as above), vol. II (Turin, 1966), pp. 110–14; G. Lombardi, 'Giovanni Vitelleschi nei giudizi di alcuni contemporanei', *I Vitelleschi*, ed. Mencarelli, pp. 23–36 (pp. 27–28), cites the critical edition by O. Merisalo (Helsinki, 1993).

93　M. Miglio, 'Valla e l'ideologia municipale romana nel de falso credita et emendita Constantini donatione', in *Italia e Germania: Liber Amicorum Arnold Esch* (Tübingen, 2001), pp. 226–33.

94　M. Mallett, *Mercenaries and their Masters: Warfare in Renaissance Italy* (London, 1974), p. 156.

95　L.B. Alberti, transl. J. Leoni, *Ten Books on Architecture* (London, 1955), lib. X (Preface), quoted by J.R. Hale, 'The Early Development of the Bastion', in *Europe in the Later Middle Ages*, ed. J.R. Hale et al., p. 472.

## CHAPTER 3

1　*Tractatus* in *Opera Inedita*, ed. G. Cugnoni (Rome, 1883), p. 581, quoted by Prodi, *The Papal Prince*, p. 1.

2　A.S. Piccolomini, ed. A. van Heck, *De viris illustribus* (Vatican City, 1991), p. 82.

3　B. Platina, ed. G.C. Zimolo, *Vita Pii II*, *RIS*, vol. III (3) (Città di Castello, 1964), p. 118.

4　Ibid., p. 159.

5　Pius II, *Commentarii*, lib. 1 p. 97; lib. V, p. 310; transl. Gragg and Gabel, *Commentaries*, pp. 92, 359.

6    Ibid, lib. V, p. 313; transl. Gragg and Gabel, *Commentaries*, p. 363.
7    Ibid., lib. IV, p. 294 ; transl. Gragg and Gabel, *Commentaries*, p. 344.
8    Giacomo d'Arezzo to Barbara of Brandenburg, Rome, 23 October 1463 (ASMn AG b. 842 c. 114r).
9    Pius II, *Commentarii*, lib. XII, p. 770; transl. Gragg and Gabel, *Commentaries*, p. 822.
10   Ibid., p. 774; transl. Gragg and Gabel, *Commentaries*, p. 826. See above p. 10.
11   Ibid., lib. XI, p. 691; transl. Gragg and Gabel, *Commentaries*, p. 748.
12   Ibid., lib. V, p. 343 ('quid pulchrius castrorum acie ordinata?'); transl. Gragg and Gabel, *Commentaries*, p. 393.
13   Carlo Franzoni to Barbara of Brandenburg, Tivoli, 17 August 1461 (ASMn AG b. 841 c. 405).
14   Pius II, *Commentarii*, lib. XIII, p. 793; transl. Gragg and Gabel, *Commentaries*, p. 845.
15   Ibid., lib. III, pp. 198–99; transl. Gragg and Gabel, *Commentaries*, p. 225.
16   Ibid., lib. IV, pp. 271–73; transl. Gragg and Gabel, *Commentaries*, pp. 322–24.
17   Ibid., lib. XII, pp. 766–69; transl. Gragg and Gabel, *Commentaries*, pp. 819–22; quoted by Housley, *Later Crusades*, p. 261.
18   P. Pagliucchi, *I Castellani di Castel Sant' Angelo* (Rome, 1906–9; repr. 1973), vol. I, pp. 126–33.
19   A. Ratti, 'Quarantatre lettere originali di Pio II relative alla guerra per la successione nel reame di Napoli 1460–63', *ASL*, ser. 3, vol. XIX, 1903, pp. 263–93 (esp. nos II–III, pp. 270–71, no. IX, pp. 274–75, no. XIII, pp. 277–78).
20   Pius II, *Commentarii*, lib. III, pp. 203–4 ('coactis subito copiis'); transl. Gragg and Gabel, *Commentaries*, pp. 231–32.
21   Theiner, *Corpus*, vol. III, no. CCCLXIII, p. 417.
22   G. Soranzo, *Pio II e la politica italiana nella lotta contro I Malatesta 1457–63* (Padua, 1911), pp. 248–49; Pius II, *Commentarii*, lib. V, pp. 354–55; transl. Gragg and Gabel, *Commentaries*, pp. 404–5. See also below.
23   Pius II, *Commentarii*, lib. IV, p. 256, lib. V, p. 315; transl. Gragg and Gabel, *Commentaries*, pp. 308, 365.
24   Cardinal F. Gonzaga to Marquis L. Gonzaga, Sant' Anna in Campareno (near Pienza), 23 September 1462 (ASMn, AG, b. 841, c. 475), quoted by Soranzo, *Pio II e la politica*, p. 318.
25   Same to Barbara of Brandenburg, Rome, 28 April 1462 (ASMn AG b. 841 c. 441r). According to Bartolomeo Marasca, the cardinal's maggiordomo, writing to Barbara on 27 April, a third effigy was burnt on the Capitol (ASMn AG, b. 841, c. 688r).
26   Same to same, Pienza, 18 August 1462, ASMn, AG, b. 861, c. 461r; Soranzo, *Pio II e la politica*, p. 303 n. 2.
27   Soranzo, *Pio II e la politica*, p. 308; G. Beani, *Niccolò Forteguerri cardinale di Teano: notizie storiche* (Pistoia, 1891), p. 25 (letter dated at Siena, 6 August 1460); also on Forteguerri's career, A. Esposito, *DBI*, vol. 49 (Rome, 1997), pp. 156–59.
28   Beani, *Forteguerri*, pp. 25–27; twenty letters from Pius to Forteguerri in October–November 1460, mostly about military operations in progress, are in the appendix (pp. 139–57), transcribed from Florence, Bib. Laurenziana Cod, 138, Plut. 90 sup.
29   Ibid., pp. 145–47, 152–57.
30   Cardinal Forteguerri to Francesco Sforza, S. Vittorino (Aquila), 3 August 1461; same to same, Avezzano, 5 August 1461 (ASMil, Sforzesco, PE (Napoli), cart. 207).
31   Same to same, 'ex castris apud oppidum Albi', 1 September 1461 (ibid.).
32   Same to same, Castellucio, 25 October, 2 November 1461 (ibid.).
33   Amy A. Bernardy, 'Il cardinale Teano e la Repubblica di San Marino', *Bulletino storico pistoiese*, IV, 1902, pp. 112–20.
34   J. Petersohn, *Ein diplomat des Quattrocento: Angelo Geraldini (1422–86)* (Tübingen, 1985), pp. 88, 92–93, 96.

35 ASMil, Sforzesco PE (Romagna), cart. 162 c. 28 (dated at Sant' Arcangelo, 22 November 1462).
36 G. Zaccagnini, 'Il cardinale di Teano nelle Marche secondo i biografi di Federico d'Urbino', *Bulletino storico pistoiese*, IV, 1902, pp. 49–60.
37 Beani, *Forteguerri*, pp. 35–37.
38 Platina, ed. Zimolo, *Vita Pii II*, p. 113.
39 'Io. Antonius Campanus. De Machina appelata Victoria' (BAV, MS Chigi I. VII. 260 fol. 155v).
40 E. Müntz, *Les arts à la cour des papes pendant le 15e et le 16e siècle* (Paris, 1878), vol. I, pp. 232, 246–47.
41 Bonatti to Marquis L. Gonzaga, Rome, 20 April 1461 (ASMn AG b. 841 c. 54r).
42 Same to same, Rome, 28 April 1461 (ASMn AG b. 841 c. 59r).
43 Same to same, Rome, 1 May 1461 (ASMn AG b. 841 c. 62r).
44 Same to Barbara of Brandenburg and L. Gonzaga, Rome, 20 May 1461 (ibid., cc. 74r, 75r).
45 Same to L. Gonzaga, Rome, 21 May 1461 (ibid., c. 76r).
46 Same to same, Rome, 24 May 1461 (ibid., c. 79r).
47 Carlo Franzoni to Barbara of Brandenburg, Rome, 27 May 1461 (ibid., c. 401).
48 B. Bonatti to Barbara of Brandenburg, Rome, 3 June 1461 (ibid., c. 96r).
49 C. Franzoni to Barbara of Brandenburg, Rome, 10 June 1461 (ibid., c. 402r).
50 Pius II, *Commentarii*, lib. V, p. 338; transl. Gragg and Gabel, *Commentaries*, pp. 388.
51 Otto of Carretto to Francesco Sforza, Rome, 11 July 1461, quoted in Beani, *Forteguerri*, pp. 28–29; Carlo Franzoni to Barbara of Brandenburg, Rome, 1 July 1461 (ASMn AG b. 841 c. 403r) .
52 C. Franzoni to same, Rome, 13 July 1461 (ASMn AG b. 841 c. 404r).
53 Ibid., lib. X, p. 609; transl. Gragg and Gabel, *Commentaries*, pp. 669–70.
54 Johannes Advocatus to Francesco Sforza, Montefiore, 7, 18 October 1462, ASMil, PE (Romagna), cart. 162, cc. 204, 231r.
55 Pius II, *Commentarii*, lib. II, p. 135; transl. Gragg and Gabel, *Commentaries*, pp. 143–44.
56 Ibid., lib. V, p. 349; transl. Gragg and Gabel, *Commentaries*, p. 398.
57 As below, n. 65.
58 Pius II, *Commentarii*, lib. V, p. 351; transl. Gragg and Gabel, *Commentaries*, p. 400.
59 ASMil. Sforzesco, PE (Romagna), cart. 162 c. 215r.; Soranzo, *Pio II e la politica*, p. 287n.
60 Pius II, *Commentarii*, lib. V, p. 355; transl. Gragg and Gabel, *Commentaries*, p. 404; Soranzo, *Pio II e la politica*, pp. 248–49.
61 Johannes Advocatus to Francesco Sforza, Mondavio, 2 October 1462 (ASMil, Sforzesco, PE (Romagna), cart. 162 c. 200r).
62 Pius II, *Commentarii*, lib. X, p. 608; transl. Gragg and Gabel, *Commentaries*, p. 668.
63 Same to same, 7 October.
64 Same to same, in camp near Verucchio, 1 November 1462, ASMil, Sforzesco, PE (Romagna), cart. 162 c. 5r; also Federico di Montefeltro to Francesco Sforza, Verucchio, 28 October 1462 (ibid. c. 248r); Soranzo, *Pio II e la politica*, pp. 336–409 passim.
65 Pius II, *Commentarii*, lib. XII, pp. 730, 767; transl. Gragg and Gabel, *Commentaries*, pp. 783, 819.
66 Ibid., lib. XII, pp. 719–29; transl. Gragg and Gabel, *Commentaries*, pp. 773–83.
67 Cardinal Forteguerri to Duke Francesco Sforza, 'ex felicibus castris apud Fanum', 16 June 1463 (ASMil, Sforzesco, PE (Marche) cart. 146).
68 Soranzo, *Pio II e la politica*, p. 424, quoting B. Pusterla to F. Sforza, 11 September 1463.
69 Pius II, *Commentarii*, Lib. XII pp. 730–31; transl. Gragg and Gabel, *Commentaries*, pp. 783–84.

70    Bartolomeo da Pusterla to F. Sforza, Pesaro, 17 September 1463, in Soranzo, *Pio II e la politica*, doc. 41, pp. 503–36.

71    Cardinal Forteguerri to Pius II, Fano, 25 September 1463, in Soranzo, *Pio II e la politica*, doc. 42, p. 580.

72    Setton, *Papacy and the Levant*, vol. II, pp. 24–25. Pius refers briefly to this in *Commentarii*, lib. IV, p. 270; transl. Gragg and Gabel, *Commentaries*, pp. 321–22.

73    Cornides, *Rose und Schwert* pp. 94–96; also Pius II, *Commentarii*, lib. XIII, pp. 795, 805–6; transl. Gragg and Gabel, *Commentaries*, pp. 847, 856.

74    Cited by G.B. Picotti, *La Dieta di Mantova e la politica de' veneziani* (Venice, 1912), p. 105; M. Pellegrini, 'Pio II, il Collegio cardinalizio e la Dieta di Mantova', in *Il sogno di Pio II e il viaggio da Roma a Mantova*, ed. A. Calzona et al. (Città di Castello, 2003), p. 65.

75    ASMn, Fondo Portioli, b. 13 'Libro giornale, 1459' cc. 61v, 66r, 83r, 88r (cf. D.S. Chambers, 'Spese del soggiorno di papa Pio II a Mantova', *Il sogno di Pio II*, pp. 391–402 (esp. 394–95)).

76    Cardinal Isidore to Marquis L. Gonzaga, Ancona, 31 May 1460 (ASMn AG b. 840 c. 410r); on 1 May 1461 Bonatto reported to the same that Isidore was gravely ill 'muto e senza intellecto' (ASMn AG b. 841 c. 62r). His death was reported by Cardinal Francesco Gonzaga on 27 April 1463 (ASMn AG b. 842 c. 3r). On his career, see Setton, *Papacy and the Levant*, vol. II, pp. 3–4, n. 5.

77    A. Esch, 'Importe in das Rom der Frührenaissance', *Studi in memoria di Federigo Melis*, vol. III (Naples, 1978), p. 413. On Prospero, see F. Petrucci in *DBI*, vol. 27 (Rome, 1982), pp. 416–18.

78    Beani, *Forteguerri*, pp. 37–39; Giacomo d'Arezzo to Ludovico Gonzaga, Rome, 4 July 1464 (ASMn AG b. 842 c. 372v).

79    Letter of G.P. Arrivabene, Nemi, 29 October 1463 (ASMn AG b. 842 c. 156r), quoted in D.S. Chambers, 'Virtù militare del cardinale Francesco Gonzaga', *Guerre, Stati e città: Mantova e l'Italia Padana*, ed. C.M. Belfanti et al. (Mantua, 1988), pp. 215–29 (at p. 216); repr. in idem, *Renaissance Cardinals and their Worldly Problems* (Aldershot, 1997).

80    Chambers, *A Renaissance Cardinal*, pp. 93–94.

81    Chambers, 'Virtù militare', p. 217.

82    L. D'Ascia, *Il Corano e la tiara: L'Epistola a Maometto II di Enea Silvio Piccolomini (papa Pio II)* (Bologna, 2001).

83    Jacobus Trottus to Borso d'Este, Rome 6 September 1469 (postscript inserted in letter of 5 September (ASMod., Estense, Ambasciatori, Roma, b. 1), quoted by Pastor, ed. Antrobus, vol. IV, p. 148).

84    I. Robertson, 'Pietro Barbo – Paul II: *Zentilhomo de Uenecia e Pontifico*', in *War, Culture and Society in Renaissance Venice: Essays in Honour of John Hale*, ed. D.S. Chambers, C.H. Clough, M.E. Mallett (London, 1993), pp. 147—72 (esp. pp. 165–71); idem, *Tyranny under the Mantle of St Peter: Pope Paul II and Bologna* (Turnhout, 2002), esp. pp. 6–9, 207–13.

85    Beani, *Forteguerri*, pp. 41–44.

86    Contemporary accounts in *Le vite di Paolo II di Gaspare da Verona e Michele Canensi*, ed. G. Zippel, *RIS*, vol. III, xvi (Città di Castello, 1904), pp. 41, 124–26.

87    De Vincentiis, *Battaglie di Memoria*, p. 92.

88    Iacopo Ammannati, ed. P. Cherubini, *Lettere (1444–79)*, vol. II (Rome, 1997), no. 161 (p. 741) to Goro Lolli, Rome, 28 July 1465; no. 169 (at p. 765) to Cardinal F. Piccolomini, Campagnano, third week in August 1465.

89    R. Bianchi, ed., *L'Eversana Deiectio di Iac. Ammannati Piccolomini* (Rome, 1984), prints the text from BAV, MS. Vat. Lat. 4063, showing differences from Ammannati's *Commentarii*, lib. 2.

90    Ammannati, ed. Cherubini, *Lettere*, vol. II, no. 363 (p. 1197); vol. III, no. 696 (pp. 1766–73).

91    Pastor, ed. Antrobus, vol. IV, p. 159.

92    I. Robertson, 'The Return of Cesena to the Direct Dominion of the Church after the Death of Malatesta Novello', *Studi Romagnoli*, 16, 1965, pp. 123–61.

93    Jones, *Malatesta*, pp. 245–48; Robertson, 'Pietro Barbo–Paul II', pp. 160–71.

94    Mallett, *Mercenaries and their Masters*, p. 157.

95    G. Zorzi, 'Un vicentino alla corte di Paolo II' (*Nuovo Archivio Veneto*, 30, 1915, pp. 369–434), which includes 'Il trattatello della milizia di Chiereghino Chiericati' (at p. 425).

96    See R. Trame, *Rodrigo Sánchez de Arévalo (1404–70): Spanish Diplomat and Champion of the Papacy* (Washington, DC, 1958).

97    W. Benziger, *Zur Theorie von Krieg und Frieden in der italiensichen Renaissance. Die 'Disputatio de pace et bello' zwischen Bartolomeo Platina und Rodrigo Sánchez de Arévalo und andere anlässlich der Pax Paolina (Rom 1468) entstandene Schriften* (Frankfurt-am-Main etc., 1996), esp. pp. 32–40 (edition of texts, in Latin and German translation at end; note pp. 41–43).

98    G. Valentini, 'La sospensione della crociata nei primi anni di Paolo II (1464–68), *AHP*, XIV, 1976, pp. 71–101.

99    Setton, *Papacy and the Levant*, vol. II, pp. 304–5.

## CHAPTER 4

1    Sigismondo de' Conti, ed. F. Racioppi, *Libri historiarum sui temporis* (Latin text with Italian transl.) (Rome, 1883), vol. I, pp. 3, 22. For Sigismondo's career, R. Ricciardi in *DBI*, vol. 28 (Rome, 1983), pp. 470–75.

2    Ibid., vol. I, pp. 5, 211.

3    Ibid., vol. II, p. 53.

4    Mantua, Biblioteca Comunale, MS 1019 fol. 30v, quoted by R. Signorini in *Il Sogno di Pio II*, ed. Calzona, pp. 334–35.

5    J.W. O'Malley, *Giles of Viterbo on Church Reform: A Study in Renaissance Thought* (Leiden, 1968), pp. 110–12.

6    S. Infessura, ed. O. Tommasini, *Diario della città di Roma* (Rome, 1890), p. 76. On Carafa, P. Petrucci, *DBI*, vol. 19 (Rome, 1976), pp. 588–96.

7    Setton, *Papacy and the Levant*, vol. II, pp. 316–18.

8    BAV, MS Ottob. Lat. 1938 cc. 1–6v (poem by the Venetian Pietro Orseolo 'Oliverii Cardinalis Neapolis Itinerarium').

9    P. Paschini, *Il carteggio fra Marco Barbo e Giovanni Lorenzi* (Vatican City, 1969), pp. 215–18'; cf. J.A.F. Thomson, *Popes and Princes 1417–1517* (London, 1980), p. 241 (n. 25).

10    Hill, *Corpus*, nos 751, 752.

11    Pastor, ed. Antrobus, vol. IV, pp. 343–47; Setton, *Papacy and the Levant*, vol. II, pp. 371–72; on Fregoso, M. Cavanna Ciappina in *DBI*, vol. 50 (Rome, 1998), pp. 427–32.

12    P. Farenga, '*Monumenta Memoriae*: Pietro Riario fra mito e storia', in *Un pontificato ed una città: Sisto IV*', ed. M. Miglio et al. (Vatican City, 1986), pp. 179–216.

13    Pastor, ed. Antrobus, vol. IV, pp. 231, 270; C. Shaw, *Julius II: The Warrior Pope* (Oxford, 1993), pp. 16–18 and passim.

14    Pastor, ed. Antrobus, vol. IV, pp. 262–69; Sigismondo de' Conti, *Libri historiarum*, vol. I, p. 9; Shaw, *Julius II*, pp. 20–24.

15    Cardinal F. Gonzaga to Marquis L. Gonzaga, 9 July 1474 (ASMn AG b. 845 c. 231r).

16    Same to same, 30 July 1474 (ibid. c. 236r).

17    Same to same, 19 August 1474 (ibid. c. 237r).

18    The confession, printed in G. Capponi, *Storia della Repubblica di Firenze* (Florence, 1930), vol. 2, Appendix III, pp. 509–23, is discussed at length in L. Martines, *April Blood: Florence and the Plot against the Medici* (London, 2003), Chapter 9.

19 V. Rees, 'Ficino's Advice to Princes', in *Marsilio Ficino: his Theology, his Philosophy, his Legacy*, ed. M.J.B. Allen, V. Rees with M. Davies (Leiden etc., 2001), pp. 339–57 (at pp. 353–54).

20 M. Simonetta, *Carteggio degli oratori mantovani alla Corte Sforzesca (1450–1500)*, vol. XI (*1478–79*) (Rome, 2001), p. 28 n. 65: this is from the *trattatello* 'Del modo de regere et regnare' by Antonio Cornazzano (New York, Pierpont Morgan Library MS 731), noted and quoted by Simonetta, pp. 22–23, nn. 46–47.

21 Cardinal F. Gonzaga to Marquis Federico Gonzaga, Bologna, 24 July, 13 August 1478 (ASMn AG b. 1141 cc. 524r, 539r).

22 Same to Zaccaria Saggi, Bologna, 3 September 1478 (ibid., c. 549r).

23 Same to Alfonso, Duke of Calabria (ASMn AG b. 2896 lib. 96 cc. 7r–7v).

24 Pastor, ed. Antrobus, IV pp. 350–52; E. Piva, *La guerra di Ferrara del 1482: Periodo Secondo* (Padua, 1894); Infessura, *Diario*, p. 89; M. Mallett, ed., *Lorenzo de' Medici: Lettere*, vol. VI (*1481–82*) (Florence, 1990), pp. 345–61: 'Excursus: le origini della guerra di Ferrara'; idem, 'Venice and the War of Ferrrara', in *War, Culture and Society in Renaissance Venice*, ed. D.S. Chambers et al. (London, 1993), pp. 57–72.

25 Infessura, *Diario*, pp. 100–1.

26 Ibid., p. 102.

27 D. Toni, ed., *Il Diario Romano di Gaspare Pontani, RIS*, vol. III (2) (Città di Castello, 1907–8), p. 21.

28 Pastor, ed. Antrobus, vol. IV, pp. 366–69.

29 F. Caglioti and T. Montanari, 'The tombs in St Peter's', in *The Basilica of St Peter in the Vatican*, ed. A. Pinelli (*Mirabilia Italiae*, vol. 10 [Modena, 2000]), pp. 359–65 (at p. 362).

30 Chambers, 'Virtù militare', p. 218.

31 Ibid., p. 219; letter to Marchesa Margarita Gonzaga, Bologna, 11 August 1479 (ASMn AG b. 1142).

32 ASMn AG b. 2900 lib. 114.

33 ASMn AG b. 1231 c. 5r.

34 Chambers, *A Renaissance Cardinal*, p. 85, fig. 5.

35 Ibid., p. 157, no. 443.

36 Cardinal F. Gonzaga to F. Maffei, Ferrara, 10 January 1483 (ASMn AG b. 2900 lib. 114 cc. 21v–3v: at c. 22r).

37 Same to G. Riario, Ferrara, 13 January, 1483 (ibid., cc. 32r–33r).

38 Same to G.G. Trivulzio and to the officer in charge of the *guastatori*, Ferrara, 13 January 1483 (ibid. cc. 35r–6r).

39 Same to F. Maffei, Ferrara, 14, 16 January 1483 and to Sixtus IV, 16 January (ibid., cc. 37r–7v, 39r–40v).

40 Same to G. Riario, Ferrara, 18 January 1483 (ibid., c. 43r).

41 Same to F. Maffei, 27 January 1483 (ibid., cc. 74r–75v).

42 Same to F. Maffei, Ferrara, 2 February 1483 (ibid., c. 86r).

43 Same to G. Riario, 4 February 1483 (ibid., cc. 92r–v).

44 Same to Sixtus IV, Ferrara, 1 January 1483 (ibid., cc. 45v–6v), and to F. Maffei, 10 February 1483 (ibid., cc. 113v–14v).

45 C. Bonatti, 'La Dieta di Cremona', *ASL*, XXXV, 1908, pp. 258–67.

46 R. Cessi, 'Il convegno di Cesena del 1484', *ASRSP*, LXVIII, 1908, pp. 75–95; D. S. Chambers, 'What made a Renaissance cardinal respectable? The case of Cardinal Costa', *Renaissance Studies*, 12, 1998, pp. 87–108 (at pp. 92–93).

47 Piva, *La guerra*, p. 44 (quoting ASV, Secr. Sen. xxxi, 10 June 1483).

48 Cardinal F. Gonzaga to Marquis F. Gonzaga, Ferrara, 18 March 1483 (ASMn AG b. 2900 lib. 114 cc. 154v–55r; original in b. 1231 c. 27r).

49 Same to same, Ferrara, 12 April, 15 May 1483 (b. 1231 cc. 32–3, 49).

50 Bartolomeo Erba to Marquis Federico Gonzaga, Mantua, 16 September 1483 (ASMn AG b. 2430 c. 535).

51    Sigismondo de' Conti, *Libri historiarum*, vol. I, p. 204; M. Mallett, ed., *Lorenzo de' Medici: Lettere*, vol. VII (*1482–84*) (Florence, 1998), pp. 505–15.
52    Infessura, *Diario*, p. 134.
53    Ibid., p. 142.
54    Ibid., p. 148.
55    Ibid., pp. 147–48.
56    Ibid. p. 165.
57    Infessura, *Diario*, pp. 107–19, 139–42; P. Cherubini, 'Tra violenza e crimine di stato: la morte di Lorenzo Colonna', in Miglio, ed., *Un pontificato ed una città*, p. 360.
58    F. Isoldi, ed., *Il 'Memoriale' di Paolo dello Mastro, RIS*, vol. XXIV (2) (Città di Castello, 1912), p. 100.
59    N. Machiavelli, ed. L.A. Burd, *Il Principe* (Oxford, 1891), Chapter XI, p. 249.
60    M. Pellegrini, *Ascanio Maria Sforza: la parabola politica di un cardinale-principe del Rinascimento*, 2 vols (Rome, 2002), vol. I, pp. 169–71.
61    J.P. Arrivabene to Marquis F. Gonzaga, Rome, 18 July 1485; cited by Pastor, ed Antrobus vol. 5, p. 252n., presumably ASM. AG b. 847 c. 318, but this letter records that Innocent ordered the rebellious barons to disarm.
62    Shaw, *Julius II*, pp. 63–64.
63    G.P. Arrivabene to Marquis F. Gonzaga, Rome, 30 August 1485 (ASMn AG b. 847 cc. 337–38).
64    Ibid., pp. 177–80.
65    G. Vespucci to the Dieci, 8 September 1485, in E. Pontieri, 'La guerra dei baroni in dispacci diplomatici fiorentini', *Archivio storico per le province napoletani*, 88 (1970), pp. 95–347 (no. 37 at p. 263).
66    G.P. Arrivabene to Marquis F. Gonzaga, Rome, 25 October 1485 (ASMn AG b. 847 c. 382).
67    Pastor, ed. Antrobus, vol. V, pp. 256–58; Pellegrini, *Ascanio Sforza*, vol. I, pp. 184–86; 198–203.
68    BMV, MS Lat. X, 175 (3622) fols. 79r–80v; cited by Petersohn, *Geraldini*, pp. 240–42.
69    Papal brief of 2 January 1486, quoted in Petersohn, *Geraldini*, p. 245 n. 65.
70    MS cited above, fol. 80v.
71    J. Burckardus, ed. E. Celani, *Liber Notarum, RIS*, vol. XXXII (1) (Città di Castello, 1907–10), vol. I, p. 155; Petersohn, *Geraldini*, p. 264 n. 62.
72    Pellegrini, *Ascanio Sforza*, vol. I, p. 202.
73    Pastor, ed. Antrobus, vol. V, pp. 264–65.
74    Letters in BMV, MS lat. Cl. X, 175 (3622); microfilm pos. 222. Some are cited by Shaw, *Julius II*, pp. 71–75.
75    MS cited, c. 30r ; Shaw, *Julius II*, p. 75; Sigismondo de' Conti, *Libri historiarum*, vol. I, p. 255; Branda Castiglione to the Duke of Milan, Rome, 16 May 1487 (ASMil., Sforzesco, PE (Roma), cart. 100).
76    M. Pellegrini, *Congiure di Romagna: Lorenzo de' Medici e il duplice tirannicidio a Forlì e a Faenza nel 1488* (Florence, 1999), pp. 33, 42–43, 47–50.
77    M. Mallett, *The Borgias* (London, 1969), p. 129.
78    Sigismondo de' Conti, *Liber historiarum*, vol. II, p. 201.
79    Mallett, *The Borgias*, pp. 129–30.
80    Shaw, *Julius II*, pp. 89–93.
81    Pellegrini, *Ascanio Sforza*, vol. II, pp. 518–25.
82    Burckardus, ed. Celani, *Liber Notarum*, vol. I, p. 531; W.H. Woodward, *Cesare Borgia* (London, 1913), p. 63.
83    Burckardus, ed. Celani, *Liber Notarum*, vol. I, pp. 564–65; Pastor, ed. Antrobus, vol. V, pp. 450–61
84    Woodward, *Cesare Borgia*, pp. 78–80.
85    Ibid., pp. 83–86;

86  Shaw, *Julius II*, p.100.
87  Pellegrini, *Ascanio Sforza*, vol.II, p.573.
88  Woodward, *Cesare Borgia*, p.101.
89  Shaw, *Julius II*, pp.101–13.
90  Sigismondo de' Conti, *Libri historiarum*, vol.II, p.166; Pellegrini, *Ascanio Sforza*, vol.II, p.611.
91  Sigismondo de' Conti, *Liber historiarum*, vol.II, pp.171–72; Woodward, *Cesare Borgia*, pp.98–100. Mallett contends that it was not wholly a defeat (*The Borgias*, pp.145–50).
92  G. Ouy, 'Le papa Alexandre VI a-t-il employé les armes chimiques?', *Recueil de travaux offerts a C. Brunel*, vol.II (Paris, 1955), pp.321–34 (at pp.327–28), cited, but without the full story, by Mallett, *The Borgias*, p.150.
93  Mallett, *The Borgias*, p.171.
94  Ibid., p.180.
95  P. Villari, ed., *Dispacci di Antonio Giustinian* (Florence, 1876), vol.I, no.53, p.69 (24 July 1502); no.56, p.72 (27 July 1502); no.57, p.76 (28 July 1502); no.58, p.76 (29 July 1502).
96  Ibid., vol.I, no.210, pp.283–84 (23 December 1502).
97  Ibid., vol.I, no.219, pp.296–97 (31 December 1502).
98  A. Gottlob, *Aus der Camera Apostolica* (Innsbruck, 1889), pp.228–29.
99  Mallett, *The Borgias*, p.192.
100  Idem, pp.180, 236–37.
101  Giustinian, *Dispacci*, vol.I, no.146, p.170 (24 October 1502).
102  Mallett, *The Borgias*, pp.207–8 (the source for this is uncertain).
103  Setton, *Papacy and the Levant*, vol.II, pp.520–34.
104  Exhibition catalogue entry with bibliography by 'C.C.' in *Titian* (National Gallery, London, 2003), pp.78–79.
105  Mallett, *Mercenaries and their Masters*, p.141; but cf. below Chapter 7 n.30.
106  G. Barbieri, *Industria e Politica Mineraria nello Stato Pontificio dal '400 al '600* (Rome, 1940), esp. pp.35–41.
107  Hale, 'The Early Development of the Bastion', pp.481–82.
108  Gianlucido Cataneo to Marquis Francesco Gonzaga, Rome, 17 November 1489 (ASMn AG b.848 c.93); quoted by Shaw, *Julius II*, p.79.
109  Chambers, 'What made a Renaissance Cardinal respectable?', pp.96 n.70, 98.
110  Hale, 'Early Development of the Bastion', pp.480–83 and passim.
111  G. Satzinger, *Antonio da Sangallo die Ältere* (Tübingen, 1999), pp.125–29.
112  M. Tosi, *Il Torneo di Belvedere in Vaticano e i Tornei in Italia nel Cinquecento* (Rome, 1946), pp.46–48.
113  Burckardus, ed. Celani, *Liber Notarum*, vol.I, pp.401–2, n.3 for Valori's text; Pellegrini, *Ascanio Sforza*, vol.I, p.419.
114  Discussed by D.S. Chambers, 'Postscript on the worldly affairs of Cardinal Francesco Gonzaga and other worldly cardinals', in idem, *Renaissance Cardinals*, esp. pp.11–18; Pellegrini, *Ascanio Sforza*, p.47 and passim.
115  Pellegrini, *Ascanio Sforza*, vol.I, pp.98–99.
116  Ibid., vol.I, p.284.
117  Ibid., vol.II, pp.520–24.
118  Ibid., vol.II, p.560, quoting letter of Benedetto Capilupi, 12 February 1495 (ASMn AG b.1630 c.464).
119  Ibid., vol.II, pp.609, 611.
120  Ibid., vol.II, pp.757–63, 768–71.
121  Letter of August 1499 quoted by C.M. Ady, *Milan under the Sforza* (London, 1907), p.172, from L.G. Pélissier, *Louis XII et Lodovic Sforza 1498–1500* (Paris, 1896), vol.I, p.196.
122  G. Bologna, 'Un fratello del Moro letterato e bibliofilo: Ascanio Maria Sforza', in various authors, *Milano nell'età di Ludovico il Moro* (Milan, 1983), pp.293–332

(at p.297); illustrated in *Enciclopedia Italiana*, vol. IV (Milan, 1929), p.489, under the heading 'Armi'. Enquiries addressed to the Armeria Reale in Turin received no reply.

123 G.B. Picotti, *La giovinezza di Leone X* (Milan, 1928; repr. Rome, 1981), pp.200–4 and passim.

124 Pellegrini, *Ascanio Sforza*, vol.I, p.356.

125 Ibid., vol.I, pp.320–64.

126 Picotti, *La giovinezza*, p.298 n.11 (p.342) refers to this passage from Alamani's letter (now ASF MAP filza LII c.145bis), more fully summarised (but also without the precise wording) by M. Pellegrini, 'Il profilo politico-istituzionale del cardinalato', in *Roma di fronte ad Europa al tempo di Alessandro VI*, ed. M. Chiabo (Rome, 2001), vol.I, p.179 n.7.

127 BL, MS Add. 8443 fol. 190v.

128 Pellegrini, *Ascanio Sforza*, vol.I, p.379.

129 P. Partner, *The Pope's Men* (Oxford, 1990), p.205.

130 M. Pellegrini, 'Da Iacopo Ammannati Piccolomini a Paolo Cortesi: lineamenti dell'Ethos cardinalizio in Età rinascimentale', *Roma nel Rinascimento*, 1998, pp.23–44. The 1468 letter is in P. Cherubini, ed., Iacopo Ammannati Piccolomini, *Lettere*, 3 vols (Rome, 1997), vol.II, p.1195, vol.III, pp.1874–75.

131 Ammannati, ed. Cherubini, *Lettere*, vol.III, no.755, pp.1874–75.

132 Pellegrini, 'Da Iacopo Ammannati', pp.34–35 (Ammannati, ed. Cherubini, *Lettere*, vol.III), no.696, pp.1767–73.

133 P. Cortesi, *De Cardinalatu* (Castro Cortesio, i.e. San Gimignano, 1510), passim. On the book's purpose, see also M. Ferraù, 'Politica e cardinalato in un età di transizione: il De Cardinalatu di Paolo Cortesi', in *Roma Capitale (1447–1527)*, ed. S. Gensini (Rome, 1994), pp.519–40.

134 Cortesi, *De Cardinalatu*, lib.II (Oeconomicus), cap. 2 (De Domo), transl. K. Weill-Garris and J. D'Amico, *The Renaissance Cardinal's Ideal Palace: A Chapter from Paolo Cortesi's De Cardinalatu* (Rome, 1989), pp.45–123.

135 Aldobrandino Guidoni to Ercole d'Este, Florence, 25 April 1488, AS Modena, Estense, Cancelleria, Ambasciatori, Firenze, b.5; cited in Pastor, ed. Antrobus, vol.V p.273; Pellegrini, *Congiure di Romagna*, pp.48–49 n.74, gives part of the text of this important letter.

136 Machiavelli, ed. Burd, *Il Principe*, Chapter XI, pp.248–50.

137 F. Guicciardini, ed. R. Palmarocchi, *Storie Fiorentine* (Bari, 1931), Chapter XXIV, p.265, quoted by Prodi, *Il sovrano pontefice*, p.105; cf. Prodi, *The Papal Prince*, p.203, n.45, where the translation differs slightly.

## CHAPTER 5

1 Machiavelli, ed. Burd, *Il Principe*, XI, pp.251–52.

2 F. Guicciardini, ed. S. Menchi, *Storia d'Italia*, Lib. XI, (Turin, 1971), p.1115.

3 *DMS*, vol.IX, cols 567–70 (568).

4 P. Villari, ed., *Dispacci di Antonio Giustinian*, vol.II, nos 614, 630, pp.279, 292–93 (1, 13 November 1503; 31 January 1504).

5 Shaw, *Julius II*, p.149.

6 Antonio Magistrellus to Marquis Francesco Gonzaga, Rome, 1 August 1506 and Federico Cribello to the same, Rome, 14 September 1506 (ASMn AG b.857 cc.131v, 196r); Shaw, *Julius II*, p.151.

7 N. Machiavelli, ed. S. Bertelli, *Legazioni e Commissarie*, vol.II (Milan, 1968), pp.955–92 passim.

8 Paris de Grassis (papal master of ceremonies), ed. L. Frati, *Le Due Spedizioni militari di Giulio II tratte dal Diario di Paride de' Grassi Bolognese* (Bologna, 1886), pp.40–48 (entry into Perugia), 63 (Forlì).

9    Pastor, ed. Antrobus, vol. VI (London, 1923), pp. 279–80; Frati, *Spedizioni militari*, pp. 79–80.
10   Erasmus to Servatius Rogerus, Florence, 4 November; Bologna, 16 November 1506, in *Opus Epistolarum Des Erasmi*, vol. I, ed. P.S. Allen (Oxford, 1906), nos 200, p. 431; 203, p. 433; *Collected Works of Erasmus*, vol. I, transl. R. A. R. Mynors and D.F.S. Thomson (Toronto and Buffalo, 1974), pp. 123, 125; Erasmus to Nicholas Varius, Basel, 20 September 1526, in *Opus Epistolarum*, ed. Allen, vol. VI (Oxford, 1926), no. 1756, p. 418; *Collected Works*, vol. 12, transl. A. Dalzell (Toronto and Buffalo, 2003), pp. 369–70.
11   A. Condivi, *Vita di Michelangelo Buonarroti*, ed. G. Nencioni (Florence, 1998), p. 29; G. Vasari, ed. G. Milanesi, *Opere*, vol. VII (Florence, 1876), pp. 170–72 (see footnotes); documentation in B. Podesta, 'Intorno alle due statue erettte in Bologna a Giulio II distrutte nei tumulti del 1511', *Atti e Memorie della R. deputazione di storia patria per le province di Romagna*, vol. VII (1868), pp. 107–30.
12   S.A. Setchfield, *Civitavecchia and its fortifications 1431–1549: a study of the political and economic role of a papal port*, M.Phil. thesis, University of London, 1989, esp. pp. 146–75.
13   On his career see C.H. Clough, 'Clement VII and Francesco Maria della Rovere, Duke of Urbino', in *The Pontificate of Clement VII: History, Politics, Culture*, ed. K. Gouwens and S.E. Reiss (Aldershot and Burlington, Vt, 2005), pp. 75–108.
14   G. Gozzadini, 'Di alcuni avvenimenti in Bologna e nell' Emilia dal 1506 al 1511 e dei Cardinali Legati A. Ferrerio e F. Alidosi', vol. I, *Atti e Memorie della R. deputazione di storia patria per le province di Romagna*, 3rd ser., vol. IV (1886), pp. 67–176 (esp. pp. 106–38); G. de Caro in *DBI*, vol. 2 (Rome, 1960), pp. 373–76.
15   Gozzadini, 'Alcuni avvenimenti' (1), p. 128; Sigismondo de' Conti, *Liber historiarum*, II, p. 392.
16   Gozzadini, 'Alcuni avvenimenti' (1), pp. 128–31; C. Ghirardacci, *Historia di Bologna, RIS*, vol. XXXIII (1) (Città di Castello, 1915–29), pp. 394– 96.
17   Gozzadini, 'Alcuni avvenimenti', doc. XXX, p. 170.
18   Ibid. p. 131; doc. XXXII, p. 170.
19   Ibid., pp. 136–37; Hill, *Corpus*, no. 610, p. 156.
20   Sigismondo de' Conti, *Liber historiarum*, vol. II, p. 392.
21   Alessandro Cardinalis to Isabella d'Este, Urbino, 29 March 1509 (ASMn AG b. 1077 c. 245r, quoted in D.S. Chambers, 'The Enigmatic Eminence of Cardinal Sigismondo Gonzaga', *Renaissance Studies*, 16, 2002, pp. 330–54 (at p. 340 n. 70).
22   Papal brief of 5 May 1509 to Cardinal S. Gonzaga (ASDMn, AMV, Pergamene no. 71); Cardinal S. Gonzaga to Marquis F. Gonzaga, Ancona, 18, 25 May 1509 (ASMn AG b. 858 cc. 265r, 271r).
23   Cardinal S. Gonzaga to Isabella d'Este, 25 May; same to Marquis F. Gonzaga, Ancona, 31 May 1509 (ASMn AG b. 858 cc. 269–70, 273–75; Chambers, 'Enigmatic Eminence', p. 341).
24   L. Byatt in *DBI*, vol. 43 (Rome, 1993), pp. 361–67.
25   R. Finlay, 'Venice, the Po Expedition and the End of the League of Cambrai', *Studies in Modern European History and Culture* (2), 1976, pp. 37–72.
26   Duke A. d'Este to Isabella d'Este, 'ex castris', 22 December 1509 (ASMn AG b. 1892, unnumbered).
27   Cardinal I. d'Este to Isabella d'Este, 'ex castris', 22 December 1509 (ASMn AG b. 1892,); quoted by A. Luzio, 'La Reggenza d'Isabella d'Este durante la prigionia del marito (1509–10)', *ASL*, ser. 4, XIV, 1910, pp. 5–104 (at p. 35).
28   G. F. Di Bagno to Isabella d'Este, 'ex castris', 22 December 1509 (ASMn AG b. 1892, cf. Luzio, 'La Reggenza', p. 35).
29   Same to same, 'ex castris', 23 December 1509 (ASMn AG b. 1892, cf. Luzio, 'La Reggenza', pp. 35–36).
30   L. Ariosto, ed. C. Segré, *Tutte le Opere*, vol. III (Milan, 1984), p. 138.

31   L. Ariosto, *Orlando Furioso*, vol. XV, p. 2.
32   Luzio, 'La Reggenza', p. 36; Finlay, 'Venice, the Po Expedition', p. 55.
33   Tommaso da Gallarate to Cardinal I. d'Este, Milan, 2 November 1510 (ASMod, Estense, Cancelleria ducale, Ambasciatori, b. 19).
34   Frati, *Spedizioni militari*, p. 230.
35   Gozzadini, 'Alcuni avvenimenti' (2), p. 166.
36   Cardinal F. Alidosi to Marquis Francesco Gonzaga, Cento, 27, 31 August 1510 (ASMn AG b. 1242 cc. 866–68).
37   Frati, *Spedizioni militari*, pp. 193–95, 199–201.
38   L.A. Rebello da Silva, ed., *Corpo Diplomatico Portuguez*, vol. I (Lisbon, 1862), p. 133.
39   *DMS*, vol. XI, col. 367.
40   Frati, *Spedizioni militari*, pp. 202–3; *DMS*, vol. XI, col. 552; Gozzadini, 'Alcuni avvenimenti' (2), p. 175.
41   *DMS*, XI, cols 596, 600–2, 626, 644. On Corner, see G. Gullino in *DBI*, vol. 29 (Rome, 1983), pp. 255–57.
42   Ibid., col. 670.
43   Frati, *Spedizioni militari*, p. 211; Gozzadini, 'Alcuni avvenimenti' (2), p. 183.
44   Marco Vigerio to Marquis F. Gonzaga, Rome, 3 March 1505 (ASMn AG b. 856 c. 580).
45   Frati, *Spedizioni militari*, p. 184.
46   Stazio Gadio to Marquis F. Gonzaga, Bologna, 29 December 1510 (ASMn AG b. 859 c. 163r).
47   Frati, *Spedizioni militari*, p. 226.
48   ASMn AG b. 3351 c. 167r.
49   Chambers, 'Enigmatic Eminence', pp. 343–44.
50   Stazio Gadio to Isabella d'Este, Bologna, 31 December 1510 (ASMn AG b. 859 c. 165v; Chambers, 'Enigmatic Eminence', p. 353).
51   Floriano degli Uberti, Cronaca, BUB, MS 430 fol. 871v.
52   *DMS*, XI, col. 721; Frati, *Spedizioni militari*, pp. 225–26; N. Perotus (papal commissary) to Marquis F. Gonzaga, Venetian camp at Concordia, 2 January 1511 (ASMn AG b. 1340 c. 228r).
53   Antonio da Gatego to Marquis F. Gonzaga, Dosso, 5 January 1511 (ASMn AG b. 1340 c. 189; cited by A. Luzio, 'Federico Gonzaga ostaggio alla corte di Giulio II', *ASRSP*, 9, 1886, pp. 509–82 [at p. 569]).
54   *DMS*, XI, col. 721.
55   Ibid., cols 722–23.
56   Augustus Hare, ed. M. Barnes, *The Years with Mother: Being an Abridgement of the first three volumes of the Story of My Life* (2nd edn, London, 1984), p. 238.
57   Pastor, ed. Antrobus, vol. VI, p. 340n; cf. Pastor, ed. Mercati, vol. III (Rome, 1959), p. 768 n. 1.
58   Carlo De Vita, 'Il Museo Storico Vaticano', in C. Pietrangeli, ed., *Il Palazzo Apostolico Lateranense* (Rome, 1991), pp. 305–14 (at p. 306).
59   Stazio Gadio, to Marquis F. Gonzaga, Bologna, 1 January 1511 (ASMn AG b. 1147; quoted by A. Luzio, 'Isabella d'Este di fronte a Giulio II negli ultimi tre anni del suo pontificato' (1), *ASL*, ser. 4, XVII, 1912, pp. 245–334 (at p. 281 n. 1).
60   Joannes Gazius to Marquis Francesco Gonzaga, Venetian camp at Concordia, 13 January 1511 (ASMn AG b. 1340 c. 253, cited by Luzio, as above, p. 285 n. 3).
61   Ibid.; *DMS*, XI, cols 738, 747.
62   *DMS*, XI, col. 195.
63   Ibid., cols 755, 766.
64   Ibid., col. 755.
65   Ibid., col. 766; BUB Ms 430 fol. 871v.
66   *DMS*, XI, col. 745.

67  Marquis Francesco Gonzaga to A. Gabbioneta and L. Brognolo, Mantua, 21 January 1511 (ASMn AG b.2918 lib.215 fol. 6v).

68  J.F. Pico to Marquis F. Gonzaga, Mirandola, 21 January 1511 (ASMn AG b. 1332, c.253).

69  Antonio da Gatego to Marquis F. Gonzaga, Dosso, 26 January 1511 (ASMn AG b.1340 c.218; noted in Luzio, 'Isabella d'Este di fronte a Giulio II', I, p.286 n.1.

70  Chambers, 'Enigmatic Eminence', pp.343–44.

71  *DMS*, XI, col. 800; letters from Ludovico da Camposampiero to Isabella d'Este, Bologna, 4, 11 February 1511 (ASMn AG b.1147), noted in Luzio, 'Isabella d'Este di fronte a Giulio II', I, p.287, but not at present traceable.

72  *DMS*, XI, col. 776.

73  Frati, *Spedizioni militari*, p.232; *DMS*, XI, col. 800; G. Gullario in *DBI*, vol.29 (Rome, 1983), pp.255–57.

74  *DMS*, XII, cols 11–14.

75  *DMS*, XI, cols 837–38; 843; Frati, *Spedizioni militari*, pp.234–35; Gozzadini, 'Alcuni avvenimenti' (2), *Atti e Memorie…per le province de Romagna*, vol. VII (1889), pp.204–5.

76  Frati, *Spedizioni militari*, p.240; *DMS*, XII, cols 12–13, 24.

77  D.S. Chambers, *Cardinal Bainbridge in the Court of Rome* (Oxford, 1965), pp.82–86.

78  Chambers, *Cardinal Bainbridge*, p.86.

79  Ludovico da Camposampiero to Marquis F. Gonzaga, Bologna, 4 May 1511 (ASMn AG b.1147 c.463r); Americhus to the same, Bologna, 5 May 1511 (ibid., c.393r); Chambers, *Cardinal Bainbridge*, p.87.

80  Chambers, *Cardinal Bainbridge*, pp.87–92.

81  Ercole Sabbadini to Isabella d'Este, Bologna, 8 April 1511 (ASMn AG b.1147 c. 428); Frati, *Spedizioni militari*, pp.261–62.

82  Sabbadino degli Arienti to Isabella d'Este, Bologna, 23 May 1511 (ASMn AG b.1147 c.435).

83  G. Vasari, ed. G. Milanesi, *Opere*, vol.VII (Florence, 1906; repr. 1998), p.172n; Floriano degli Ubaldi, *Cronaca*, BUB, MS. 430 fols. 907v–8r, quoted in Podesta, 'Intorno alle due statue', p.123. The dubious source is A. Frizzi, *Memorie per servire alla storia di Ferrara*, vol.IV (Ferrara, 1791), pp.240–41.

84  Podesta, 'Intorno alle due statue', pp.114–17.

85  E.g. Machiavelli, *Discorsi*, lib.III, cap. ix.

86  *DMS*, XII, cols 197–200; Frati, *Spedizioni militari*, pp.275–80; Gozzadini, 'Alcuni avvenimenti' (2), pp.214–25; Pastor, ed. Antrobus, vol.VI, pp.348–51.

87  Frati, *Spedizioni militari*, pp.310–12.

88  Ibid., p.311.

89  Ibid., pp.310–12.

90  A. Büchi, *Korrespondenzen und Akten zur Geschichte des Kardinals Matthäeus Schiner*, vol.I (Basel, 1920), no.160, pp.126–27; idem, *Kardinal Matthäeus Schiner als Staatsmann und Kirchenfürst* (Zurich, 1923), p.279; Frati, *Spedizioni militari*, pp.312–13.

91  *DMS*, XIV, cols 230–31, 279–80; Büchi, *Matthäeus Schiner*, pp.280–81.

92  Julius II to Cardinal Schiner, 18 April 1512 (Büchi, *Korrespondenzen und Akten*, vol.I, no.173, pp.138–39); *DMS*, XIV, cols 260–64, 295, 297.

93  Büchi, *Korrespondenzen und Akten*, vol.I, no.352, p.287.

94  Frati, *Spedizioni militari*, p.321; Büchi, *Matthäeus Schiner*, pp.290–98.

95  Papal brief to Cardinal Sigismondo Gonzaga, 29 April 1512 (quoted in A. Luzio, 'Isabella d'Este di fronte a Giulio II negli ultimi tre anni del suo pontificato' (2), *ASL*, ser. 4, XVIII, 1912, pp.55–144, 393–456 [at p.82]).

96  Paris de Grassis, *Diarium*, BL MS Add. 8443 fol. 190v.; P. Giovio, transl. L. Domenichi, *Le Vite di Leon Decimo etc.* (Venice, 1549), pp.163–74.

97  J. D'Atri to Marquis F. Gonzaga, Bles (=Blois?), 19 April 1512 (ASMn AG b.633, quoted without provenance in Luzio, 'Isabella d'Este di fronte a Giulio II' (2), at pp.80–81).

98  Frati, *Spedizioni militari*, pp.314–16; Chambers, 'Enigmatic Eminence', p.349.

99  Frati, *Spedizioni militari*, pp.327–30.

100  Pastor, ed. Antrobus, vol.VI, pp.420–22; on the Matildine legacy claim Shaw, *Julius II*, p.306 cites C. Santoro, *Gli Sforza* (Milan, 1968), p.350, but Santoro gives no reference. The quotation about the legal claims of the Church being beyond dispute is from Folenghino's letter of 15 August 1512 noted below.

101  Folenghino to Marquis F. Gonzaga, Rome, 15, 19, 28 August 1512 (ASMn AG b.860 cc.281v, 283r, 291r). See also Luzio, 'Isabella d'Este di fronte a Giulio II' (2), pp.135–37; *DMS* XIV, col. 454.

102  Condivi, ed. Nencioni, *Vita di Michelagnolo*, pp.22–25, 47; cf. Vasari, ed. Milanesi, *Opere*, vol.VII, pp.164–65.

103  R. Jones and N. Penny, *Raphael* (New Haven, Conn. and London, 1980), pp.113–17, pl.131–33, 137; J. Shearman, 'The Expulsion of Heliodorus', *Rafaello a Roma* (Rome, 1986), pp.75–88. But see discussion, rejecting allusions to specific events, in C. Hope, 'Aspects of criticism in art and literature in sixteenth-century Italy', *Word and Image Conference Proceedings*, IV (1), 1988, pp.1–9 (esp. pp.6–7).

104  J. Shearman, *Raphael in Early Modern Sources, 1483–1692* (New Haven, Conn. and London, 2003), pp.159–60.

105  Stazio Gadio to Isabella d'Este, 15 August 1512 (ASMn AG b.860 cc.116r–116v; extract in Luzio, 'Isabella d'Este di fronte a Giulio II' (2), p.123).

106  Il Grossino to Isabella d'Este, 26 September 1512 (ASMn AG b.860 c.222r; extract in Luzio, 'Isabella d'Este di fronte a Giulio II' (2), p.123n) .

107  Stazio Gadio to Isabella d'Este, 4 February 1513 (ASMn AG b. 861 cc. 39v–40v).

108  Pandolfo Pico to Marquis F. Gonzaga, Ancona, 16 June 1509 (ASMn AG b.858 c.298r).

109  Cardinal S. Gonzaga to Marquis F. Gonzaga and Isabella d'Este, Ancona, 10 June 1509 (ASMn AG b.858, cc.278v, 280r; cited in Luzio, 'La Reggenza d'Isabella d'Este', p.41).

110  Luzio, 'Isabella d'Este di fronte a Giulio II', I, p.291.

111  Gomez, *De rebus gestis*, quoted by W.H. Prescott, *History of the Reign of Ferdinand and Isabella* (London, 1886), p.709, and by H. Kamen, 'Clerical violence in a Catholic Society: the Hispanic World 1450–1720', in Sheils, ed., *The Church and War*, pp.201–16 (at p.203).

112  Cortesi, *De Cardinalatu*, lib.I, cap. 1 ('de vario bellorum genere suscipiendo'), pp.VIr–VIIv .

113  Catherine Mary Curtis, *Richard Pace on pedagogy, counsel and satire* (PhD thesis, University of Cambridge, 1997).

114  Ibid., p.193 and passim.

115  Chambers, *Cardinal Bainbridge*, p.119; e.g. Appendix II, nos 4, 7, 8.

116  Ibid., p.119.

117  Setton, *Papacy and the Levant*, vol.III, p.1367.

118  M.A. Di Cesare, *Vida's Christiad and Vergilian Epic* (New York, 1964), p.3.

119  R. Bellarmine, *Tractatus de potestatate S. Pontificis in rebus temporalibus*, lib. V, cap. xi, quoted by Prodi, *The Papal Prince*, p.28.


## CHAPTER 6

1  *DMS*, XVI, cols 163, 684–85; Pastor, ed. R.F. Kerr (London, 1923), vol.VII, pp.35–43.

2     *Carmina apposita ad Pasquillum* (BL pressmark 11426 c. 104; Italian verses, ibid. c. 71); J. Shearman, *Raphael's Cartoons in the Collection of HM the Queen and the Tapestries for the Sistine Chapel* (London, 1972), pp. 18–19, 77–78 discusses the theme of 'Christus Medicus' and the name Leo.

3     E.g. Guicciardini, ed. Palmarocchi, *Storie Fiorentine*, Chapter IX.

4     Erasmus to Cardinal Rafaelle Riario, May 1515; *Opus Epistolarum*, ed. P.S. Allen, vol. II (Oxford, 1910), ep. 335, p. 69; *Collected Works*, vol. III, p. 86; M. Reeves, *The Influence of Prophecy in the Later Middle Ages* (Oxford, 1969), pp. 268–70.

5     Antonio De Beatis to Isabella d'Este, Rome, 11 May 1518 (ASMn AG b. 863, cc. 629r–v); Pastor, ed. Mercati, vol. IV (2) (Rome, 1956), p. 680.

6     Ludovico Guerrieri to Marquis F. Gonzaga, Rome, 13 March 1513 (ASMn AG b. 861 c. 384r).

7     Cardinal S. Gonzaga to Isabella d'Este, Rome, 11 April 1513 (ibid., c. 236r).

8     Gabbioneta to Marquis F. Gonzaga, Rome, 10 June 1513 (ASMn AG b. 861, c. 156); Bainbridge to Henry VIII, 6 June 1513, quoted in Chambers, *Cardinal Bainbridge*, p. 45; Pastor, ed. Kerr, vol. VII, pp. 49–53.

9     Chambers, *Cardinal Bainbridge*, pp. 46–47.

10    F. Vettori to N. Machiavelli, Rome, 12 July 1513 (N. Machiavelli, ed. F. Gaeta, *Lettere* [Milan, 1961], no. 132, pp. 267–68).

11    Machiavelli to Vettori, 20 December 1514, 31 January 1515 (Machiavelli, *Lettere*, nos 159, 162; pp. 364–65, 374–75).

12    Jones and Penny, *Raphael*, pp. 117, 121, 133 152; pls 131–33, 157, 159; Hope, 'Aspects of Criticism', pp. 6–7.

13    Cardinal Giulio to Lorenzo de' Medici, Bologna, 27, 29 August 1515, in G. Canestrini and A. Desjardins, *Négotiations diplomatiques de la France avec la Toscane*, vol. II (Paris, 1861), nos xii, xxiii, pp. 725, 728.

14    Paris de Grassis, *Diarium* (BL, MS Add. 8443 fols. 166r–v).

15    Pastor, ed. Kerr, vol. VII, p. 126.

16    *DMS*, XXIV, col. 94.

17    Cardinal I. d'Este to Marquis F. Gonzaga, Eger, 21 February, 4 March 1518; 20 December 1519 (ASMn AG b. 533).

18    P. Giovio, transl. L. Domenichi, *Le vite di Leone Decimo e d'Adriano Sesto Sommi Pontifici e del Cardinale Pompeo Colonna* (Florence, 1549); F. Petrucci in *DBI*, vol. 27 (Rome, 1987), pp. 407–12

19    On these events see Clough, 'Clement VII and Francesco Maria della Rovere', pp. 85–92.

20    A. Da Mosto, 'Ordinamenti militari delle soldatesche dello stato romano nel secolo XVI', *QF*, vol. VI, 1904, pp. 72–133 (at pp. 98–100).

21    P. Balan, *Roberto Boschetti e li avvenimenti italiani dei suoi tempi (1494–1529)* (Modena, 1877), pp. 111–17. Clough, as above, pp. 85–92.

22    F. Vettori, ed. E. Niccolini, *Sommario della Storia d'Italia* (Bari, 1972), p. 181.

23    *DMS*, XXIV, cols 149–247.

24    G.L. Moncallero, *Il Cardinale Bernardo Dovizi da Bibbiena* (Florence, 1953), pp. 441–59 (at p. 446); idem, *Epistolario di Bernardo Dovizi da Bibbiena* (Florence, 1955), vol. II, pp. 101–3 (letter of 18 April 1517).

25    G. Gheri to Francesco Guicciardini, Reggio, 27 and 29 July 1517 (R. Palmarocchi, ed., *Carteggi di Francesco Guicciardini*, vol. II (Bologna, 1939), no. 192, pp. 163–64).

26    J. Dennistoun, *Memoirs of the Dukes of Urbino* (London, 1851), vol. II, p. 382; Moncallero, *Il Cardinale B. Dovizi*, p. 458.

27    R. Devonshire-Jones, 'Lorenzo de' Medici, Duca d'Urbino', in *Studies on Machiavelli*, ed. M.P. Gilmore (Florence, 1972), pp. 299–315.

28    Pastor, ed. Kerr, vol. VII p. 215

29    Ardinghelli on behalf of Cardinal Giulio de' Medici to Antonio Pucci, 17 November 1517 (Setton, *Papacy and the Levant*, vol. III, p. 174, from E. Guasti,

ed., 'I Manoscritti Torrigiani donati allo R. Archivio Centrale di Stato di Firenze', *ASI*, 3rd ser., XXI, 1875, p. 194).

30    F. Guicciardini to G. Gheri, Reggio, 18 November 1517 (Palmarocchi, ed., *Carteggi*, vol. II, no. 260, p. 217).

31    Pastor, ed. Kerr, vol. VII, pp. 230–35; Setton, *Papacy and the Levant*, vol. III, pp. 172–80.

32    Guicciardini, *Storia d'Italia*, lib. 16, Chapter III.

33    Ibid., quoted by R. Ridolfi, transl. C. Grayson, *The Life of Francesco Guicciardini* (London, 1967), pp. 86, 90.

34    R. Zapperi in *DBI*, vol. XI (Rome, 1965), pp. 492–95.

35    Pastor, ed. Kerr, vol. VIII, pp. 5–8; Angelo Germanello to Marquis F. Gonzaga, Rome, 17, 24 March 1520 (ASMn AG b. 864 c. 610v, c. 616r).

36    B. Castiglione to Marquis Federico Gonzaga, Rome, 10 July, 12 August 1521 (ASMn AG b. 865 cc. 206v, 245r).

37    Same to same, Rome, 19 August 1521 (ibid., c. 250r).

38    Same to same, Rome, 23 August 1521 (ibid., c. 256r).

39    Same to same, Rome, 24 August 1521 (ibid., c. 259r).

40    Same to same, 28 August, 14 September, 19 September 1521 (ibid., cc. 261r, 273v, 278r).

41    Same to same, Rome, 2 October 1521 (ibid. c. 290).

42    Same to same, Rome, 7 October 1521 (ibid., c. 297r).

43    Same to same, 30 October 1521 (ibid., c. 324r).

44    *DMS*, XXXII, col. 162.

45    Pastor, ed. Kerr, vol. VIII, p. 55n.

46    Guicciardini, *Storia d'Italia*, vol. XI, p. 8.

47    B. Castiglione to Marquis Federico Gonzaga, Rome, 27 November 1521 (ASMn AG b. 865 c. 355r).

48    Pastor, ed. Kerr, vol. IX, p. 63.

49    Ibid., p. 57.

50    Ibid., pp. 160–61; Jones, *Malatesta*, p. 337.

51    Ibid., pp. 206–8; Setton, *Papacy and the Levant*, vol. III, pp. 206–14.

52    Ibid., pp. 211–14.

53    Guicciardini, *Storia d'Italia*, lib. II, Chapter XI.

54    *State Papers*, vol. VI (Royal Commission, London, 1844), p. 89.

55    N. Machiavelli, ed. F. Gaeta, *Lettere* (Milan, 1961), pp. 413–14. On Cardinal Salviati see P. Hurtubise, *Une famille témoin: les Salviati* (Vatican City, 1985), esp. pp. 152–60, 240–48.

56    Pastor, ed. Kerr, vol. IX, pp. 265–68.

57    Gianmatteo Giberti to Cardinal Giovanni Salviati, legate to the camp, Rome, 26 February 1526 (Canestrini and Desjardins, *Négotiations*, vol. II, pp. 832–33). On Giberti, see A. Turchini in *DBI*, vol. 54 (Rome, 2000), pp. 623–29.

58    P. Guicciardini, ed., *Scritti inediti di Francesco Guicciardini sopra la politica di Clemente VII dopo la battaglia di Pavia* (Florence, 1940), pp. 105–13 (esp. pp. 111–13); Ridolfi, *Francesco Guicciardini*, p. 147.

59    Pastor, ed. Kerr, vol. IX, p. 317.

60    Ibid., pp. 317–24.

61    On his actions and motivations see Clough, 'Clement VII and Francesco Maria della Rovere', esp. pp. 101ff.

62    Pastor, ed. Kerr, vol. IX, pp. 313–16, 351–53.

63    Giovio, transl. Domenichi, *Vite di Leone X etc.*, pp. 560–97, 630–31.

64    Pastor, ed. Kerr, vol. IX, Appendix 45.

65    *DMS*, XLII (Venice, 1895), col. 681; J. Hook, *The Sack of Rome, 1527* (London, 1972), p. 103.

66    J. R. Hale, *Artists and Warfare in the Renaissance* (New Haven, Conn., and London, 1990), Chapter 2, 'The German Image of the Soldier', passim.

67 Hook, *Sack of Rome*, p. 186.
68 C. Milanesi, ed., *Il Sacco di Roma del MDXXVII: narrazioni di contemporani* (Florence, 1867), pp. 474, 477; Hook, *Sack of Rome*, pp. 168–70.
69 Hook, *Sack of Rome*, pp. 228–34, 236–37.
70 J.E. Longhurst, ed., *Alfonso de Valdés and the Sack of Rome: Dialogue of Lactancio and an Archdeacon* (Albuquerque, N. Mex., 1952), p. 34.
71 E. Costantini, *Il cardinale di Ravenna al governo di Ancona* (Pesaro, 1891), pp. 24–45, 64–85.
72 Ibid., p. 414.
73 L. Fiumi, 'La legazione del Cardinale Ippolito de' Medici nell' Umbria', *Bollettino della regia deputazione di storia patria per l'Umbria*, 5 (1899), pp. 481–587.
74 *DMS*, LVI, col. 817; Pastor, ed. Mercati, vol. IV (2), p. 429 (quoting letter of Peregrini, 21 June 1532).
75 *DMS*, LVI, cols 927, 960
76 Vasari, ed. Milanesi, *Opere*, VII, pp. 441–42: '... [Tiziano] ritrasse ancora ... il detto cardinale Ippolito de Medici con abito all'ungherese, ed in un'altro quadro più piccolo, il medesimo tutto armato.'
77 *DMS*, LVI, col. 968; Pastor, ed. Mercati, vol. IV, p. 437.
78 F. Peregrino to Duke Federico Gonzaga, Rome, 25 October 1532 (ASMn AG b. 881); *DMS*, LVII, cols 46, 97, 133, 197.
79 Same to same, 17 October 1534 (ASMn AG b. 883 cc. 798r-v.)
80 Frati, *Spedizioni militari*, pp. 43, 123, 222, 254–56.
81 A. Antonovics, 'Counter-Reformation Cardinals 1534–90', *European Studies Review*, 2, 1972, pp. 301–28.
82 F. Peregrino to Duke Federico Gonzaga, 2 February 1537 (ASMn AG b. 887).
83 Same to same, 9 February 1537 (ASMn AG b. 887 c. 16r).
84 Fiumi, 'La legazione del Cardinale Ippolito de' Medici', pp. 568–69; Pastor, ed. Mercati, vol. V (Rome, 1959), pp. 196–97.
85 Peregrino to Duke Federico Gonzaga, Rome, 21 August 1535 (ASMn AG b. 885, c. 478r); P. Pellini, ed. L. Faina, *Della Historia di Perugia*, vol. III (Perugia, 1970), pp. 572–76; Pastor, ed. Mercati, vol. V, pp. 216–21, 726–27.
86 Peregrino to Duke Federico Gonzaga, Rome, 18 April, 18 May 1540 (ASMn AG b. 888 cc. 25r, 32r). On Gambara's military experience, G. Brunelli in *DBI*, vol. 52 (Rome, 1999), pp. 63–68.
87 Pellini, *Historia di Perugia*, vol. III, pp. 626–33; cf. C.F. Black, 'Perugia and Papal Absolutism', *EHR*, 96 (1981), pp. 626–33; G. Bacile di Castiglione, 'La Rocca Paolina di Perugia', *L'Arte*, VI (1903), pp. 347–67.
88 Peregrino to Duke Federico Gonzaga, Rome, 11 August 1536 (ASMn AG b. 886 c. 89r); Pastor, ed. Mercati, vol. V, pp. 201–4, 211–13. On Cardinal Filonardi see R. Becker in *DBI*, vol. 47 (Rome, 1997), pp. 819–25.
89 C. Capasso, *Il papa Paolo III, 1534–49* (Messina, 1924), vol. II, p. 438.
90 Peregrino to Duke Federico Gonzaga, Rome, 14 January 1535 (ASMn AG b. 885 c. 356r).
91 Peregrino to Duke Federico Gonzaga, Rome, 13 August 1535 (ASMn AG b. 885 c. 471).
92 Same to same, Rome, 11 August 1536 (ASMn AG b. 886 c. 89r); Pastor, ed. Mercati, vol. V, pp. 201–4.
93 Same to same, Rome, 12 June 1537 (ASMn AG b. 887 c. 56r).
94 Same to same, 25 June, 3 July 1537 (ASMn AG b. 887 c. 71r).
95 Same to same, Rome, 6, 16 August 1537 (ASMn AG b. 887 cc. 80r, 84r).
96 Setton, *Papacy and the Levant*, vol. III, p. 447 (quoting ASV, Senato Secreta, 59 fol. 16r).
97 Peregrino to Duke Federico Gonzaga, Rome, 11 January 1538 (b. 887 c. 525r).
98 P. Paschini, 'La flotta papale alla Prevesa 1538', *Rivista di storia della Chiesa in Italia*, vol. V (1951), pp. 55–74.

99  Capasso, *Paolo III*, vol.II, pp.512–17, 522–23; Pastor, ed. Mercati, vol.V, p.538; C. Robertson in *DBI*, vol.45, p.57.
100  See fig. 1 above. It was reproduced in R.H. Bainton, *Erasmus of Christendom* (Fontana edn, London, 1972), p. 133, and as fig. 22 in L. Partridge and R. Stern, *A Renaissance Likeness. Art and Culture in Raphael's Julius II* (Berkeley, Los Angeles and London, 2003). I am grateful to Liz McGrath and Opher Mansour for these references.
101  A. Chastel, transl. B. Archer, *The Sack of Rome, 1527* (Princeton, 1983), passim; some of the *Passional* woodcuts are reproduced there on pp.70–72.
102  R.B. Scribner, *For the Sake of Simple Folk. Popular Propaganda for the German Reformation* (Cambridge, 1981), pp.148–57.
103  Warburg Institute Photographic Collection (Religious Satire).
104  *Luther's Works*, ed. R.C. Schultz (Philadelphia, 1967), vol. 46, pp.168–69 (*Martin Luthers Werke*, 30 (2), Weimar 1909, p.115). I am grateful to Professor Norman Housley for the reference, part of which he quotes in *The Later Crusades*, p.380.
105  Pastor, ed. Mercati, vol.V, pp.222–27.
106  C. Robertson, *Il gran cardinale: alessandro Farnese, Patron of the Arts* (New Haven, Conn., and London, 1992), pp.65–67.
107  R. Harpath, *Papst Paul III als Alexander der Grosse* (Berlin and New York, 1978), pp.27–35.
108  Annibal Caro, ed. A. Greco, *Lettere familiari* (Florence, 1957–61), vol.II, p.372, quoted by Robertson, *Il gran cardinale*, p.67.
109  Various authors, *Le Palais Farnèse* (Rome, 1980), pp.254–59; pls 210a, 213b.
110  L.W. Partridge, 'Divinity and Dynasty at Caprarola: Perfect History in the Room of Farnese Deeds', *Art Bulletin*, LX, 1978, pp.494–530 (at pp.518–19).
111  Scribner, *For the Sake of Simple Folk*, pp.158–59, fig. 129.
112  Pastor, ed. Mercati, vol.VI (Rome, 1963), pp.90–98; P. Balan, *Gli assedii della Mirandola di Papa Giulio II nel 1511 e di Papa Giulio III nel 1551 e 1552* (Mirandola, 1876), esp. pp.44–45.
113  Pastor, ed. Mercati, vol.VI, pp.380, 392.
114  E. Gibbon, ed. J.B. Bury, *History of the Decline and Fall of the Roman Empire* (London, 1914), vol.VII, p.308.
115  Pastor, ed. Mercati, vol.VI, pp.397–402.
116  Ibid., p.403. On Carlo, see A. Prosperi, *DBI*, vol.19 (Rome, 1976), pp.497–509.
117  Francesco Tonina to Duke Guglielmo Gonzaga, 22, 29 July 1564 (ASMn AG b. 894 cc.161r, 166r; Pastor, ed. Mercati, vol.VII, doc. 72, p.632, gives incorrect date).
118  Pastor, ed. Mercati, vol.VII (Rome, 1950), pp.62–64, 395–97, 528; Setton, *Papacy and the Levant*, vol.IV (Philadelphia, 1984), pp.852–65.
119  Tosi, *Il Torneo di Belvedere*, pp.54, 71–112 (contemporary text, pp.126–64).

## CHAPTER 7

1  G. Lutz, 'Das päpstliche Heer im Jahre 1667: apostolische Kammer und Nepotismus, römisches Militärbudget in der frühen Neuzeit', *AHP*, 14, 1976, pp.163–217 (at pp.175 n.12, 205–6, 212).
2  J. Delumeau, *Vie économique et sociale de Rome dans la seconde moitié du XVIe siècle*, vol.II (Paris, 1959), pp.756–60.
3  Lutz, 'Das päpstliche Heer', pp.170–75, 182–92.
4  Pastor, ed. Mercati, vol.VIII (Rome, 1964), pp.325–34.
5  C. Hirschaeur, *La politique de St Pie V en France (1566–72)* (Paris, 1922), pp.21–25, 30–49.
6  A. Herz, 'The Sixtine and Pauline Tombs: Documents of the Counter Reformation', *Storia dell'Arte*, 41, 1981, pp.241–62 (at pp.257–58, 261); E.

Borsellino, 'Il monumento di Pio V in Santa Maria Maggiore', in M. Fagiolo and M.L. Madonna, *Sisto V*, vol.I (Rome, 1992 ), pp.837–50, fig. 6; C. Pietrangeli, *La Basilica romana di Santa Maria Maggiore* (Florence, 1987), p.234.

7    Setton, *The Papacy and the Levant*, vol.IV, p.904.

8    Ibid., pp.1015–16; Pastor, ed. Mercati, vol.VIII, p.549.

9    Pastor, ed. Mercati, vol.VIII, pp.530–31.

10   Castagna to Cardinal Alessandrino, Madrid, 27 January 1571 (L. Serrano, *Correspondencia diplomatica entre Espana y la Santa Sede durante el Pontificado de Pio V* (Madrid, 1914), vol.IV, pp.170–71).

11   Pastor, ed. Mercati, vol.VIII, pp.574–76.

12   N.M. Sutherland, *The Massacre of St Bartholomew and the European Conflict 1559–72* (London, 1973), passim; but cf. A. Lynn Martin, 'Papal Policy and the European Conflict 1559–72', *Sixteenth Century Journal*, 11, 1980, pp.35–48.

13   P. Hurtubise, 'Comment Rome apprit la nouvelle du massacre de la Saint-Barthélemy', *AHP*, X (1972), pp.187–209 (at p.193); Pastor, ed. Cenci, vol.IX (Rome, 1955), pp.354–66.

14   P. Fehl, 'Vasari's "Extirpation of the Huguenots": the Challenge of Pity and Fear', *Gazette des Beaux Arts*, 84 (2) (1974), pp.257–83 (the subtitle of Fehl's shorter article in German, 'Gedanken über das Schreckliche in der Kunst', *Mitteilungen der Technischen Universität Carolo-Wilhelmina zu Braunschschweig*, IX, heft III/IV, 1974, pp.71–85, seems more to the point).

15   Ibid., p.264, fig. 7; Sutherland, *The Massacre*, p.55.

16   P. Renold, ed., *Letters of William Allen and Richard Barret 1572–78* (London, 1967), pp.285–86.

17   Herz, 'The Sixtine and Pauline Tombs', pp.256, 261, fig. 20; Pietrangeli, *La Basilica*, p.234.

18   Pastor, ed. Cenci, vol.X (Rome, 1955), pp.390–95.

19   Ibid., pp.549–50.

20   P. Bartl, 'Marcione verso Constantinopoli: zur Turkenpolitik Klemens VIII', *Saeculum*, XX, 1969, pp.44–66.

21   B. Barbiche, 'La politique de Clément VIII à l'égard de Ferrare et l'excommunication de César d'Este', *Mélanges d'Archéologie et d'Histoire*, LXXIV, 1962, pp.290–328; L. von Ranke, transl. E. Foster, *History of the Popes* (Bohn edn, London, 1880), vol.II, pp.69–76.

22   Pastor, ed. Cenci, vol.IX, p.607.

23   Gibbon, ed. Bury, *Decline and Fall of the Roman Empire*, vol.VII, p.307.

24   Herz, 'The Sixtine and Pauline Tombs', pp.256–62, figs. 11–14, 19; Pietrangeli, *La Basilica*, pp.264, 266–67.

25   T. Campanella, *Monarchia Messiae: con due Discorsi della libertà e della felice suggezione allo stato ecclesiastico*, 1633, facsimile ed. L. Firpo (Turin, 1973), esp. Chapter X.

26   Giovanni Magno to Duke Vincenzo I Gonzaga, Rome, 26 August 1606 (ASMn, AG b.981 c.328r).

27   W.J. Bouwsma, *Venice and the Defense of Republican Liberty* (Berkeley Calif. and London, 1984) pp.374–77, 390–91.

28   G. Botero, *Della...republica veneta e Discorso intorno allo stato della Chiesa* (Venice, 1605), pp.110–22.

29   Von Ranke, transl. Foster, *History of the Popes*, vol.III, Appendix 23, pp.326–27.

30   Barbieri, *Industria e Politica Mineraria*, p.51 (letter of 23 June 1629, BAV, MS Vat. Urb. 1099 fols. 369v–70r).

31   Pastor, ed. Cenci, vol.XIII (Rome, 1961), pp.865–67; on Cardinal Barberini, A. Merola in *DBI*, vol.7 (Rome, 1964), pp.156–60.

32   L. Gambi and A. Pinella, eds, *La Galleria delle Carte Geografiche in Vaticano*, Mirabilia Italiae 1 (Modena, 1994), pp.398, 400–3.

33  Pastor, ed. Cenci, vol. XIII, p. 304.
34  Ibid., pp. 271–73; Giacinto Gigli, ed. G. Riccioti, *Diario romano 1608–70* (Rome, 1958), p. 121; Dennistoun, *Memoirs of the Dukes of Urbino*, vol. III (London, 1851), pp. 203–10, 232–33.
35  Gigli, *Diario*, pp. 200–1.
36  Pastor, ed. Cenci, vol. XIII, pp. 883–95; Gigli, *Diario*, pp. 212–20, 243.
37  BAV, MS Barberini lat. 6157, fols 20r–36v (noted by Pastor, ed. Cenci, vol. XIII, p. 898). I am grateful to Letizia Panizza for information about Ferrante Pallavicino.
38  Lutz, 'Das päpstliche Heer', pp. 182–92.
39  Prodi, *The Papal Prince*, pp. 158, 179; O. Chadwick, *The Popes and European Revolution* (Oxford, 1981), pp. 254–55.
40  Pastor, ed. Cenci, vol. XV, pp. 27–54; Chadwick, *The Popes and European Revolution*, p. 276.
41  I. Raulich, 'Il cardinale Alberoni e la repubblica di San Marino', *ASI*, XXXIX (1907), pp. 352–95 (esp. pp. 370–81).
42  G. Filippone, *Le Relazioni tra lo Stato Pontificio e la Francia rivoluzionaria: Storia Diplomatica del Trattato di Tolentino*, vol. I (Milan, 1961), pp. 22–30 (letter to Catherine the Great noted p. 25 n. 12); cf. Lutz, 'Das päpstliche Heer', p. 211.
43  Pastor, ed. Cenci, vol. XVI (3) (Rome, 1955), pp. 548–49.
44  Filippone, *Le Relazioni*, vol. II (Milan, 1967), Appendix 15, p. 679.
45  Ibid., pp. 582–86, 608–16, 628.
46  Ibid., pp. 629–33.
47  Ibid., Appendix 24, pp. 689–90.
48  Pastor, ed. Cenci, vol. XVI (3) (Rome, 1955), pp. 633–34; G. Gendry, *Pie VI: Sa Vie. Son Pontificat* (Paris, 1906), pp. 308–10; on Consalvi, A. Roveri in *DBI*, vol. 28 (Rome, 1983), pp. 33–43.
49  D. Sachinelli, *Memorie storiche sulla vita del cardinale Fabrizio Ruffo: tutte le contestazioni dell'abate Sanfedista* (Naples, 1833; repr. 1999), pp. 127–28.
50  B. Croce, ed., *Lettere del cardinale Ruffo: la riconquista del Regno di Napoli nel 1799* (Bari, 1943; repr. Naples, 1999), pp. 16, 29, 53, 70.
51  Sachinelli, *Memorie storiche*, pp. 196–97.
52  Ibid., pp. 191–92.
53  A. Latreille, *Napoléon et le Saint Siège (1801–8): l'Ambassade du Cardinal Fesch à Rome* (Paris, 1935), passim.
54  Ibid., pp. 433–583.
55  On the careers of Bernetti and Benvenuti, G. Pignatelli in *DBI*, vol. 9 (Rome, 1967), pp. 338–43; idem in *DBI*, vol. 8 (Rome, 1966), pp. 667–71.
56  O. Chadwick, *A History of the Popes 1830–1914* (Oxford, 1998), pp. 2–3.
57  L. Pàsztor, 'I cardinali Albani e Bernetti e l'intervento austriaco nel 1831', *Rivista di storia della Chiesa in Italia*, 8, 1954, pp. 95–115; idem, 'L'intervento austriaco nello Stato pontificio nel 1832 e i cardinali Albani e Bernetti', *Studi romagnoli*, VIII, 1957, pp. 529–95.
58  Ibid., p. 68.
59  P. Pirri, 'L' Amnistia di Pio IX nei documenti ufficiali', *Rivista di storia della Chiesa in Italia*, 8, 1954, pp. 207–32.
60  Chadwick, *History of the Popes*, pp. 77–79.
61  Ibid., pp. 80–83.
62  G.M. Trevelyan, *Garibaldi's Defence of the Roman Republic* (London, 1907; library edn, 1921), pp. 92–93, 189–90.
63  R. Aubert, *DBI*, vol. 3 (Rome, 1961), pp. 484–93; Chadwick, *History of the Popes*, pp. 92–94 and passim.
64  N. Blakiston, ed., *The Roman Question: Extracts from the Despatches of Odo Russell from Rome, 1858–70* (London, 1962), no. 11, p. 11.
65  Odo Russell to Earl of Malmesbury (Foreign Secretary), Rome, 24 June 1859; same to Lord John Russell, 7 July 1859, (ibid., nos 28, 31, pp. 28, 32–33).

66 Same to Lord John Russell, Rome, 16 September 1859 (ibid., no. 46, pp. 49–50).
67 F. Althaus, ed., transl. Mrs G.W. Hamilton, *The Roman Journals of Ferdinand Gregorovius 1852–74* (London, 1907), p. 59.
68 E.g. Odo Russell to Lord John Russell, Rome 22 July 1859 (Blakiston, *The Roman Question*, no. 36, p. 40).
69 Same to same, Rome, 3, 7, 17, 18 April 1860 (ibid., nos 93–97, pp. 96–100). On Lamoricière see also Chadwick, *History of the Popes*, pp. 149–50.
70 Same to same, Rome, 3, 12 July 1860 (ibid., nos 118, 121, pp. 115, 118–19).
71 Same to same, Rome, 25 September 1860 (ibid., no. 134, p. 131).
72 Same to Earl Russell, Rome, 26 July 1862 (ibid., no. 240, p. 236).
73 Same to the Earl of Clarendon, Rome, 10 November 1865 (ibid., no. 330, p. 318); Chadwick, *History of the Popes*, pp. 166–67.
74 Same to Lord Stanley, Rome, 26 March 1868 (ibid., no. 383, p. 351).
75 Tosi, *Il Torneo*, p. 67.
76 Chadwick, *History of the Popes*, pp. 218, 280, 345–46.

## EPILOGUE

1 Discussed by Marina Warner, 'Who's sorry now? What apology means in the modem world', *Times Literary Supplement*, 1 August 2003, pp. 10–13.
2 Erasmus, ed. A.H.T. Levi, *Querela Pacis*, in *Collected Works of Erasmus, Literary and Educational Writings*, vol. 5 (Toronto etc., 1986), p. 307.

# Bibliography

Because of this book's long time time-span, unevenly covered, the Bibliography is presented in three chronological parts; the second and largest of them, concerning the early fifteenth to the mid-sixteenth century, corresponds to the central and most detailed sections of the book (later parts of Chapter 2 to Chapter 6). Although not every title cited in the endnotes is given here, most of those cited more than once, and all titles relevant to more than one chapter (noted below with an asterisk*), are included.

N.B. Full references to titles are given in the endnotes for a first or single reference, followed by abbreviated titles for subsequent references.

The only work cited throughout the book is the *Dizionario biografico degli italiani** (vol. 1, Rome, 1960), which reached in 2005 vol. 65 (to Lorenzetti). Individual entries from the *DBI* appearing in endnote references are not, however, included separately in this Bibliography, nor are entries from the *Dictionnaire d'Histoire et de Géographie Ecclésiastiques** (vol. I, Paris, 1913), which barely reached in 2004 vol. 28 (the letter 'K'). It should be noted that C. Eubel et al., *Hierarchia Catholica Medii…et Recentioris Aevi,** 7 vols (Münster, 1901–Padua, 1998), is the essential reference work for dates and appointments of popes, cardinals and Catholic bishops.

The most indispensable secondary work, cited throughout, except in Chapter 1, remains L. Pastor, *History of the Popes from the Close of the Middle Ages** (English and Italian versions).

Unpublished sources are listed separately at the end of the Bibliography.

## I. MEDIEVAL (CHAPTER 1, PARTS OF CHAPTER 2, TO CA. 1430)

Broderick, J.F., 'The Sacred College of Cardinals: Size and Geographical Composition', *AHP*, 25 (1987), pp. 7–71*
Ciaccio, L., *Il cardinale legato Bertrando del Poggetto in Bologna 1327–34* (Bologna, 1902)
Cornides, E., *Rose und Schwert im päpstlichem Zeremoniell von den Anfängen bis zum Pontificat Gregors XIII* (Vienna, 1967)
Cowdrey, H.E.J., *Pope Gregory VII, 1073–85* (Oxford, 1998)
Duchesne, L., ed., *Le Liber Pontificalis*, 3 vols (Paris, 1981), vol. 1
Dupré Theseider, E., *Santa Caterina da Siena: Epistolario I* (Rome, 1940)
Erdmann, C., transl. Baldwin, Marshall W. and Goffat, W., *The Origins of the Idea of Crusade* (Princeton, 1977)

Cushing, K., 'Anselm and Coercion: A Legal Form of Persuasion', in *The Papacy and Law in the Gregorian Reformation: The Canon Law Works of Anselm of Lucca* (Oxford, 1998)

Filippini, F., *Il cardinale Egidio Albornoz* (Bologna, 1937)

Finke, H., *Acta Aragonensia*, Bd 1 (Berlin and Leipzig, 1908)

Giovanni da Legnano, ed. Erskine Holland, T., *Tractatus de bello, de represaliis et de duello* (Oxford, 1917)

Gori, G., 'L'eccidio di Cesena nel 1377', *ASI*, n.s., 8, ii (1858), pp. 3–37

Gregorovius, F., transl. Hamilton, A., *A History of the City of Rome in the Middle Ages*, 6 vols (revised edn, London, 1905; repr. New York, 2000–4)*

Holmes, G., 'Cardinal Beaufort and the Crusade against the Hussites', *EHR*, 88 (1973), pp. 721–50

Housley, N., *The Italian Crusades: The Papal–Angevin Alliance and the Crusades against the Lay Powers 1254–1343* (Oxford, 1982)*

Kantorowicz, E., transl. Lorimer, E.O., *Frederick the Second* (London, 1931)

Kuttner, S., 'Cardinalis: the Growth of a Canonical Concept', *Traditio*, 3 (1945), pp. 129–214

Marsilio of Padua, transl. Gewirth, A., *Defensor Pacis* (New York, 1956; repr. 1967)

Mollat, G., *Les papes d'Avignon* (9th edn, Paris, 1949; transl. Love, J., *The Popes at Avignon*, London etc., 1963)

Moroni, G., *Dizionario di Erudizione storica ecclesiastica*, 103 vols (Venice, 1845)*

Partner, P., *The Papal State under Martin V* (London, 1958)

Idem, *The Lands of St Peter* (London, 1972)*

Reh, F., *Kardinal Peter Capocci: ein Staatsmann und Feldherr des XIII. Jahrhunderts* (Berlin, 1933)

Soranzo, G., *La Guerra fra Venezia e la Santa Sede per il dominio di Ferrara 1308–13* (Città di Castello, 1905)

Stácul, P., *Il cardinale Pileo da Prata* (Rome, 1957)

Swanson, R., '"The Way of Action": Pierre d'Ailly and the Military Solution to the Great Schism', in Sheils, W.J., ed., *The Church and War*, Studies in Church History, 20 (Oxford, 1963)

Theiner, A., *Codex Diplomaticus Dominii Temporalis Sanctae Sedis*, vols 2–3 (Rome, 1862)*

Throop, Palmer A., *Criticism of the Crusade* (Amsterdam, 1940)

Ullmann, W., *The Growth of Papal Government in the Middle Ages* (revised edn, London, 1965)

Waley, D., 'Papal armies in the thirteenth century', *EHR*, LXXI (1957), pp. 1–30

Idem, *The Papal State in the Thirteenth Century* (London, 1961)

Westenholz, E. von, *Kardinal Rainer von Viterbo* (Heidelberg, 1912)

Wilks, M.J., *The Problem of Sovereignty in the Middle Ages* (Cambridge, 1963)

## II. RENAISSANCE (LATER PART OF CHAPTER 2 TO CHAPTER 6, CA.1430–1565)

Ammannati Piccolomini, Jacopo, ed. Cherubini, P., *Lettere*, 3 vols (Rome, 1997)

Antonovics, A., 'Counter-Reformation Cardinals 1534–90', *European Studies Review*, 2 (1972), pp. 301–28*

Balan, P., *Roberto Boschetti e li avvenimenti italiani dei suoi tempi (1494–1529)* (Modena, 1877)

Idem, *Gli assedii della Mirandola di Papa Giulio II nel 1511 e di Papa Giulio III nel 1551 e 1552* (Mirandola, 1876)

Barbieri, G., *Industria e Politica Mineraria nello Stato Pontificio dal '400 al '600* (Rome, 1940)

Beani, G., *Niccolò Forteguerri cardinale di Teano: notizie storiche* (Pistoia, 1891)

Benziger, W., *Zur Theorie von Krieg und Frieden in der italienischen Renaissance: Die Disputatio de pace et bello zwischen Bartolomeo Platina und Rodrigo Sánchez de Arévalo und andere anlässlich der Pax Paolina (Rom 1968) entstandene Schriften* (Frankfurt-am-Main etc., 1996)

Bernardy, A.A., 'Il cardinal Teano e la Repubblica di San Marino', *Bulletino storico pistoiese*, IV (1902), pp. 112–20

Black, A., *Monarchy and Community: Political Ideas in the Later Conciliar Controversy 1430–50* (Cambridge, 1970)

Büchi, A., *Korrespondenzen und Akten zur Geschichte des Kardinals Matthäeus Schiner* vol. I (Basel, 1920)

Idem, *Kardinal Matthäeus Schiner als Staatsmann und Kirchenfürst*, vol. I (Zurich, 1923)

Burckhardus, J., ed. Celani, E., *Liber Notarum, RIS*, vol. XXXII (1) (Città di Castello, 1907–10)

Calzona, A., et al., ed., *Il sogno di Pio II e il viaggio da Roma a Mantova* (Città di Castello, 2003)

Canestrini, G., and Desjardins, A., *Négotiations diplomatiques de la France avec la Toscane*, vol. 2 (Paris, 1861)

Capasso, C., *Il papa Paolo III, 1534–49*, 2 vols (Messina, 1924)

Caravale, M., and Caracciolo, A., *Lo Stato Pontificio da Martino V a Pio X* (Turin, 1978)*

Chambers, D.S., *Cardinal Bainbridge in the Court of Rome* (Oxford, 1965)

Idem, 'Virtù militare del cardinal Francesco Gonzaga', repr. in Chambers, D.S., *Renaissance Cardinals and their Worldly Problems* (Aldershot, 1997)

Idem, *A Renaissance Cardinal and his Worldly Goods: The Will and Inventory of Francesco Gonzaga (1444–83)* (London, 1992)

Idem, 'What made a Renaissance cardinal respectable? The case of Cardinal Costa', *Renaissance Studies*, 12 (1998), pp. 87–108

Idem, 'The Enigmatic Eminence of Cardinal Sigismondo Gonzaga', *Renaissance Studies*, 16 (2002), pp. 330–54

Idem, 'Tomasso Parentucelli vice-camerlengo: problemi attorno la Camera Apostolica e il governatorato di Roma', in E. Vecchi, ed., *Papato, stati regionali e Lunigiana nell'età di Niccolò V*, Atti delle giornate di studio, maggio 2000 (La Spezia, 2004), pp. 59–71

Clough, C.H., 'Clement VII and Francesco Maria della Rovere, Duke of Urbino', in Gouwens, K., and Reiss, S.E., eds, *The Pontificate of Clement VII: History, Politics, Culture* (Aldershot, 2005), pp. 75–108

Condivi, A., ed. Nencioni, G., *Vita di Michelagnolo Buonarotti* (Florence, 1998)

Cortesi, P., *De Cardinalatu* (Castro Cortese, 1510)

Costantini, E., *Il cardinale di Ravenna al governo di Ancona* (Pesaro, 1891)

Cranach., L., *Passional Christi und Antichristi* (Wittenberg, 1521)

Da Bisticci, Vespasiano da, ed. Greco, A., *Le Vite*, 2 vols (Florence, 1970–76)

Da Mosto, A., 'Ordinamenti militari delle soldatesche dello stato romano dal 1430 al 1470', *QF*, vol. V (1903), pp. 19–34

Idem, 'Ordinamenti militari delle soldatesche dello stato romano nel secolo XVI', *QF*, vol. VI (1904), pp. 72–133

De' Conti, Sigismondo, *Libri historiarum sui temporis* (Rome, 1883)

De Grassis, Paris de, ed. Frati, L., *Le Due Spedizioni militari di Giulio II tratte dal Diario di Paride de' Grassi Bolognese* (Bologna, 1886)

De Vincentiis, A., *Battaglie di Memoria: gruppi, intellectuali testi e la discontinuità del potere papale* (Rome, 2002)

Della Tuccia, N., in Ciampi, I., ed., *Cronache e statute della città di Viterbo* (Florence, 1872)

Delumeau, J., *Vie économique et sociale de Rome dans la seconde moitié du XVIe siècle*, 2 vols (Paris, 1957–59)*

Dennistoun, J., *Memoirs of the Dukes of Urbino*, 3 vols (London, 1851)*

Erasmus, Desiderius, ed. Mynors, R.A.B., *Collected Works in English: Letters*, vols. 1, 3, 12 (Toronto and Buffalo, 1974–2003); ed., Levi, A.H.T, *Collected Works in English:*

*Literary and Educational Writings*, vol. 27 (Toronto, Buffalo and London, 1986), 'Julius Excluded from Heaven: A Dialogue', transl. Heath, M.J., pp.155–97

Esch, A., 'Importe in Rom der Frührenaissance', *Studi in memoria di Federigo Melis*, vol. III (Naples, 1978)

Finlay, R., 'Venice, the Po Expedition and the End of the League of Cambrai', *Studies in Modern European History and Culture*, 2 (1976), pp.37–72.

Fumi, L., 'La legazione del Cardinal Ippolito de' Medici nell'Umbria', *Bollettino della regia deputazione di storia patria per l'Umbria*, 5 (1899), pp.481–587

Giovio, P., transl. Domenichi, L., *Le vite di Leone Decimo e d'Adriano Sesto Sommi Pontefici et del Cardinal Pompeo Colonna* (Florence, 1549)

Giustinian, Antonio, ed. Villari, P., *Dispacci*, 3 vols (Florence, 1876)

Gomez-Canedo, L., *Un Español al Servicio de la Santa Sede: Don Juan de Carvajal, Cardinal de Sant' Angelo, legato en Alemania y Hungria (1392–1469)* (Madrid, 1947)

Gottlob, A., *Aus der Camera Apostolica* (Innsbruck, 1889)

Gozzadini, G., 'Di alcuni avvenimenti in Bologna e nell'Emilia dal 1506 al 1511 e dei Cardinali Legati A. Ferrerio e F. Alidosi', *Atti e Memorie della R. deputazione di storia patria per le province di Romagna*, 3rd ser., IV (1886) pp.67–176 (Part 1); VII (1889), pp.161–267 (Part 2)

Guasti, E., 'I Manoscrittti Torrigiani donati allo R. Archivio Centrale di Stato di Firenze', *ASI*, 3rd ser., XXI (1875)

Guicciardini, F., ed. Palmarocchi, R., *Carteggi*, vol.2 (Bologna, 1939)

Idem, ed. Menchi, S., *Storia d'Italia* (Turin, 1971)

Idem, ed. Guicciardini, P., *Scritti inediti di Francesco Guicciardini sopra la politica di Clemente VII dopo la battaglia di Pavia* (Florence, 1940)

Hale, J.R., 'The Early Development of the Bastion', in Hale, J.R., et al., eds, *Europe in the Later Middle Ages* (Oxford, 1965)

Hankins, J., 'Renaissance crusaders: humanist crusade literature in the age of Mehmed II', Dumbarton Oaks Papers, 29 (1955), pp.111–201

Hill, G., *A Corpus of Italian Medals before Cellini* (London, 1930)

Infessura, S., ed. Tommasini, O., *Diario della città di Roma* (Rome, 1890)

Jones, P.J., *The Malatesta of Rimini and the Papal State* (Cambridge, 1974)

Law, J.E., 'Giovanni Vitelleschi: "prelate guerriero"', *Renaissance Studies*, 12 (1998), pp.40–66

Luzio, A., 'La Reggenza d'Isabella d'Este durante la prigionia dl marito (1509–10)', *ASL*, ser. 4, XIV (1910) pp.5–104

Idem, 'Federigo Gonzaga ostaggio alla corte di Giulio II', *ASRSP*, 9 (1886), pp.509–82

Idem, 'Isabella d'Este di fronte a Giulio II negli ultimi tre anni del suo pontificato', (1) *ASL*, ser. 4, XVII (1912), pp.245–334; (2) XVIII (1912) pp. 55–144, pp. 392–456

Machiavelli, N., ed. Burd, A., *De Principe* (Oxford, 1891)

Idem, ed. Bertelli, S., *Legazioni e Commissarie*, 3 vols (Milan, 1968)

Idem, ed. Gaeta, F., *Lettere* (Milan, 1961)

Mallett, M., *Mercenaries and their Masters: Warfare in Renaissance Italy* (London, 1974)

Idem, *The Borgias* (London, 1969)

Manetti, G., ed. Muratori, L., *Vita Nicholai Quinti*, RIS, vol.III, 2 (Milan, 1724); Modigliano, A., transl. and ed., *Vita di Nicolò V* (Rome, 1999)

Mencarelli, G., ed., *I Vitelleschi: fonti, realtà e mito* (Tarquinia, 1998)

Miglio, M., ed., *Un pontificato ed una città: Sisto IV* (Vatican City, 1986)

Idem, 'Valla e l'ideologia municipale romana nel De falso credita et emendita Constantini donatione', in *Italia e Germania: Liber Amicorum Arnold Esch* (Tübingen, 2001), pp.226–33.

Moncallero, G.L., *Il Cardinale Bernardo Dovizi da Bibbiena* (Florence, 1953)

Idem, *Epistolario di Bernardo Dovizi da Bibbiena*, 2 vols (Florence, 1955)

Müntz, E., *Les arts à la cour des papes pendant le 15e et le 16e siècle*, vol.I (Paris, 1878)

Pagliucchi, P., *I Castellani di Castel Sant' Angelo* (Rome, 1906–9; repr. 1973)

Partner, P., *The Pope's Men* (Oxford, 1990)

Partridge, L., and Starn, R., *A Renaissance Likeness: Art and Culture in Raphael's Julius II* (Berkeley, Los Angeles, London, 1980)

Paschini, P., *Lodovico Cardinal Camerlengo* (Rome, 1939)

Idem, 'La flotta papale alla Prevesa', *Rivista di storia della Chiesa in Italia*, 5 (1951), pp. 55–74

Idem, *Il carteggio fra Marco Barbo e Giovanni Lorenzi* (Vatican City, 1969)

Pastor, L., *Geschichte der Papste seit der Ausgang des Mittelalters* (1st German edn, vol. 1, 1884); transl. and ed. (from 6th German edn) by Antrobus, F., vols I–VI, vols. VII–VIII, by R.F. Kerr (London, 1923); revised Italian version, vols I–VIII, ed. Mercati, A., *Storia dei Papi* (various dates, Rome, 1950–64); vols IX–XVI, transl. and ed. P. Cenci (Rome, 1955–58)

Pellegrini, M., *Congiure di Romagna: Lorenzo de' Medici e il duplice tirannicidio a Forlì e a Faenza nel 1488* (Florence, 1999)

Idem, 'Il profile politico-istituzionale del cardinalato', in Chiabo, M., ed., *Roma di fronte ad Europa al tempo di Alessandro VI* (Rome, 2001)

Idem, *Ascanio Maria Sforza: la parabola politica di un cardinale-principe del Rinascimento*, 2 vols (Rome, 2002)

Petersohn, J., *Ein diplomat des Quattrocento: Angelo Geraldini (1422–86)* (Tübingen, 1985)

Piccolomini, Aeneas Silvius, see Pius II

Picotti, G.B., *La Dieta di Mantova e la politica de' veneziani* (Venice, 1912)

Idem, *La giovinezza di Leone X* (Milan, 1928; repr. Rome, 1981)

Pietrangeli, C., ed., *Il Palazzo Apostolico Lateranense* (Rome, 1991)

Pius II, ed. van Heck, A., *Commentarii*, 2 vols (Vatican City, 1984); ed. and transl. Gragg, F.A., and Gabel, L.G., *The Commentaries of Pius II*, Smith College Studies in History, Northampton, Mass., 1937–57.

Piva, *La guerra di Ferrara del 1482: Periodo Secondo* (Padua, 1894)

Platina, B., ed. Zimolo, G.C., *Vita Pii II*, *RIS*, vol. III (3) (Città di Castello, 1964)

Prodi, P., *Il sovrano pontefice* (Bologna, 1982; repr. 1999); transl. Haskins, S., *The Papal Prince: One Body and Two Souls: the Papal Monarchy in Early Modern Europe* (Cambridge, 1987)*

Ratti, A., 'Quarantatre lettere originali di Pio II relative alla Guerra per la successione nel reame di Napoli 1460–63', *ASL*, ser. 3, XIX (1903), pp. 263–93

Rees, V., 'Ficino's advice to Princes', in Allen, M.J.B., et al., eds, *Marsilio Ficino: his Theology, his Philosophy, his Legacy* (Leiden, 2001) pp. 339–57

Robertson, C., *Il gran cardinale. Alessandro Farnese, Patron of the Arts* (New Haven, Conn., and London, 1992)

Robertson, I., 'Pietro Barbo – Paul II: *Zentilhomo de Venecia e Pontifico*', in Chambers, D.S., et al., eds, *War, Culture and Society in Renaissance Venice* (London, 1993)

Idem, *Tyranny under the Mantle of St Peter: Pope Paul II and Bologna* (Turnhout, 2002)

Sanudo, Marin, ed. Fulin, R. et al., *I Diarii*, 57 vols (Venice, 1879–1903; repr. Bologna, 1969–70)

Scribner, R., *For the Sake of Simple Folk. Popular Propaganda for the German Reformation* (Cambridge, 1981)

Setton, K., *The Papacy and the Levant*, 4 vols (Philadelphia, 1978–84)*

Shaw, C., *Julius II: The Warrior Pope* (Oxford, 1993)

Sigmund, P.E., *Nicholas of Cusa and Medieval Political Thought* (New Haven, Conn., 1963)

Soranzo, G., *Pio II e la politica italiana nella lotta contro i Malatesta 1457–63* (Padua, 1911)

Tosi, M., *Il Torneo di Belvedere in Vaticano e I Tornei in Italia nel Cinquecento* (Rome, 1946)

Valentini, G., 'La sospensione della crociata nei primi anni di Paolo II (1464–68): Chiereghino Chiericati e il suo trattatello della Milizia', *AHP*, XIV, 1976, pp. 71–101.

Vasari, G., ed. Milanesi, G., *Opere*, vol. VII (Florence, 1876; repr. 1906, 1998)\*
Woodward, W.H., *Cesare Borgia* (London, 1913)
Zorzi, G., 'Un vicentino alla corte di Paolo II', *Nuovo Archivio Veneto*, 30 (1915), pp. 369–434.

## III. LATER (TO 1870)

Barbiche, B., 'La politique de Clément VIII a l'égard de Ferrare et l'excommunication de César d'Este', *Mélanges d'Archéologie et d'Histoire*, 74 (1962), pp. 290–328
Blakiston, N., *The Roman Question: Extracts from the Despatches of Odo Russell from Rome 1858–70* (London, 1962)
Botero, G., *Della...republica veneta e Discorso intorno allo stato della Chiesa* (Venice, 1605)
Campanella, T., *Monarchia Messiae: con due Discorsi della libertà e della felice suggezione allo stato ecclesiastico*, 1633 (facsimile ed. Firpo, L., Turin, 1973)
Chadwick, O., *The Popes and European Revolution* (Oxford, 1981)
Idem, *A History of the Popes 1830–1914* (Oxford, 1998)
Croce, B., ed., *Lettere del cardinale Ruffo: la riconquista del Regno di Napoli nel 1799* (Bari, 1943; repr. Naples, 1999)
Delumeau, J., *Vie économique et sociale de Rome dans la seconde moitié du XVIe siècle*, 2 vols (Paris, 1957–59)\*
Fehl, P., 'Vasari's "Extirpation of the Huguenots": the Challenge of Pity and Fear', *Gazette des Beaux Arts*, 84 (2) (1974), pp. 257–83
Filippone, G., *Le relazioni tra lo Stato pontificio e la Francia rivoluzionaria: Storia Diplomatica del Trattato di Tolentino*, 2 vols (Milan, 1961, 1967)
Gambi, L., and Pinella, A., eds, *La Galleria delle Carte Geografiche in Vaticano*, Mirabilia Italiae, I (Modena, 1994)
Gigli, G., ed., Riciotti, G., *Diario romano 1608–70* (Rome, 1958)
Latreillé, A., *Napoléon et le Saint Siège (1801–08): l'Ambassade du Cardinal Fesch à Rome* (Paris, 1935)
Pastor, L., as above, *Storia dei papi*, Mercati, A., ed., vol. VIII (Rome, 1964); Cenci, P., ed., vols IX–X (Rome, 1955), XIII (Rome, 1961), XVI, 3 (Rome, 1955)
Pásztor, L., 'I cardinali Albani e Bernetti e l'intervento austriaco nel 1831', *Rivista di storia della Chiesa in Italia*, 8 (1954), pp. 95–115
Idem, 'L'intervento austriaco nello Stato pontificio nel 1832 e i cardinali Albani e Bernetti', *Studi romagnoli*, 8 (1957), pp. 529–95
Pietrangeli, C., *La Basilica romana di Santa Maria Maggiore* (Florence, 1887)
Ranke, L. von, transl. Foster, E., *History of the Popes*, 3 vols (Bohn edn, London, 1880)\*
Raulich, I., 'Il cardinal Alberoni e la repubblica di San Marino', *ASI*, 39 (1907), pp. 352–95
Sachinelli, D., *Memorie storiche sulla vita del cardinale Fabrizio Ruffo: tutte le contestazioni dell'abate Sanfedista* (Naples, 1833; repr., 1999)

## UNPUBLISHED SOURCES

London, British Library
Additional MS 8443

Mantua, Archivio di Stato
Archivio Gonzaga
*Busta* 533 (Corrispondenza Estera: Ungheria)
*Busta* 663 (Francia)
*Buste* 840–981 (Roma): 840 c. 410; 841 cc. 54, 59, 62, 74–6, 79, 96, 401–5, 410, 441, 475, 688; 842 cc. 3, 156, 372; 845 cc. 231, 236–37; 848 c. 93; 856 c. 5; 857

cc. 131, 196; 858 cc. 265, 269, 270–75, 278, 280, 298; 859 cc. 163, 165; 860
cc. 116, 222; 861 cc. 39–40, 156, 236, 384; 863 c. 629; 864 cc. 610, 616; 865
cc. 206, 245, 250, 256, 259, 261, 273, 278, 290, 297, 324, 355; 883 c. 798; 885
cc. 47, 356, 471; 886 c. 89; 887 cc. 16, 71, 80, 84, 525; 888 cc. 25, 32; 894 cc. 161,
166; 981 c. 328
*Busta* 1077 (Urbino)
*Busta* 1141 (Bologna) cc. 524, 539, 549; 1142 c. 464; 1147 cc. 428, 435
*Busta* 1231 (Ferrara) cc. 27, 32–33, 49; 1242 cc. 866–68
*Busta* 1332 (Mirandola) cc. 253; 1340 cc. 189, 218, 228, 253
*Busta* 1630 (Milano)
*Busta* 1892 (Corrispondenza colla Marchesa Isabella d'Este )
*Busta* 2430 (Lettere da Mantova) c. 535
*Busta* 2896, lib. 96 (Copialettere) fol. 7
*Busta* 2900, lib. 114 (Copialettere) fols 21–3, 32–40, 3, 51, 74–75, 86, 92, 113–14,
154–55; 2918, lib. 215, fol. 6
3351 (Brevia etc.)
Fondo Portioli:
*Busta* 13

Mantua, Archivio Diocesano
Archivio Mensa Vescovile
Pergamene no. 71

Milan, Archivio di Stato
Archivio Sforzesco: Potenze Estere
*Cartella* 100 (Roma)
*Cartella* 146 (Marche)
*Cartella* 162 (Romagna) cc. 5, 28, 200, 204, 215, 231
*Cartella* 207 (Napoli)

Modena, Archivio di Stato
Archivio Estense: Cancelleria ducale, Ambasciatori
Roma *busta* 1
Firenze *busta* 5
Milano *busta* 19

Vatican City, Biblioteca Apostolica Vaticana
MS Chigi, I. VII. 260

# Index